Socially Responsible Accounting

Socially Responsible Accounting

M. R. Mathews

Faculty of Business Studies
Massey University
New Zealand

CHAPMAN & HALL
London · Glasgow · New York · Tokyo · Melbourne · Madras

Published by Chapman & Hall, 2–6 Boundary Row, London SE1 8HN

Chapman & Hall, 2–6 Boundary Row, London SE1 8HN, UK

Blackie Academic & Professional, Wester Cleddens Road, Bishopbriggs, Glasgow G64 2NZ, UK

Chapman & Hall, 29 West 35th Street, New York NY 10001, USA

Chapman & Hall Japan, Thomson Publishing Japan, Hirakawacho Nemoto Building, 6F, 1–7–11 Hirakawa-cho, Chiyoda-ku, Tokyo 102, Japan

Chapman & Hall Australia, Thomas Nelson Australia, 102 Dodds Street, South Melbourne, Victoria 3205, Australia

Chapman & Hall India, R. Seshadri, 32 Second Main Road, CIT East, Madras 600 035, India

First edition 1993

© 1993 M. R. Mathews

Phototypeset in Great Britain by Intype, London
Printed in Great Britain by the University Press, Cambridge

ISBN 0 412 47340 2

A catalogue record for this book is available from the British Library

Library of Congress Cataloging-in-Publication data

Mathews, M. R. (M. Reg)
  Socially Responsible Accounting / M.R. Mathews.
    p. cm.
  Includes bibliographical references and index.
  ISBN 0–412–47340–2
  1. Social accounting. I. Title.
HB141.5.M38 1993
657–dc20   92–38135
                                                       CIP

Contents

Preface

Modern accounting has roots which are firmly planted in 19th and 20th century industrial and commercial developments. The growth of accounting has, therefore, been concerned with reporting to investors (shareholders and creditors) on the stewardship of managers, while the interests of other groups in society have been largely ignored. If accounting is the language of business, then both the spoken and the written word have had a narrow vocabulary.

Social accounting (and more recently, environmental accounting) attempts to broaden the scope of the discipline by addressing the issues and audiences which have been neglected by traditional mainstream accounting developments. The issues addressed include employee- and product-related matters and externalities (market failures) and the environment; the audiences include employees, consumers and the general public.

We may justify the employment of alternative (additional) accounting disclosures in terms of attempts to influence the capital markets, but more properly in terms of the notions of organizational legitimacy and the social contract of business (and government) with society. The various types of social and environmental accounting are classified herein, in order to assist the reader to address the very wide dimension covered by the social view of the accounting function. Nevertheless, the ultimate unity of the discipline should not be forgotten.

Proponents of social and environmental accounting argue that eventually conventional financial and management accounting will be perceived as a subdivision of a wider approach to accounting; whereas the present position is that of social and environmental accounting being attached as an appendage to conventional accounting.

The approach taken in this book is not revolutionary but evolutionary; nevertheless, the existing perspectives of many readers will be challenged. The book incorporates both philosophical discussion and details of models and approaches which have been proposed or adopted by accountants in a number of attempts to provide information which is not provided by conventional accounting.

The problems to be addressed by socially responsible accounting are universal and international, as reflected by much of the content (and origin) of this book. The basic framework is that employed for a thesis presented to Loughborough University of Technology in 1987. The content reflects the author's residence in Australia and New Zealand and extensive visits to Canada and the United States, as well as his British origins.

I am pleased to acknowledge the long-term influence, through discussion and scholarly publication, which Professor R. H. Gray, now of the University of Dundee, has had on my thinking, and the assistance received from Mr Alan Nelson of Chapman & Hall. Extensive updating and revision has taken place during a period of study leave at the University of Montana in the United States. The opportunities provided by Dean L. Gianchetta and Professor B. P. Budge were very much appreciated.

The last and most significant acknowledgement is to my wife Rita, who has spent countless hours on word-processing, proof-reading and general encouragement. It is to her that this book is dedicated.

M. R. Mathews
Massey University, New Zealand.

Introduction to socially responsible accounting

1

INTRODUCTION

The history of accounting and record-keeping may be traced for over 6000 years. From the clay tablet records of the Mesopotamians (Keister, 1965, pp. 18–24) through the government-centred accounting systems of the Chou dynasty (Fu, 1971), the temple and estate records of the Greeks and Romans (Chatfield, 1977), to the charge and discharge activities of manorial accounting (Goldberg, 1971), various accounting practices contributed to the smooth functioning of society (that is, to social welfare) in the ancient world and up to the Middle Ages. The advent of modern record-keeping systems in the Italian states, so ably publicized by Pacioli (Goldberg, 1971, p. 12), required a particular level of societal development as well as the incentive of trade (Littleton, 1966, pp. 13–21).

Despite some disagreement about whether double-entry bookkeeping may have caused the capitalistic form of societal structure (Sombart, 1924) or was the product of pressures and demands within the existing society (Yamey, 1949, 1964; Winjum, 1970, 1971), it is generally agreed that the relationship between the development of accounting and the society in which it is situated is close and continuing.

Subsequent influences on the development of accounting include the Industrial Revolution and the development of the railways (Chatfield, 1977; Crossman, 1953), the legislative changes of the 19th century (Baxter and Davidson, 1977), the imposition of taxation (particularly in this century) and the events of the depression years. The accounting principles and practices which evolved were subsequently codified during the period 1920–40. This process has continued into recent decades (Mathews and Perera, 1991).

The relationship between accounting and the host society has been summed up very well by Goldberg:

This evolution has followed the pattern of responses to external influences which is present in all organic development and, as in the growth of organisms, the essence of later developments has been present in earlier stages of existence. It seems most unlikely that this evolution has reached its end; as we work and study new phases of development appear to be arising. Thus, economists and statisticians are beginning to explore the social implications of the techniques of accounting and the economic influences of its concepts and procedures, and the social responsibilities of accountants are continually increasing. (Goldberg, 1971, pp. 36–7)

The purpose of this book is to show the directions which have to be followed to illustrate what these social responsibilities are.

Accounting is a social construct and the relationship between the stage of development of the accounting discipline and the needs and preferences of society cannot be allowed to get too far apart if accounting (and accountants) are not to lose the standing that they have gained over many years. The reputation gained by accountants as preparers and auditors of company accounts and advisers to management, on both internal and external matters, is well known. Taxation accounting, internal auditing, the control of the electronic data-processing function, strategic and operational planning using mathematical models and, for some, a role in government activities have all been added over the past few decades. There are a number of common themes running through most of these activities;

1. *Traditional reporting.* Shareholders and management are the main constituents involved in preparing traditional external reports, and management the normal target of internal reporting (FASB, 1978). A narrow view of users is adopted and groups such as employees, consumers and the general public are not given adequate consideration in the reporting process, although recent developments show that some accountants recognize the needs of other constituencies (ASSC, 1975; HMSO, 1977).
2. *Reporting in monetary terms.* The method of reporting traditionally uses monetary aggregates with relatively little concern for non-monetary accounting and socially related measurements.
3. *Public costs.* Probably as a result of historical developments and the difficulties inherent in measurement, the measures used to capture the costs of production and operations do not take public costs into account. Only private (internal) costs are currently of interest to accountants and the management of entities. Externalities have been ignored by most accountants. The situation cannot continue for much longer, not least because

externalities in the form of pollution and industrial waste have now reached serious proportions in many industrialized societies (Galbraith, 1958; Beams and Fertig, 1971; Estes, 1972; Gray, 1990).

4. *The role of the accountant.* The involvement of accountants in government (at various levels) appears generally to have been limited to the traditional management and stewardship roles. However, recently introduced management techniques are now pointing the way towards the use of efficiency and effectiveness audits and performance measurements in non-traditional areas. Accountants must be part of these developments if they are to retain or extend their influence (Likierman and Creasey, 1985; Mayston, 1985).

These common themes are often associated with undisclosed values, including a belief in private property, in the efficiency of capital markets to effect resource allocation and the transfer of resources between parties, and the limitation of government intervention to external and macro control activities. In total these values amount to support for the capitalist system of ownership of production and distribution, and a restricted view of the rights of parties not involved in the market place.

The four themes identified above are subject to change. Societal changes indicate that the accounting discipline will need to change. Accountants will need to recognize additional interests in the form of new constituents; allow for non-monetary aggregates and different reporting styles; consider the external costs of operations; and, where appropriate, become involved in aspects of performance evaluation of government activities and publicly funded projects.

These changes could be accomplished without discarding the traditional philosophical values underlying the accepted accounting systems, although some strains may become apparent, particularly when considering the inclusion of externalities. These themes are all included within this book under the general heading of social accounting. New constituents, non-monetary aggregates and different reporting styles, the external costs of operations, and the areas of more socially relevant government accounting and reporting form the substance of socially responsible accounting. In each case an extensive literature was found to exist, although the extent to which this literature has influenced practice is frequently minimal. However, when compared with the total history of the development of accounting, the period of development taken up by social accounting has been very short. Social accounting is regarded by many academics and most practitioners as outside the general area of accounting, although support for some features of more socially responsible accounting has been found in a number of surveys (Barnett and Caldwell, 1974; Stiner, 1978; Mathews and Gordon, 1984).

GENERAL ORGANIZATION OF THE BOOK

The general stance taken in this work is that there is a case to be made for social accounting as a natural extension of the existing discipline, in line with changes in societal conditions and expectations. As such, social accounting may be considered as inevitable because as society changes, demanding greater and different degrees of accountability from managers of both public and private enterprises, accounting systems must evolve to satisfy these demands. If appropriate accounting systems do not evolve, other parties will organize themselves to fill the gap and thereby remedy the deficiency. This reaction would weaken the role and structure of accounting, perhaps with potentially serious and negative consequences for the discipline and the profession.

However, mere assertion of inevitability in the development of social accounting could be condemned as just normative theorizing which is currently out of favour. Clearly, we do not want to rely upon the sort of arguments that produced the following rebuke: 'Until recently, accounting theory largely consisted of a set of competing *a priori* arguments about the relative merits of alternative accounting measurements' (AAA, 1971, p. 77).

However, for some potential developments it is difficult to provide a case which is not at least partially normative. This point is considered by Gray, Owen and Maunders, who state that in relation to what they have termed corporate social reporting:

> The normative deductive theories attempt to answer the questions: 'How well does accounting practice satisfy objective X?' (e.g. users' needs), or 'How might accounting practice be improved in order to satisfy objective X?' They are thus more evaluative and are deduced from both our empirical knowledge of accounting practice and from some objective *held for* the accounting activity. As a result of being goal/objective-oriented, the normative-deductive theories are claimed to be more value-laden than the inductive theories in that they start from a value-judgement such as 'accounting activity *should* satisfy users' needs'. (Gray, Owen and Maunders, 1987, p. 65)

This study is mainly normative-deductive, although in many places reference is made to empirical work, where an understanding of the present state of the development of social accounting is required.

A case has to be made which justifies the development of social accounting (including the costs imposed on shareholders, customers, taxpayers and other parties). After justifying the concern with new forms of accounting and establishing the case for social accounting, it is necessary to consider the organization and administration of the procedural aspects, since accounting theories cannot be meaningful if divorced from a practical context.

Chapter 2 deals with justifications for the interest shown in social accounting. These are divided into three groups. The first form of justification is to provide information of value to shareholders and financial markets. In other words, social accounting disclosures have information content and can affect the prices of securities in share markets. The second justification is by means of a philosophical argument resting on the social contract between business and society as recognized by business ethicists. The notion of a social contract is used to argue the case for the wider disclosure of socially related information to the general public and employees, rather than only to shareholders and capital markets. This section provides some interesting features not commonly found in the accounting literature. Similar arguments can be made in respect of citizens and government bodies. Indeed, the origin of the social contract lies in the relationship between the government and the governed. The application of the social contract approach is complicated by the cultural differences which exist between national and sub-national groups. Considerable evidence for the existence and importance of cultural effects in accounting is considered at this point, together with the importance of these developments for socially responsible accounting.

The third justification for social accounting research and development rests upon a radical paradigm. Social structures are seen as exploitative; society consists of one social group oppressing another social group. Critical theorists argue the need for radical political change which, some argue, may be assisted by developments in social accounting. It is contended in this chapter that many of the arguments found in the literature of the radical paradigm are likely to be dysfunctional, in the search for a means of encouraging the acceptance and development of a more socially relevant accounting. This point is emphasized by showing that there is a basic lack of congruence between the radical paradigm and the political condition of current Anglo-American society. The fundamental value-systems of accountants would be violated by the radical paradigm. However, there is a place for radical paradigms in research and education, particularly to ensure that accounting does keep pace with the remainder of society and avoids simply conforming to the status quo.

Chapters 3 to 7 outline the development of social accounting across a wide spectrum. The dimensions covered include private and public sectors, the short, medium and long terms and the use of financial and non-financial measurements. The five classifications used to facilitate consideration are: social responsibility accounting; total impact accounting; socio-economic accounting; social indicators accounting; and societal accounting. The literature relating to each area is considered.

The final chapter summarizes the area covered in the book and notes probable future developments in the field.

THE EVOLUTIONARY POSITION

One of the features of the radical literature is that scholars are urged to make clear their philosophical positions in order that their contributions may be fully evaluated. This imperative is accepted by the author and consequently it must be stated that this book is based upon existing socio-economic conditions of a managed mixed economy and is evolutionary rather than revolutionary in orientation. The position argued is that a more socially responsible accounting may be justified and should be implemented, not to radically change society but to modify and improve our present system, by including measurement and reporting relationships which are currently excluded.

The overall contribution to the discussion of socially responsible accounting lies in providing arguments to justify the development and implementation of many aspects of social accounting which would meet the deficiencies perceived in the traditional model. The market is accepted with modification, and property ownership is supported provided that the longer rather than shorter-term perspective is adopted.

SUMMARY

This introductory chapter has set out briefly the development of accounting over a lengthy period of time, in response to societal needs and changes. The position of accounting as a social construct means that changes in society should logically lead to developments in accounting and reporting.

A number of the limitations of current accounting systems were identified, including the restriction of most reporting to shareholders; reliance on the use of only monetary measurements; the exclusion of externalities; and the need to extend modern accounting developments into the government and non-profit areas.

The general organization of the book and the philosophical position adopted by the author were reviewed. The work is evolutionary rather than revolutionary, normative-deductive in nature and concerned with two main themes: justifying the allocation of resources to new developments such as social accounting, and providing a structure or classifi-cation whereby the area known as social accounting may be more clearly understood and implemented.

Justifications for additional disclosures 2

INTRODUCTION

A number of early writers in the area of social accounting attempted to establish a need for the development of this sub-discipline. Davis (1973) presented the cases for and against the involvement of business in matters of social responsibility, a process which he regarded as inevitable (1976). Prakash (1975) provided a framework within which corporate social performance may be analysed, and Spicer (1978b) compared and contrasted classical, managerial and activist views of social performance. Other attempts to examine the notion of corporate social responsibility have included Fitch (1976), Dalton and Cosier (1982), and Lawrence (1982). References to public-interest matters and the accounting profession can be found in Neubauer (1971), Zeisel and Estes (1979) and Skousen (1982).

During the 1970s a series of reports by committees of the American Accounting Association dealt with measures of effectiveness for social programmes (1972), environmental effects of organizational behaviour (1973a), human resource accounting (1973b), the measurement of social costs (1974), accounting for social performance (1976), and social costs (1975). This activity reflected the social climate of the period and the position of the US economy which could afford additional accounting reports. The National Association of Accountants (NAA) also set up a committee to look at accounting for corporate social performance. This Committee reported in February and September 1974 (NAA, 1974a, 1974b).

Perhaps as a result of the greater maturity of the subject area, it is now quite common for advocates of social accounting and its many variants to make two, often implicit, assumptions. These are, first, that revised systems of accounting are desirable, justified and would fill a demonstrated need, and second, that the reader knows what these newer forms of accounting are. After studying the literature it is clear that neither assumption should really be made. The first assumption, that the various forms of social accounting are desirable, justified and fill a demonstrated need, is examined in this chapter.

Three broad groups of arguments which may be used to justify the use of scarce resources in making further accounting disclosures are examined. These are market-related, socially related and radically related arguments. Market-related arguments are used to advance the case for additional disclosures on the basis that shareholders and creditors will benefit from a more responsive market which is influenced by the information content intrinsic in the disclosures. This aspect of the problem is discussed in the first section and consists of the review of a number of market studies which seek to associate social responsibility disclosures with changes in earnings or share prices.

Socially related arguments are used where additional disclosures would be made to establish the moral nature of the corporation, to satisfy the implicit social contract between business and society and to legitimate the organization in the eyes of the public. In this case, the groups for whom the information is intended include employees, customers, the general public and government agencies. Shareholders and creditors may also find this information of benefit but the primary motivation is not to report to those groups.

Radically related arguments are those put forward by critical theorists who believe in an alternative model for society, including a different role for accounting. As previously stated, the basis of this book is evolutionary rather than revolutionary. Nevertheless, it is appropriate to note the important literature of the radical theorists.

MARKET-RELATED JUSTIFICATIONS: THE ASSOCIATION OF SOCIAL ACCOUNTING DISCLOSURES WITH THE FREE MARKET SYSTEM

INTRODUCTION

Proponents of a free market system of economic exchange normally argue against the imposition of social responsibility requirements on corporations. Furthermore, any assumption of social responsibility objectives by the management of corporations would be regarded by some as an improper use of shareholders' funds. It is usual in these cases to quote a number of economists, from Adam Smith to Milton Friedman, on the benefits of the 'invisible hand' in the maximization of aggregate social satisfaction through the use of an open market system. For example, Friedman (1962, p. 133) objects to the notion that corporate officers have moral responsibilities:

It shows a fundamental misconception of the character and nature of a free economy. In such an economy, there is one and only one social responsibility of business – to use its resources and engage in activities designed to increase its profits so long as it stays within the rules of the game, which is to say, engages in open and free competition without deception or fraud.

There are at least two deficiencies in the view put forward by Freidman. First, there is no such thing as a free economy since all presently operating economic systems have constraints on freedom of action. Secondly, it must be recognized that the 'rules of the game' will vary between different time periods and economic situations. If the 'rules of the game' includes the existing legal framework, then it might be argued that a Friedmanite approach to corporate management would probably result in greater government intervention, the opposite of what is desired by the advocates of a free market approach.

In contrast to the Freidmanite position, there are a number of arguments which may be advanced in support of at least some social responsibility (and hence socially responsible accounting) by corporations in a relatively free market system. These are:

1. A free market will be more efficient if more information is available to participants;
2. Empirical research has demonstrated that a measure of social responsibility by management may correlate with higher corporate income;
3. There is some evidence that share prices may be influenced by the social responsibility disclosures of corporations.

The first argument may affect all market participants. The others directly concern the welfare of the shareholders towards whom management have a stewardship-reporting relationship. These positions, relating to general disclosure, corporate income and shareholder wealth, are discussed below.

It should be noted that the discussion in this section is not concerned with rights, duties, obligations or any other moral concern. These matters are discussed in a later section.

INCREASING THE FLOW OF INFORMATION TO THE MARKET

The increased quantity of information sought by those advocating socially responsible accounting could serve to make the market more efficient. The conditions necessary for the (unattainable) perfect market include perfect information, that is, all participants know everything at the same time. Furthermore, there is no cost to the information, which is costless to the recipient. If the modern Freidmanite free market is to approximate the ideal of perfect competition, then the more information that is generally available, the more efficient the market should be. This approach, together with the legal/stewardship arguments, can be applied to the financial disclosures required of all corporations.

The advocates of social accounting argue for increased financial, non-financial, quantitative and qualitative disclosures in respect of employment practices, environmental impact, product safety, energy usage and community relations. All these may be relevant to interested parties, such as actual and potential employees, customers, regulatory bodies, shareholders and debtholders.

The majority of the information that is currently produced relates to the internal costs of the firm. There is another class of disclosure called externalities which, although more difficult to measure and value, has considerable potential for changing market behaviour. Externalities, such as pollution, mean that private costs are being allowed to cross into the public domain. These costs are not being included in the total cost of the good or service. In most firms the cost of production bears some relationship to the desired selling price, and selling price affects demand for the product (and vice versa) through the market. Consequently, a failure to capture all the manufacturing costs results in a lower total cost and may lead to a lower price and a greater quantity sold in the market place. This may not matter, but on the other hand, if the externality which leads to the lower costs (because it is not counted) is going to cause environmental damage, then the consumer is gaining a lower-priced product at the expense of the whole of society (both consumers and non-consumers). From this perspective a free market for securities cannot function properly in the absence of additional accounting measurements and disclosures because resource allocation is disrupted. Firms with higher pollution costs to society may currently have higher returns to investors and vice versa, leading to a diversion of resources. The capital maket is not as efficient as some would have us believe, because externalities are not included.

Arguments against the increase in information flow appear to rest on the grounds of confidentiality and the cost of producing and disclosing the information. Confidentiality arguments are concerned with the opportunities which competitors allegedly have to discover more about the organization than they already know. This is a weak argument since the disclosures are of material which would be known to most competitors if the market place is working efficiently. The cost argument may have more merit although, as demonstrated in the next section, the cost of the information may be considered as an investment by the organization in better public relations.

THE RELATIONSHIP BETWEEN SOCIAL RESPONSIBILITY ACCOUNTING
DISCLOSURES AND MARKET PERFORMANCE

The relationship between social accounting disclosures in annual reports and measures of market performance has been examined in a number of studies. The results have been mixed, with some researchers, for example Bowman and Haire (1975, pp. 49–53), establishing an interesting positive relationship between the two variables. Other studies have found no relationship, or even a negative correlation. Tables 2.1 to 2.5, which are modelled on a survey article by Arlow and Gannon (1982, pp. 235–41), provide a summary of much of the relevant research.

The research making up the market studies part of the social accounting literature attempts to relate some measure of social responsibility to measures of market performance. The choice of a measure of social responsibility varies widely as shown in Table 2.1. The four groups are reported separately as Tables 2.2 to 2.5 respectively. A reasonable amount of detail is provided, sufficient to identify the main features of each study and the results obtained.

Sturdivant and Ginter (1977) examined the connection between the performance of organizations on both traditional (earnings per share) and corporate social responsiveness bases and the attitude of corporate management. The corporations selected came from the list of those cited by Moskowitz as 'best' or 'worst' in terms of social performance. A third group of 'honourable mention' companies was added, giving three groups. There were 18, 29 and 20 firms in each group respectively.

A management attitude survey instrument was developed and tested. Factor analysis showed significant differences between the responses

Table 2.1 Choice of social responsibility measure

	Method	Studies
1.	Subjective ratings of corporation performance	Parket and Eilbirt (1975) Sturdivant and Ginter (1977)
2.	Quasi-objective ratings based on annual report content or structural analysis	Bowman and Haire (1975) Vance (1975) Alexander and Bucholz (1978) Ingram (1978) Abbott and Monsen (1979)
3.	Pollution measures as reported by companies themselves	Belkaoui (1976) Mahapatra (1984)
4.	Pollution measures as reported by parties other than the companies	Folger and Nutt (1975) Spicer (1978a) Stevens (1982) Shane and Spicer (1983) Freedman and Stagliano (1984)

Table 2.2 Studies using subjective ratings of corporate performance. From Mathews and Perera (1993)

	Study	Sample	Indicator of social performance	Indicator of market performance	Outcome of study
1.	Parker and Eilbirt (1975)	80 firms in 1971 Forbes Roster of Biggest Corporations	Author's judgement	NI NI as a percent of sales, NI as a percent of shareholders equity, EPS	Socially responsible firms (80) have greater median values on all dimensions compared to 1973 Fortune 500 list
2.	Sturdivant and Ginter (1977)	28 corporations in 1975 Fortune 500	Moskowitz's ratings of best or worst, and author's rating	Growth in EPS relative to industry average 1967–74	Best and honourable mention significantly higher growth in EPS than worst-rated corporations

Table 2.3 Studies using quasi-objective ratings based upon annual reports or structural analysis. From Mathews and Perera (1993)

	Study	Sample	Indicator of social performance	Indicator of market performance	Outcome of study
1.	Bowman and Haire (1975)	88 firms in food processing in 1973 Moody's and Standard and Poor industries indices	Percent of prose in annual report on social responsibility	Mean or median ROE, 1968–72 or 1969–73	Both mean and median ROE higher for firms with some discussion than none. Medium mention firms have significantly greater median ROE than either high or low mention
2.	Vance (1975)	45 and 50 major corporations	Ratings by students and executives in 1972 *Business and Society Review*	Per share stock price 1/1/75 as percent 1/1/74 price	Average ratings of both groups negatively correlated with 1974 stock market performance. No significant relationships
3.	Alexander and Bucholz (1978)	41 firms from Vance (1975)	Same as Vance (1975)	Risk adjusted ROE 1970–4 and 1971–3	No significant relationships
4.	Abbott and Monsen (1979)	450 corporations in 1975 *Fortune 500*	Social Involvement Disclosure Scale (number of social action disclosures in annual reports)	Total returns to investors 1964–74	No meaningful difference in total returns to investors for high and low involvement firms
5.	Ingram (1978)	387 *Fortune 500* companies (1970–6)	SRA Disclosures Annual Reports	Computsat price dividends earnings tape	Information content of firms' social responsibility disclosures conditional upon market segment rather than a general cross-section of firms

Table 2.4 Pollution measures as reported by companies. From Mathews and Perera (1993)

	Study	Sample	Indicator of social performance	Indicator of market performance	Outcome of study
1.	Belkaoui (1976)	Two groups of 50 US corporations from different industries	Pollution control expenses at least 1% of sales plus control group disclosures Standard and Poor 500	Monthly closing stock prices 18 months before and after expenditures	Substantial but temporary positive effect on stock market prices for companies disclosing pollution data
2.	Mahapatra (1984)	67 firms from six industries, 60 firms as control group	Expenditure on pollution control	Compstat PDE tape	Pollution control expenditure and high profitability not positively associated. Expenditures for pollution control do not automatically lead to higher market returns

Table 2.5 Pollution measures not reported by companies. From Mathews and Perera (1993)

	Study	Sample	Indicator of social performance	Indicator of market performance	Outcome of study
1.	Folger and Nutt (1975)	Nine paper companies	Government pollution indices	P/E ratio. Mutual fund purchases (in dollars). Common stock price. (Data from selected quarters 1971–2)	No positive relationships
2.	Spicer (1978a)	18 firms in pulp and paper industry 1968–73	CEP studies of pollution control developed into a pollution index, related to productive capacity and plant numbers	Profitability, size, total risk, systematic risk, price/earnings ratio	Companies with better pollution control records tend to have higher profitability, larger size, lower total risks, lower systematic risks and higher price/earnings ratio than companies with poorer pollution control records. Relatively short-lived phenomena
3.	Stevens (1982)	54 firms in four industries subject to CEP reports	CEP pollution reports	Effect of CEP reports of pollution status of corporation on earnings per share	Cumulative average excess returns for portfolios of firms with *high* estimated expenditures for pollution control are consistently below the returns for portfolios of firms with *low* estimated expenditures

4.	Shane and Spicer (1983)	72 firms in four industry areas	CEP pollution reports	Share prices over a six-day period before and after publication of CEP reports	Sample firms' large negative abnormal returns on two days immediately prior to newspaper reports of release of CEP studies. Low rankings associated with more negative returns on publication
5.	Freedman and Stagliano (1984)	27 weaving, finishing and knitting mills (1984)	OSHA dust disclosures through SEC 10K reports	Stock price movements	Disclosures on impact of new cotton dust emission standard do not have significant information content for investors

by managers of corporations in the various groups. The performance characterization of corporations, over a ten-year period, compared to the industry average, was set against the social performance rating, and the test results showed no difference between 'best' and 'honourable mention' firms. However, statistically significant differences were obtained at the 0.01 level between 'best'/'honourable mention' and 'worst' performers.

Sturdivant and Ginter (1977, p. 38) concluded:

> While the findings certainly will not support the argument that socially responsive companies will always outperform less responsive firms in the long run, there is evidence that, in general the responsively managed firms will enjoy better economic performance. It would be simple minded, at best, to argue a one-on-one cause-effect relationship. However, it would appear that a case can be made for an association between responsiveness to social issues and the ability to respond effectively to traditional business challenges.

Table 2.3 repeats the same general approach but utilizes measures of social responsibility performance which appear to be more objective, although still relying on judgement to a considerable extent.

In a 1975 study Bowman and Haire investigated the association between social responsibility disclosures and shareholder benefits in the form of increased income to the organization. The search for a relationship between these two variables was directed towards the development of a strategic posture by management. The sample consisted of the 1973 annual reports of 82 food-processing companies. The return-on-equity figure used was an average of the period 1969–73 (in a few cases 1968–72) taken from Moody's or Standard and Poor's published indices. The surrogate measure for social responsibility was the proportion of prose devoted to social responsibiity matters in the annual report. This measure was investigated by comparing the disclosure of social responsibility items by companies accepted by critics as socially responsible with the performance of a random sample of companies. The results of this test showed the measure to be capable of separating these companies into two groups on the basis of their demonstrated social responsibility.

Using the proportional measure of social responsibility items reported as an indication of social responsibility, Bowman and Haire (1975) found a statistically significant relationship when associated with income. A medium ranking, on a scale of low-medium-high for social responsibility disclosures, was associated with the highest return on equity (using the previous five years).

The authors were most concerned to avoid unintended interpretations of their work:

> We are reporting an association of two measures; we are not implying a directional causal relationship. It does not follow, simply, from these data, that more discussion of corporate responsibility (and inferentially, on the basis of our tests of the measure, more activity in this area) causes greater profits. At the same time, it is perfectly clear that more corporate social responsibility is not associated with less profits.   (Bowman and Haire, 1975, p. 52)

The association is explained in terms of the type of management involved. Social responsibility accounting disclosures are 'a signal of the presence of a style of management that extends broadly across the entire business function and leads to more profitable operation' (ibid. p. 54). Unfortunately, the position is more complex than reported by Bowman and Haire, since other studies do not report comparable findings.

Ingram extended the range of social responsibility measures used to include environmental, fair business, personnel, community and product-related matters. The results were only significant when the sample of firms was partitioned into segments. The associations were of a limited nature since: 'Apparently, combining the segments . . . washes out the effects of the disclosures on security returns' (Ingram, 1978, p. 283).

The influence of the market segment is particularly important:

> These findings suggest that it may be important to evaluate information content by analyzing the impact of the signals on market segments (or segments identified by firm-specific characteristics), rather than on a general cross-section of firms.   (Ibid., p. 283)

The results set out in Table 2.3 show considerable variation, with Bowman and Haire (1975) showing a positive relationship, especially for medium social responsibility rated companies, and Ingram (1978) showing positive results when using a market segment approach. However, the other contributors found either no relationship or a negative relationship. It should be noted that a negative relationship still demonstrates information content to market participants, but would not support (justify) the use of resources to produce socially orientated information.

Table 2.4 shows the results of studies which have used pollution-related measures supplied by the companies themselves. Belkaoui found some short-term increases in share prices as a result of the disclosure of pollution expenditure:

> In general, this study refutes the suggestion that the worst offenders in the reporting of social costs will be rewarded more in the capital market. In fact, on the basis of these results, managers may be advised to allocate a proportion of their resources to pollution control and to report these expenditures to the stockholders. (Belkaoui, 1976, p. 30)

Mahapatra demonstrated that the 'ethical investor' was not active at the time this study was undertaken, since the results were consistent with the existence of a 'rational economic investor':

> The conclusion is that the investors view pollution control expenditure, legally or voluntary, as a drain on resources which could have been invested profitably, and do not 'reward' the companies for socially responsible behaviour. Thus an average investor is not an 'ethical investor' and industries and investors left to themselves do not have any incentive to spend for pollution and manifest socially desirable behaviour. (Mahapatra, 1984, p. 37)

The next group of studies are perhaps the most important in the series. They are generally more recent and more sophisticated in the analysis and have a uniform data base, namely, the reports on pollution activities of industries and companies supplied by outside parties, as shown in Table 2.5.

Results may be described as mixed since although Folger and Nutt (1975) did not find any positive relationships, Spicer (1978a) found that for a limited sample of pulp and paper companies the disclosures by an outside body (the Council on Economic Priorities) were associated with profitability, size of company, total risk, systematic risk and price-earnings. All associations were in the direction favouring disclosure. In other words, shareholders would benefit if companies worked towards better pollution-control records. This study was criticized by Chen and Metcalf (1980) on a number of methodological grounds. In his reply Spicer stressed the findings as **associations** between variables and not **caused relationships**:

> My primary objective was to determine whether a perceived association between corporate social performance . . . and the investment worth of corporations' securities . . . was borne out by observation. (Spicer, 1980, p. 178)

Folger and Nutt (1975) used a reduced sample of nine companies (in order to obtain stable earnings histories and avoid the results of merger activity). They developed indices of pollution and related these to quarterly price-earnings ratios from March 1971 to March 1972. No significant relationship was found for either short- or long-run performance.

The citing of major paper producers as polluters did not affect the market price of their stock. The following explanation may still be important:

> Yet, the results are in agreement with the expected results in an efficient capital market composed of a majority of 'return' conscious investors – that is, while socially conscious investors might sell the shares of less socially responsible companies, such sales would be viewed as bargains by the return conscious investors.   (Folger and Nutt, 1975, p. 159)

The reaction of the investing public is likely to vary from time to time and from place to place in line with evolving social preferences. Gray (1990) has noted the potentially important development of investment for 'ethical investors' and Owen (1992) includes references to 'green investing'.

Stevens found that 'high' estimated expenditures for pollution control were associated with lower cumulative average excess returns, in comparison to 'low' estimated expenditure where the cumulative average excess returns were not reduced. The disclosures had information content but the current shareholders would suffer a loss of capital value as the information became available to the market. In the longer term, however, shareholders should benefit:

> The data examined in this study represent a source of information which may have been previously unavailable to the market. As such, its publication could provide meaningful data for assessing the timing and magnitude of future cash flows.   (Stevens, 1982, p. 25)

Shane and Spicer demonstrated that the use of externally produced and publicized environmental information may have an effect on the share prices of polluting corporations, when the disclosures are first made. In a manner similar to Stevens', this study demonstrated the information effect of the disclosures, although to the short-term discomfort of the present shareholders. However, given the importance of the efficient market and the manner in which the marginal investor reacts, it is interesting that:

> The reported results also are consistent with investors using the information released by the CEP to discriminate between companies with different pollution-control performance records.   (Shane and Spicer, 1983, p. 535)

In the longer term this should achieve environmental goals of lower pollution levels.

Freedman and Stagliano (1984) found no evidence of information content since there was no positive or negative association of share prices with the particular pollution disclosures under investigation. The authors offered a number of possible explanations, including an efficient market which had already impounded the information before it was disclosed or a sub-market for particular firms that was not efficient at all (p. 318).

OTHER APPROACHES

Belkaoui (1980) conducted an experiment to determine the impact of socio-economic statements on an investment decision. Sets of accounts were prepared in which the treatment of pollution costs was varied from conventional (that is to say, none) to footnote exposure of pollution control costs to full disclosure of the costs and their effects. Professional groups of accountants and bankers were then asked to 'invest' in the two companies (that is, to vary the portfolio held). The investment strategy was also varied between investing for capital gains or for income. In conclusion Belkaoui reported that:

> The findings attest to the general relevance of socio-economic accounting information for the bankers under any investment strategy, and for the accountants only under an investment strategy focussing on capital gains.   (Belkaoui, 1980, p. 280)

and went on to make the important point that:

> The significant interaction effects between the three examined factors provide a warning about any generalisations to be derived from a similar field experiment. In other words the informational content of any new information, e.g. socio-economic accounting information, is to be ascertained in terms of its relations to relevant environmental variables.   (Ibid.)

SECTION SUMMARY

This section has considered the results of a number of studies which were aimed at establishing the existence of any relationship between social responsibility accounting disclosures and measures of market performance. The findings from a number of studies are conflicting, although it may be argued that the overall weight lies towards the view that disclosure of non-traditional information does have utility for shareholders and the security market because information content is established regardless of the direction in which share prices move. Those advocating a market-related approach to justifying additional expenditure on disclosures should derive support from these studies because a concrete relationship between disclosure and share price effect was being established. This concrete relationship would assist managers and investors to make more rational economic decisions.

The market-related studies, as applied to accounting research, are concerned with the traditional relationship of managers and investors. Any justification for social accounting which falls within this approach must establish that shareholders could make better decisions and benefit economically in the long term from having the additional information. The results of the studies reviewed (a reasonable cross-section of the total number available) suggest that the issue is complicated by intervening variables and the need to employ sophisticated techniques in order to establish statistically significant relationships. The relationships detected are characterized as associations and not caused relationships.

Although potential benefits may have been indicated by the work outlined in this section the associated costs have not been determined and, therefore, a cost-benefit interrelationship cannot be established. Nevertheless, it is argued that social accounting may be justified to shareholders as an aid to market efficiency and improved decision making.

SOCIALLY RELATED ARGUMENTS; SOCIAL ACCOUNTING, THE SOCIAL CONTRACT AND ORGANIZATIONAL LEGITIMACY

INTRODUCTION

The arguments in favour of forms of social accounting that are derived from market studies will not necessarily be relevant to a wider audience. Share-market reaction to social accounting disclosures is less meaningful to non-equity holders, employees, customers and the general public than to shareholders and creditors. To interest these groups in social accounting disclosures it is necessary to look at the basic functioning of industrial and commercial activities, and to enter the moral debate surrounding the notions of a social contract between business and society. This approach to justify the expenditure of resources on social accounting falls within the area of socially related arguments.

The notion of the social contract has been expressed by Shocker and Sethi (1974, p. 67) as follows:

> Any social institution – and business is no exception – operates in society via a social contract, expressed or implied, whereby its survival and growth are based on:

(i)   the delivery of some socially desirable ends to society in general and,

(ii) the distribution of economic, social, or political benefits to groups from which it derives its power.

In a dynamic society, neither the sources of institutional power nor the needs for its services are permanent. Therefore, an institution must constantly meet the twin tests of legitimacy and relevance by demonstrating that society requires its services and that the groups benefiting from its rewards have society's approval.

Although it is not difficult to find references to the need for corporations to be accountable to a wider audience (Nader, 1973; Galbraith, 1974), the moral position of the corporation is much more difficult to establish. It is only after satisfactorily answering questions about the moral position of the corporation that the notion of a social contract can be considered.

THE MORAL POSITION OF THE CORPORATION

Several contrary positions may be examined, in particular the moral-person view and the structural-restraint view. The most simplistic approach is the moral-person view which argues that corporations are moral persons and therefore are moral agents: consequently corporations are morally responsible for their actions. There are clearly difficulties in establishing this case, since corporations cannot act intentionally by themselves or exercise the normal functions of persons. The legal personality of the corporation is a convenient fiction, the person-related functions are exercised by directors or managers on behalf of the corporation.

It has been argued that corporations cannot be held to be morally at fault because they are not physical persons (French, 1979; Ladd, 1970). Manning has made the point that if corporations are moral persons they have to be treated fairly, which may have an effect on the ability of society to find fault with the actions of the corporation:

If we accept the view that moral persons have a right to be treated fairly and corporations are moral persons, then they have the right to be treated fairly. The right to be treated fairly requires that we refrain from making moral fault attributions of the person who has the right, unless we can show that certain conditions are met.   (Manning, 1984, p. 79)

These conditions are utilitarian, are not related to fairness and are associated with determining causal effect, compensation for those who may suffer injury and prevention of any recurrence of the action which caused the breach in the first place (ibid., pp. 82–4).

The opposite view is that corporations cannot be moral agents of any kind, because their actions are controlled by their structures and, therefore, moral freedom often cannot be exercised. If taken to an extreme position the structural restraint view would mean that the only way in which the actions of corporations could be controlled (in any moral sense) would be by extensive legislation. However, corporations vary considerably in size, type and public stance on many issues. These differences allow the specification of certain conditions by which a corporation may qualify as a moral agent.

Donaldson (1982, p. 30) outlined these conditions as follows:

> In order to qualify as a moral agent, a corporation would need to embody a process of moral decision-making. On the basis of our previous discussion, this process seems to require, at a minimum:
>
> 1. The capacity to use moral reasons in decision-making;
> 2. The capacity of the decision-making process to control not only overt corporate acts, but also the structure of policies and rules.

Corporations may qualify as moral agents (but not moral persons) if they subscribe to the conditions above. If they do not, then there would seem to be support for a structural restraint view (which in turn may mean increased legislative control and restraint).

Donaldson (1982) suggests that one of the conditions for qualifying as a corporation (presumably as a legal entity) should be that an organization meets the conditions of moral agency. This view is reinforced by the rights and responsibilities which corporations possess and which point to conditions of moral agency being associated with conditions of corporate status. Corporate rights are granted in most developed industrial countries and include limited liability for the shareholders, and unlimited life, the ability to sue and be sued, and contractural rights for the corporation as of a natural person. In return, the responsibilities owed by corporations to the rest of society (including other corporations) include a number of direct and indirect moral obligations.

The direct obligations of corporations are specified explicitly by statute, case law regulation and contract and involve shareholders, employees, suppliers and customers. The indirect obligations are not formally specified and involve parties with whom the corporation has no direct contractual relationship, including competitors, local communities and the general public. Some parties will be included in both sets of obligations, for example, employees may be customers, employees and members of the general public.

Breaches of direct obligations are usually identifiable and may be settled through legal action or by adverse publicity (probably leading to legislation), if not through the specified terms of the contract. It is the indirect obligations that cause problems, because they are not readily identifiable, may not be agreed between the parties to disputes, and frequently give rise to measurement and valuation problems, even where their existence can be agreed upon. The indirect obligations give rise to the notion of a social contract between business and society. These issues underlie many of the problems of accounting for externalities.

THE SOCIAL CONTRACT OF BUSINESS WITH SOCIETY

In a speech to the Harvard Business School in 1969, Henry Ford II is reported to have stated:

> The terms of the contract between industry and society are changing . . . Now we are being asked to serve a wider range of human values and to accept an obligation to members of the public with whom we have no commercial transactions. (Donaldson, 1982, p. 36)

The notion of a social contract originated in political philosophy, where it is argued that society in general accepts an overriding control over individual freedoms in order to achieve collective goals. However, a social contract underlies the arrangement, and the failure to deliver the expected outcomes may justify a revolt on the part of the general society. Consequently:

> The political social contract provides a clue for understanding the contract for business. If the political contract serves as a justification for the existence of the state, then the business contract by parity of reasoning should serve as the justification for the existence of the corporation. (Ibid., p. 37)

The social contract would exist between corporations (usually limited companies) and individual members of society. Society (as a collection of individuals) provides corporations with their legal standing and attributes and the authority to own and use natural resources and to hire employees. Organizations draw on community resources and output both goods and services and waste products to the general environment. The corporation has no inherent rights to these benefits, and in order to allow their existence, society would expect benefits to exceed the costs to society.

There are a number of potential drawbacks to the operation of the social contract, where customers and employees may both be affected by non-performance. Social costs for consumers (and non-consumers) include the depletion of natural resources and increasing environmental pollution. A less easily recognized, but equally important, cost occurs because of the 'diffusion of individual moral responsibility which sometimes occurs in productive organizations' (ibid., p. 50).

Employees may feel responsible to their superiors within the hierarchy, but not to the end-user of the product or service. Profit-seeking organizations accumulate power as well as wealth, which enables them to interact with government in a manner which may be to the disadvantage of the ordinary consumer. The generation and enhancement of monopoly power may result from these interactions. Employees may suffer as a result of their work in productive organizations, including alienation and an inability (in the case of lower-level employees) to control their working conditions. Furthermore, in some cases the design of the productive system may lead to monotony and the dehumanization of workers.

In addition to the maximization of the benefits and the minimization of the problems outlined above, the social contract between productive organizations and the individual member of society would include an element of justice. As Donaldson has expressed the issue:

> the application of the concept of justice to productive organizations appears to imply *that productive organizations avoid deception or fraud, that they show respect for their workers as human beings, and that they avoid any practice that systematically worsens the situation of a given group in society.*   (Ibid., p. 53, original emphasis)

Some theorists would argue that the 'ideal' in respect of employees and the social contract would be a different relationship, that belongs in the next section dealing with the radical approach. However, the moral agency of the corporation and the social contract between a productive organization and the general public does not contain any imperative towards a change in the management or structure of the organization, beyond those necessary to reach the state of a moral agent and to maintain the contract.

THE STUDY OF BUSINESS ETHICS

The study of business ethics may be seen as the practical expression of philosophical discussions on the social contract between business and society. Henderson explored the differences between lawyers and business executives in their attitudes to business ethics which he defined thus: 'Business ethics is the continuing process of re-defining the goals and rules of business activity' (Henderson, 1984, p. 163). Henderson has offered a 'spectrum of ethicality' to enable corporate executives to

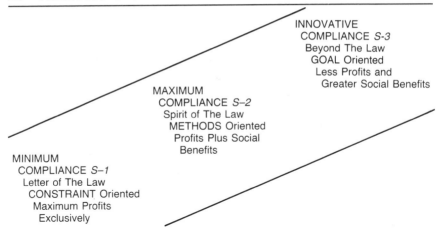

Figure 2.1 A graphic conceptualization of the spectrum of ethicality. Source: Henderson (1984, p. 169).

clarify and defend the postures they select (ibid., p. 169). This is shown in Figure 2.1.

Grcic (1985) has put forward the notion of consumer and employee representatives on the boards of directors of public corporations to promote corporate moral behaviour.

THE CORPORATE REPORT AND THE SOCIAL CONTRACT

The Corporate Report (ASSC, 1975) was the most significant of the conceptual frameworks (for socially responsible accounting) produced by committees and working groups on behalf of major accounting organizations. This document was published on behalf of the Institute of Chartered Accountants in England and Wales. The significance of this report for the socially related argument is that there was an underlying philosophical position very similar to that of the social contract of business with society. Although the social contract basis was not formally acknowledged, it appeared to underlie such statements as are identified in the basic philosophy of the report, key points of which are reproduced below:

1.1 Our basic approach has been that corporate reports should seek to satisfy, as far as possible, the information needs of users; they should be useful.

1.2 In our view there is an implicit responsibility to report publicly (whether or not required by law or regulation) incumbent on every economic entity whose size or format renders it significant.

1.3 We consider the responsibility to report publicly (referred to later as public accountability) is separate from and broader than the legal obligation to report and arises from the custodial role played in the community by economic entities.

1.4 The reporting responsibility we identify is an all-purpose one, intended for the general information of all users outside those charged with the control and management of the organisation.

1.5 In this context public accountability does not imply more than the responsibility to provide general purpose information.

1.6 Corporate reports are the primary means by which the management of an entity is able to fulfil its reporting responsibility by demonstrating how resources with which it has been entrusted have been used.

1.8 Users of corporate reports we define as those having a reasonable right to information concerning the reporting entity.

1.9 The groups we identify as having a reasonable right to information and whose information needs should be recognised by corporate reports are: The equity investor group, the loan creditor group, the employee group, the analyst-advisor group, the business contact group, the government and the public.   (ASSC, 1975, pp. 15–17)

CONCLUDING COMMENTS ON THE SOCIAL CONTRACT

The productive organization exists to satisfy certain social interests:

Productive organizations . . . are subject to moral evaluations which transcend the boundaries of the political systems that contain them. The underlying function of all such organizations from the standpoint of society is to enhance social welfare through satisfying consumer and worker interests, while at the same time remaining within the bounds of justice. When they fail to live up to these expectations they are deserving of moral criticism. When an organization, in the United States or elsewhere, manufactures a product that is inherently dangerous, or when it pushes its employees beyond reasonable limits, it deserves moral condemnation: the organization has failed to live up to a hypothetical contract – a contract between itself and society.   (Donaldson, 1982, p. 57)

If we accept this view then any techniques of data collection, analysis and disclosure that enables society to evaluate the performance of the organization are both legitimate and desirable. The socially related arguments for social accounting show how social accounting may be justified as the provision of additional information to audiences other than shareholders and creditors. However, if management is unwilling to consider the social contract as a justification for additional disclosures, they may consider organizational legitimacy as an alternative position.

ORGANIZATIONAL LEGITIMACY

An alternative view of the relationship between the corporation and society is offered by Lindblom (1984). The social contract is an abstraction, a useful device for the analysis of the role of the corporation in relation to society. The social contract is ongoing and continually renewable; furthermore, the basis of a collectivity is one of a voluntary association of individuals, any or all of whom may decide to leave the collectivity if their needs are not receiving due attention.

Lindblom used the societal context (US) of the challenge to established patterns of responsibility and control during the 1960s and 1970s to analyse the notion of corporate social responsibility. Lindblom states that there has been a change from 'not doing harm' to 'doing something positive' in terms of the expectations of society towards business. At the same time, changes in the organizational structure of developed societies are making responses to changing societal needs more difficult and time consuming:

> One interpretation of the corporate responsibility challenges of the mid 1960s to the mid 1970s might be that, as the environmental conditions of the original contract changed, the public expected business to be responsive to those changes. While business had undergone a structural change which made it less responsive to the public. (Lindblom, 1984, p. 15)

Lindblom went on to argue that the social contract leads logically to the concept of organizational legitimacy which has been defined in the following manner:

> Organizations seek to establish congruence between the social values associated with or implied by their activities and the norms of acceptable behavior in the larger social system of which they are a part. Insofar as these two value systems are congruent we can speak of organizational legitimacy. When an actual or potential disparity exists between the two value systems, there will exist a threat to organizational legitimacy. (Dowling and Pfeffer, 1975, p. 122)

Neither making a profit nor observing legal requirements will establish organizational legitimacy. This quality can only come from a reference to the norms and values of society. The notion of organizational legitimacy is not an absolute or a constant, because organizations differ considerably in their visibility to society as a whole and some are more heavily dependent than others upon social and political support.

Organizational legitimacy has been summarized by Lindblom in the following terms:

1. Legitimacy is not synonymous with economic success or legality.
2. Legitimacy is determined to exist when the organization goals, output, and methods of operation are in conformance with societal norms and values.
3. Legitimacy challenges are related to the size of the organization and to the amount of social and political support it receives with the more visible being most likely to be challenged.
4. Legitimacy challenges may involve legal, political or social sanctions. (Lindblom, 1984, pp. 20–1)

The implications which the notion of organizational legitimacy has for the management of the corporation includes better communication with society. This enlarged accounting or accountability may be essential for the continued existence of the corporation in its present form:

> To the extent, then, that the accounting profession wishes to continue to provide relevant information to external users, the legitimacy challenges serve as an indication of a need for change in the accounting function.   (Ibid., pp. 30–1)

The arguments put forward by Lindblom connect the philosophical propositions of the social contract as put forward by Donaldson with the need for corporate social disclosures, through the notion of organizational legitimacy. This pragmatic justification may be used with managers who do not necessarily accept the social contract arguments, but recognize the need to influence the general public through additional disclosures. Some decision-makers may accept the need for social accounting even though it may be for the 'wrong' reasons.

ARGUMENTS AGAINST THE SOCIAL CONTRACT PRINCIPLE

The review which follows is drawn from a monograph which looks at corporate social responsibility from a Friedmanite viewpoint. Den Uyl argues that the corporate social responsibility debate is primarily a moral issue and that demands for change were directed at 'the very values inherent in a market oriented system of production, and that makes these challenges moral challenges' (Den Uyl, 1984, p. 3). He deplores the lack of rigour of the moral debate and what he sees as the avoidance of ethical issues. Theories about the morality of corporate social responsibility are discussed within the following framework:

1. The fundamentalist theory (also called traditionalist or classical) made up of
    (a) functional theory (Levitt);
    (b) individual agreement theory (Friedman).
2. Social permission theory, which is made up of
    (a) constituency theory;
    (b) legal framework theory;
    (c) corporate citizenship theory.

The social permission school works in opposition to the fundamentalist school. The social permission approach is based upon the notion that corporation management must deal fairly with all constituents (constituency theory), be good citizens (citizenship theory) and recognize that corporations are creations of the state (legal framework theory).

The functional theory

The functional theory, which seeks to avoid dominance by any one section of society, is described by Den Uyl as conceiving of the debate in morally neutral or amoral terms:

> It cannot be denied that the position has great short term pragmatic and rhetorical appeal. But in the final analysis, the functional view cannot offer any criteria for distinguishing the legitimate claim or offer any form of consistent guidance. (Den Uyl, 1984, p. 10)

and:

> Ultimately the argument suggests that the whole issue of CSR reduces to a power game – with business currently on the losing end of the struggle. (Ibid., p. 12)

Den Uyl argues that because the functional theory is pragmatic and amoral there is no place for it in the discussion; which may account for his ignoring organizational legitimacy because the approach appears to be equivalent in moral status to the functional theory.

Social permission theory

In examining social permission theory Den Uyl rejected the arguments of those who see the corporation as created by the state (legal framework theory) although conceding that a modified view, 'the social creation approach', would make the theory stronger. His major attack was reserved for Donaldson and the social contract approach. The notion that the corporation is permitted to operate by society is rejected unless the corporation is only a trustee for societal resources and not an owner of those resources. Donaldson, it was argued, began with an assumption 'that individuals (corporate or otherwise) are entitled to their goals and holdings only so long as those goals or holdings service the interests of society' (ibid., p. 17). Den Uyl rejected this view as oppressive, and ignored many of the limitations which both individuals and corporations face when relating to the authority of the modern state. For example, restrictions on transfers of property (sales of goods) to foreign states, transfers of funds subject to exchange control regulations and the compulsory purchase of property (land) by the state for roads, airports and similar purposes, are all features of modern society.

In dealing with the legal framework theory (also referred to as the concession theory) Den Uyl did not refer to any of the specific features which make companies unique in our society, such as creation of the corporation as a legal person with unlimited life, limited liability for shareholders, differential tax rates and tax concessions, and the enormous economic and political power of the corporation. This is not surprising, since his main purpose was to provide a moral basis for supporting a Friedmanite view through the individual agreement theory.

Individual agreement theory

Den Uyl referred to the strong moral commitment represented by the sanctity of the contract, which he saw as the basis of the frequently quoted statement by Friedman that the only responsibility of business is to make profits, suject to remaining within the legal framework. The individual agreement theory argues that shareholders want to maximize profits from their investment:

> Thus, the corporation is not an end in itself, nor is it an essentially public institution despite the large numbers of persons who may be associated with it . . . It would seem to follow, then, that corporations are not creatures of the state, but are, rather, private institutions whose existence is recognised by law.   (Den Uyl, 1984, pp. 22–3)

This philosophical position would seem to be central to Den Uyl's argument and also to the fears of many people that corporations are often so large and influential that they are not under the control or influence of individual investors but of less-accountable managers. Den Uyl argued that Friedman's position does not prevent corporations pursuing moral goals, provided profitability is not reduced. He went on to discuss his theory of individual rights, the dichotomy of morality and profits, and finally put forward guidelines for what he regards as responsible behaviour.

A theory of individual rights

In addressing the theory of individual rights Den Uyl was concerned with the rights of an individual to be free from coercion by other individuals. His exposition concentrated upon the 'negative' aspects of interrelationships, because 'positive' aspects are seen as placing individuals on different levels in their dealings with one another:

> Individuals must refrain from crossing the boundaries of others. 'Positive' rights, which require the taking of the resources of some for the benefit of others, treat the ends of some persons as more significant than the ends of others. Indeed, it is virtually impossible to maintain a system of individual rights if one admits the existence of positive rights . . . (Den Uyl, 1984, pp. 25–6)

This treatment of individual rights assumes equality of all individual characteristics, not only in legal and contractual relationships but in economic and political bargaining power as well. Den Uyl assumed throughout his explanation that corporate social responsibility involves the diminution of the benefits of one group to satisfy the perceived needs of another group. This approach ignores the interrelationships which may persist between groups. For example, employees may also be shareholders. Unequal power positions render the argument that individual rights must be treated equally untenable in modern society.

The dichotomy between morality and profits

It is argued that there is no dichotomy between morality and profits because the pursuit of profit fulfils the obligations that management has towards the owners of the business. Provided that profitability is not reduced, management may engage in actions which are considered to be socially responsible. This argument overlooks or ignores any longer-term perspective.

Guidelines for responsible behaviour

In the section entitled 'Guidelines for Responsible Behaviour' Den Uyl derived three principles. The first, called the 'principle of respect for individual rights', comes from the individual agreement theory outlined previously. The second, the 'principle of responsible recommendations', comes from the position that the pursuit of profit is an obligation and, therefore, any recommendation which does not take this factor into account is not responsible. Finally, provided the first two primary principles are followed, then the effects of alternative courses of action on various parties should be evaluated. This is referred to as the 'principle of moral consideration.'

The three basic principles may be used to evaluate the actions of corporations as well as their critics:

> To summarize: 1) no action should be taken which violates another's individual rights; 2) recommendations must be responsible in the sense that they do not ignore the context, purpose, and basic contractual commitments of those to whom the recommendation is made; and 3) the moral dimension of an action should always be given serious attention.   (Den Uyl, 1984, p. 55)

Unaddressed issues

Considerable attention has been given in this section of the chapter to the review of Den Uyl because his monograph explicitly adopts the viewpoint of a Friedmanite free market approach and attempts to support this position on moral grounds. The social permission approach (especially the social contract) is criticized and guidelines for the evaluation of social responsibility recommendations have been put forward. The value systems explored by Den Uyl are relevant to an understanding of criticisms of some aspects of social accounting (for example, the valuation of externalities by Benston) which are reported in later chapters. However, a number of issues are unaddressed in the discussion leading up to the guidelines reproduced above. Organizational legitimacy was not discussed, possibly because this appears to fall into the functional theory area which is categorized by Den Uyl as amoral and consequently outside the scope of his work.

The first principle assumes that all individuals contracting with each other (and observing each others' rights) are of equal standing regardless of economic and political power, information asymmetry and wealth endowments. Individuals are assumed to be involved in only one role at a time. In particular, positive discrimination is to be ruled out under any circumstances.

The second principle is based on a discussion of profitability and with reference to the market processes. The definition of profit, and hence profitability, is problematic. What is to be included in the calculation of profit? Which gains and losses are to be recognized at any point in time? What, if anything, should one do to capture external costs? What is the period of time with which we are concerned? The difficulties of relying upon the market are discussed in the next section, by reference to a number of authorities. One does not need to be a political radical to be critical of Den Uyl and the value positions he articulates, although support for his position has been given by Valone: 'The principle virtue of the book is the rational and open way in which the author invites debate on CSR' (Valone, 1985, p. 408). He concludes:

> He points to the danger of lapsing into sermons and polemics rather than careful analyses of the economic-ethical matrix. Advocates of corporate social responsibility must appeal less to the conscience of the manager than the recognition of the ethical-social elements which condition and set the parameters of economic thinking.   (Ibid., p. 424)

Unfortunately, the rational and non-ideological nature of Den Uyl's approach leads to his rejecting many of the moves to make corporations responsible for alleviating the problems which are associated with their operations, such as pollution and environmental degradation. In this area Den Uyl rejects regulation and favours 'the practical efficiency and moral superiority of market alternatives' (Den Uyl, 1984, p. 25). This is alarming since it is the market which cannot cope with externalities in the first place.

MORAL AGENCY, THE SOCIAL CONTRACT, ORGANIZATIONAL
LEGITIMACY AND SOCIAL ACCOUNTING

Social accounting activity can be justified in terms of moral agency and the social contract, which form the socially related arguments used here, because the world is not viewed in the same way as it was by investors and potential investors in the previous section, or by the advocates of a radical political solution in the following section. The participants addressed by socially related arguments include customers, employees, the general public and those affected by the indirect responsibilities of the corporation.

Organizational legitimacy may be the practical expression of the philosophical position adopted by the social permission theorists. The norms of society change continually and organizational management must adapt to these changes. To avoid doing so may be as damaging to the legitimacy of the organization as a dynamic system as would allowing products to become outdated be to the market position of the corporation. The philosophical positions considered in this chapter can be used to justify social accounting on moral or pragmatic grounds. On moral grounds, if the manager wishes to present the corporation as acting within a social contract framework; and on pragmatic grounds, if organizational legitimacy is the motivating force. In the latter case the disclosures would be made, not because the manager believed that constituencies were entitled to have them but in order to satisfy a demand for information and legitimate the organization with the public.

Individual agreement theory attempts to provide a philosophical basis for a relatively free market approach to economic activity and, therefore, indirectly acts to restrict any extension of accounting disclosures.

THE EFFECT OF CULTURE ON THE PHILOSOPHICAL BASES OF SOCIAL ACCOUNTING

It may be argued that the philosophical basis for social accounting is relatively strong compared to that underlying free market economics. Therefore, the socially related arguments are more appropriate than those related to market studies. However, the response of the accounting profession does not appear to follow the strength of the philosophical argument. There may be several reasons for this phenomenon, including the strength of classical economics and marginalistic philosophies within many economic systems (they are based on 19th century economics), inertia, or lack of explanation and educational endeavour on the part of accounting theorists. Recent work on the effects of culture on accounting may explain why social accounting developments do not always gain the support which might be expected, and also why the level of support varies both over time and between geographical areas.

Burchell, Clubb and Hopwood examined the relationship between the inception, development and apparent decline in the use of value added statements and the changes in social and economic conditions prevailing in the UK. In their conclusion they stated that:

> We have sought to indicate how the value added event arose out of a complex interplay of institutions, issues and processes. The study of this particular accounting change has enabled us not only to move towards grounding accounting in the specific social contexts in which it operates but also to raise and discuss what we see to be some important theoretical issues which have to be faced when seeking to understand the social functioning of the accounting craft.   (Burchell, Clubb and Hopwood, 1985, p. 408).

The cultural-accounting interface they explored was within one national culture which was changing over a period of time, rather than accounting practices in different cultures at the same time.

Perera (1985) considered the cultural aspects of accounting systems, particularly as they related to developing countries. A number of dimensions of culture were examined, specifically those which might affect accounting measurement and disclosure. Perera used the cultural dimensions put forward by Hofstede (1983a) and the international classification supplied by Gray (1985) to develop a model of the relationship between accounting and culture, which is reproduced as Figure 2.2. Perera and Mathews (1991) have applied the model to the differences in the attention given to social accounting disclosures. There is

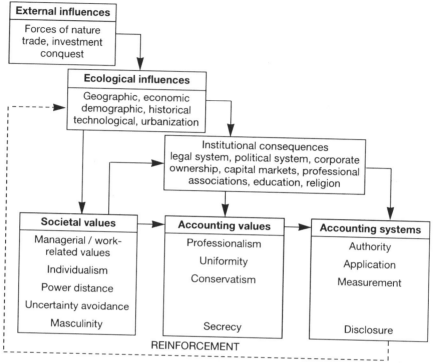

Figure 2.2 Accounting and culture. Source: Mathews and Perera (1991, p. 326).

evidence that Anglo-American accounting systems (including those of Canada, Australia and New Zealand) have different priorities for both financial and social responsibility accounting than do continental European countries. In particular, employee reporting has a far higher priority in European countries than it does amongst Anglo-American accounting systems. A number of differences are detailed by Gray, Owen and Maunders (1987).

Gambling (1977) has argued that accounting practices are akin to magic or rituals taking place within a particular environment which makes them meaningful. These rituals are often culturally specific or anthropocentric (Gambling and Karim, 1986). The effects of cultural differences on the philosophical bases of both social and conventional accounting are not known with precision, although the general direction may be predicted.

The arguments put forward by social permission theorists and those favouring a social contract or organizational legitimacy approach, on the one hand, or individual agreement theories on the other, will be perceived differently by different groups at varying times. If this effect exists, it may account for the ebb and flow of support for social accounting. The majority of social accounting theorists and researchers work in developed countries following Anglo-American or continental European systems and it is possible that their research may be incongruent with the national culture or the accounting sub-culture or both.

SECTION SUMMARY

This section has distinguished a number of philosophical bases which underlie social accounting, together with an alternative philosophy underlying free market economic thinking. In particular, the notions of the social contract and organizational legitimacy merit further attention as justifications for additional disclosures.

The important point to be made here is that the expenditure of additional resources on social accounting may be justified to share-holders and debtholders (actual and potential) through market studies and to most of the other groups in society through the socially related arguments. There may be criticism of this position from radical groups, because it contains an implicit acceptance of many of the characteristics of present societal organization and values (with limited modifications in respect of the latter). In other words, much of the status quo is maintained.

The effects of culture on the development of accounting suggests that there are a number of complicating factors which may assist or inhibit the acceptance of given philosophies. Culture has a relationship with the accounting sub-culture for financial accounting, and social accounting developments may be similarly affected.

SOCIAL ACCOUNTING AND THE RADICAL PARADIGM

INTRODUCTION

Supporters of a radical approach to the justification of social accounting are critical of many aspects of current society. They are unlikely to support social accounting as a result of the arguments put forward in the two previous sections, although some of the concepts used in developing the moral-agency view of the productive organization may be encouraged. A radical individual will only be persuaded to take an interest in social accounting by means of arguments framed in terms of the radical paradigmatic view of society. In the last few years there have been an increasing number of contributors to this debate and several of the works are reviewed in this section.

In general, the radical view concludes that accounting has supported, and continues to support, a particular view of society. It is associated with capitalistic production and marginalistic economics, which does not admit to problematic relationships between the organizations that accounting serves and society and follows a positivist approach. The radical theorists are critical of the socially related arguments used in the earlier sections of the chapter because that work envisages a plurality of approaches, the evolution of accounting and organizational developments, and the acceptance of much of the capitalist-based production and ownership systems.

The radical theorists have commented on many of the same issues as those working within the market-studies and socially related fields. The literature dealing with public interest accounting includes many of the issues which will be considered in later chapters, such as social responsibility accounting and the internalization of externalities, but from radical non-market and collectivist perspectives.

The work discussed in this section is only a small part of the voluminous literature produced by radical theorists and the proponents of critical theory (although including the most important contributions in the public interest accounting debate), and of these only a few items can be selected for discussion. The remainder of the chapter is divided into two main parts. First, a review of several items from the radical literature that are particularly relevant to the radical paradigm as a justification for developing different forms of accounting; and second, an examination of the problems which the promotion of the radical paradigm may generate for the proponents of practical social accounting.

A CONSIDERATION OF SELECTED ITEMS FROM THE RADICAL LITERATURE

Tinker, Merino and Neimark (1982)

Tinker, Merino and Neimark (TMN) have argued that all theories are normative, even where they are described as positive or empirical. There is no one reality 'out there' as is assumed by the instrumental paradigm, and all claims of reality are problematic and negotiable. The authors use a materialist theory of accounting in which the theory may come to form part of the reality by a process of reification. The purpose of their paper becomes clearer with an exposition of the arguments against a marginalist economic view of accounting, because such a view benefits only the shareholding and managerial class, without any attempt to extend the coverage to workers or customers. An analysis of the development of value theory is given, followed by a table contrasting the marginalist and classical theories.

The authors note that accounting thought has remained committed to marginalism through an emphasis on individualism (both shareholder and organization) and by attempts to preserve the fiction of objectivity by reference to objective market prices. Thus accountants, TMN argue, avoid becoming involved in social conflict between groups and classes:

> The second emphasis in the development of accounting thought is the positioning of accounting as an impartial record of historical exchange values with the corollary that the accountant bears no responsibility for affecting expectations, decisions or ultimately the distribution of income within and between classes.   (Tinker, Merino and Neimark, 1982, p. 189)

The implications for accounting and the development of research programmes are:

1. It is necessary to understand the normative basis of marginalism and the positive accounting approaches: 'the normative bias that is inherent in marginalism and its positive accounting variants: a neoconservative ideological bias that encourages us to take the 'free' market and its implicit institutional apparatus as 'given' (ibid., p. 191).
2. Radical accounting should not be construed too narrowly as 'only' accounting for trade unions and corporate accountability.
3. Accounting for social value in a wide sense is desirable.
4. Radical accounting needs to be extended into the management accounting field to investigate the effects of budgetary systems in the work-place.
5. Investigative studies are needed: 'The investigative studies, together with the general proposals for greater corporate accountability, envisage a similar role for accounting – that of an interpretor and articulator of social value, as an adjudicator in social struggles and as an instrument of social change'. (Ibid., p. 192).
6. Multinational organizations need to be investigated for their effects on developing countries.

Merino and Neimark (1982)

Merino and Neimark have questioned the conventional wisdom that the 1933 and 1934 US Securities Acts resulted in enlarged disclosure requirements. They concluded that the Acts were not fundamental changes to accounting disclosure provisions, but part of an attempt to maintain the status quo in ideological, social and economic terms. A radical paradigm is adopted, because the authors speak of a contradiction between an individualistic, market-based philosophy (atomistic competiton and the assumptions underlying a free market) and the realities of increased economic concentration (monopoly and oligopoly). This contradiction is presumably intensifying over time because the conflict continues over accounting policy and the provisions for disclosure.

The authors refer to a number of recent developments as part of the unresolved difficulties. Examples given are the different views on the degree of knowledge possessed by shareholders expressed in Trublood and SFAC 1 (American Institute of Certified Public Accountants, 1973; Financial Accounting Standards Board, 1978), the reliance of some writers on the efficient markets hypothesis, and a 'Darwinian model of competitive market regulation (by rolling back disclosure requirements)' (Merino and Neimark, 1982, p. 50). They call for consideration of 'substantive corporate regulation rather than the tokenism of legislation such as the securities acts' (ibid., p. 51).

Presumably the substantive legislation would include 'measures of corporate performance and means of control . . . that are independent of such markets and that are sensitive to the social consequences of corporate pricing policies, worldwide employment practices, waste disposal methods, and so on' (ibid.). The approach to regulating corporations (if they are permitted to exist!) is similar to the structural restraint view.

Lehman (1983)

Lehman examined the development of social responsibility over a period from the late 1960s, beginning with an attempt to define the topic area. If organizations are social as well as economic, and if there are moral considerations involved, should researchers be operating in a market context? Lehman clearly had doubts since 'Moral imperatives or quality considerations are not resolvable in an economic framework. The usual market framework cannot promote or be used to implement moral values or ensure quality of life' (Lehman, 1983, p. 3) Clearly, this view is in direct contrast to the view expressed by Den Uyl in a previous section of this chapter.

The various forms of social permission theory, as expressed through the social contract, notions of organizational legitimacy, government regulation and social audits, are based upon a consensus or harmonious view of the nature of society. In turn, the mainstream policy recommendations and research agenda reflect these assumptions. Lehman considered the outcomes from a different set of assumptions which view the world as conflictual as a result of social divisions and differences. Four models were considered: interpenetrating, public policy, general market, and financial market.

The interpenetrating model (Preston and Post, 1975) emphasized the degree to which corporations influence the public and are, in turn, influenced by the political, social and economic environment. Although apparently straightforward, this theory does not explicitly recognize the extent to which the corporation can influence the environment as a result of economic and political power. Social responsibility reports may be designed to present only one side of selected issues, ignoring other, more revealing, aspects:

> Although most accounting social responsibility researchers view the corporate influence over the public's expectations as non-problematic, they do so only by ignoring a wide body of literature that describes the influences corporations have had in this regard. (Lehman, 1987, p. 12)

Social institutions, such as the legal and education systems, influence public expectations; as does accounting, despite a widely held view that it is value-free and that the public is able to react in an independent manner to each new situation. If public expectations are conditioned by dominant groups, including corporations themselves, then 'the suggestion that public opinion and pressure can and will cause corporations to be socially responsible may be inappropriate' (ibid., p. 15).

The public policy model is based upon the use of the power of the state to influence company policy and decision-making. The general public can influence government to act because: 'The state is a free and neutral agent in this process and has the ability to act in ways that it determines rather than are determined by corporations' (ibid., p. 15).

However, a section of the literature has drawn attention to the degree to which corporations, as powerful economic interests, can lobby the legislative organs and modify any direct challenge to their authority:

> accounts suggest corporations were supportive of government regulations and laws which would monitor corporations where such regulations were necessary for the survival of the corporations (e.g., such regulations could alleviate public criticism by providing, a sometimes false, assurance that corporations would be held accountable for their actions). (Ibid., p. 17)

From the radical perspective, the public policy model suffers from the same drawback as the interpenetrating model.

The general-market model assumes that the generation of profits and the increase in value of the corporation in the market-place are desired by shareholders and accepted by the general public as the legitimate aims of business entities. The market is held to be efficient and the best means of achieving resource allocation. However, unequal wealth endowments affect the ability of both consumers and investors to enter markets and influence outcomes. Furthermore, the concentration of economic power leads to monopolistic and oligopolistic influences which detract from the resource allocation aspects of market performance. Many socially related activities lie outside the normal decision alternatives of management and they are not internalized into the market mechanism, because they do not provide guidance on socially related issues, including the social responsibility of business:

> 'Additional important social issues are also ignored by those researchers who rely, particularly, on financial market participants (stock holders) to evaluate corporate activities and to achieve corporate social responsibility . . .' (Ibid., p. 21)

The financial-market model is based upon the premiss that shareholders seek to maximize share prices and will not invest in companies whose managements are not socially responsible. Shareholders will be concerned that corporate behaviour may attract government regulation, for example action against enterprises investing in South Africa. Management will in turn be concerned to keep share prices from falling. It is also suggested that a group of ethical investors may exist and drive down selected share prices if they discover that some of their holdings are in socially non-responsible corporations. Lehman challenges the assumption by some researchers that market mechanisms can be used to achieve corporate social responsibility. In addition to the general problems of market information asymmetry and biased communication, maximizing share prices does not necessarily maximize shareholder utility. The existence of monopolistic and oligopolistic enterprises, which are less reliant on the market for capital requirements and the varied nature of shareholders, prevents any valid generalizations about overall shareholders' intentions. Furthermore, shareholders only represent one of a number of constituencies or audiences in society. The maximization of share prices does not lead automatically to corporate social policies which would maximize the overall welfare of all stakeholders.

Lehman concluded that researchers do not agree on how to define corporate social responsibility because of the view of corporations as profit-maximizing institutions:

> 'Therefore, it is necessary for researchers to move beyond economic considerations, and explore defining corporate social responsibility broadly, in terms of social, moral and quality of life considerations'. (Ibid., p. 24)

None of the models considered, Lehman suggests, can deal with these social, moral and quality of life considerations, and researchers are urged to consider administrative theory: 'This theory recognises that corporations, as social institutions, affect the political process, the quality of life, moral values, economic conditions and social relationships'. (Ibid.)

The market cannot be employed as an indicator of efficiency because it is not longer effective as a regulator and cannot be an adjudicator of moral values. The search for social indicators as a measure of corporate social responsibility must be directed towards effects on society which are not simply market-related.

Cooper and Sherer (1984)

Cooper and Sherer have argued for a political economy of accounting to replace the existing approaches to external accounting for corporate performance. The present system of accounting ignores aggregate social welfare because of a bias towards shareholders. Studies cited showed that traditional accounting reports are useful to shareholders, but these studies must be evaluated against the lack of an accepted theory of user needs. The changes in accounting policies towards disclosure (naive or knowledgeable shareholders) means the possibility of wealth redistribution between shareholding groups. The effect of such a redistribution may not lead to a more efficient capital market because 'understanding individual responses may be of interest in contributing to a general understanding of accounting (elaborating users and their settings); but it is unlikely that individual behaviour translates to aggregate market responses (Cooper and Sherer, 1984, p. 210).

Cooper and Sherer suggested that the literature relating the value of accounting reports to individual shareholders is concerned with the efficiency of the market for information rather than the efficiency of the market for securities:

> It may be that the empirical results indicate the private value (or otherwise) of information . . . But only in the most unlikely of circumstances is it possible that capital market reactions also indicate the social view of information or have implications about the desirability of alternative accounting measures or disclosure.   (Ibid., p. 210)

The usefulness of shareholder reports as a contribution towards the efficiency of the economy as a whole is questioned, together with the use of markets as a standard by which other social institutions should be judged. The authors critique both general equilibrium analysis and economic consequences analysis in much the same terms as the radical writers considered previously, before coming to their political economy of accounting approach. Political economy of accounting has three features: the recognition of power and conflict in society (which affects wealth distribution) and the logical consequences for accountants as partipants; an emphasis on the specific historical and institutional environment of society; and a more emancipated view of society: 'Attempts to resolve technical issues without consideration of this environment may result in an imperfect and incomplete resolution due to the acceptance of current institutions and practices' (ibid., p. 219). These characteristics may be reduced to three imperatives: be normative, be descriptive and be critical. Accounting researchers should be explicit about the value systems underlying their work. This would place their work within a particular paradigm and facilitate the evaluation of alternative paradigms. Researchers are encouraged to describe 'accounting in action', provided that recognition is given to descriptions beyond 'commonsense' views of the world.

Finally, the researcher needs to be 'critical', a term interpreted as looking beyond markets and established value systems in order to assess the background influences on accounting. Cooper and Sherer indicated some doubt that the last imperative could be successfully implemented:

> Whether critical theory can in practice be applied to accounting research . . . depends on whether researchers can free themselves from the attitudes and orientations which result from their social and educational training and which are reinforced by the beliefs of the accounting profession and the business community. (Ibid., p. 222)

In conclusion the authors state that:

> it may be insufficient to rely on the market for accounting research to foster research which is significantly different in approach from the existing paradigm. Rather, in order to develop a political economy of accounting normative, descriptive and critical research needs to be actively promoted and nurtured. (Ibid., p. 226)

Tinker (1985)

Tinker (1985) critiqued accounting from a Marxist position and proposed the outline of an alternative system. The book is divided into four parts, beginning with an exposé of a number of scandals involving large corporations. The purpose of this part appears to be to indicate that not all (any?) large corporations behave in a socially responsible manner and that their irresponsibility is not hindered, and indeed may be assisted, by current accounting systems.

In part two, Tinker examines value theory, which is a major contribution to the accounting literature. Accounting practice is defined as 'a means for resolving social conflict, a device for appraising the terms of

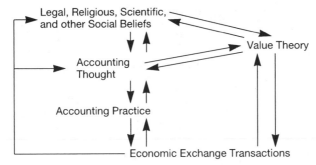

Figure 2.3 The relationship between value theory and accounting. Source: Tinker (1985, p. 83).

exchange between social constituencies, and an institutional mechanism for arbitrating, evaluating and adjudicating social choices' (Tinker, 1985, p. 81). The relationship between value theory and accounting is demonstrated in Figure 2.3.

Accounting practice is shown as affecting, and being affected by, economic exchange transactions. Value theory relates to both economic exchange transactions and accounting thought; though the latter value theory also affects accounting practice. The relationship between accounting and value theory is explored in an historical context and Tinker suggests that early forms of accounting involved labour value theory which was an early form of developed exchange. This leads into part three, which provides a detailed discussion of theories of value, especially Marxian labour theory of value, compared to the marginalist theory of private value which is criticized as providing the basis of modern accounting. The marginalist value theory adopted by modern accounting means that accounting as a discipline is not value-free; it supports the status quo and does not perform the functions attributed to it in the definition provided above.

Part four offers a conceptual outline of a new form of accounting, radical accounting, which would provide a response to a variety of problems brought about by alienation. A hierarchy of problems resulting from alienation are illustrated, together with a related hierarchy of accounting systems. These are shown in Figure 2.4.

In the discussion which takes up the last part of the book Tinker deals with social constituency accounting and emancipatory accounting. Social constituency accounting recognizes two forms of alienation which have not been considered previously, intra-class alienation and externalized alienation. The parties concerned are capital providers, local communities and neighbourhoods, customers, labour and overseas nations. The approach of social constituency accounting is to recognize externalities:

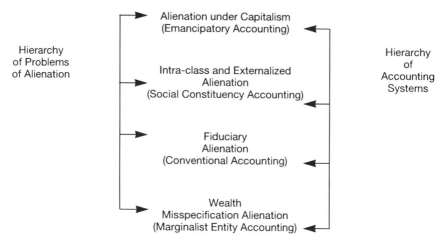

Figure 2.4 Alienation and accounting consciousness. Source: Tinker (1985, p. 178.

> Corporations may be compelled to acknowledge their external effects by fines, taxes, compensation payments and restrictions on the use of technology. These difference practices result in the externalities being internalised or impounded in the cost and profit functions of the offending corporation, thereby curtailing the anti-social (alienating) effects.   (Ibid., p. 217)

However, although some attention is given to social constituency accounting, Tinker did not consider that it was adequate for his needs: 'Marginalist entity accounting was adjudged inadequate because it ignores many of the social contradictions raised by surrounding activity; thus we find that, in the final analysis, social constituency accounting, with its marginalist underpinnings, is similarly flawed' (ibid., p. 217).

This means that the majority of the literature on social accounting which refers to additional disclosures, including those of externalities, is also considered to be deficient. Tinker responded to this perceived deficiency by introducing the further category of 'emancipatory accounting' which he intended should deal with the problem of alienation under capitalism. This form of accounting was incompletely developed, although it clearly is based upon labour theory of value, is opposed to capitalist systems of production and consumption, and consequently is revolutionary rather than evolutionary in terms of current practice. Tinker is almost silent on the content of emancipatory accounting: 'Emancipatory accounting includes information systems capable of recognising the alienating effects of capitalism and therefore is more effective in detecting capitalist alienation than any of the other accountability systems discussed previously' (ibid., p. 202). Clearly, further work is needed in this area if Tinker is going to provide substance to this particular form of accounting.

Paper Prophets has been examined from both the conventional and radical accounting positions. Johnson (1986) has suggested that the work contains several faults, including a lack of specificity in relation to what radical accounting systems would look like in practice.

A similar point has been made in a review by Laughlin and Puxty. The review was favourable to Tinker and the authors noted the difficulties inherent in providing the specification for a completely new system of accounting:

> It is hardly surprising therefore that the alternative proposed by him is not worked out in detail . . . Tinker is rejecting the basing of accounting values in market transactions. Instead, he is proposing a value system based in production. It is not clear if the balance sheet headings will remain essentially the same but the numbers attached to them would differ . . . (Laughlin and Puxty, 1986, pp. 87–8).

Alternatively, Laughlin and Puxty noted that the whole of the property-owning relationships in society may be changed. It is also noted that the mechanism by which society is to adopt a different form of accounting is not made clear; is a pluralistic society with active and energetic checks on accountability envisaged or some other scenario: 'we are not clear if he envisages his system as improving current society, or being operational only in an alternative society' (ibid., p. 89).

If others were clear about this feature of radical accounting their reactions might be different. Tinker has made a major contribution to the social accounting literature although not completely specifying his more advanced theories.

Lehman (1987)

Lehman has examined professional ethics, one of the most conservative aspects of accounting, from a radical position. In a review of accounting literature which covered the categories of discourse rather than the actual content, she concluded that:

> The preceding results suggest that ethics is denied any fundamental importance in these publications; rather ethical practices are secondary to profit maximization. The real 'lesson' taught in these publications is survival of the fittest: compete rather than co-operate; advance the individual before the community. The promotion of Social Darwinism is business, the sacrosanct status attached to individual advancement, and the valuing of ends (the bottom line)

over means inhibits critical appraisal of unethical practice. (Lehman, 1988, p. 75)

Lehman noted that the predominant mode of accounting education is connected with 'how' to do things, not with 'why' they are done and the underlying implications of the particular course of action under examination. The trend shows that business education is taking the place of studies in education and the humanities in providing the basic general education of many young graduates, and yet the level of attention given to ethical matters in business courses is very low.

The institutional call for education in ethical matters is designed to constrain the system and ensure its survival because ethical behaviour is an informal control mechanism which mitigates against the worst excesses of the market system. The radical view is that the encouragement of ethical conduct in the professional and educational arenas should not be to ensure survival of the system; it should examine the broad effects of the action of organizations on the environment; and should involve education to the extent of questioning the institutionalization of inequalities, political constraints and the role of accounting in social conflicts; finally, social and political issues should not be taught separately from accounting and business. This position is summarized by Lehman as follows:

> In contrast, the education in ethics proposed here entails: challenging old notions of ethics as good deeds of individuals, exploring the structures inhibiting socially desirable behaviour, and promoting political and institutional changes that would advance ethics. (Ibid., p. 3)

A SYNTHESIS OF THE RADICAL POSITION

The radical literature surveyed in this section serves to emphasize a number of different aspects of the radical approach. A number of basic characteristics may be distinguished:

1. The market must be de-emphasized, or even abolished, as a device for allocating resources. The efficiency which is alleged to exist benefits only a part of society.
2. Corporations are owned, organized and operated in a manner that is designed to establish and exploit power relationships.
3. The accounting profession as currently organized is engaged in wittingly or unwittingly maintaining the status quo by attaching itself to one party to social conflict (capital) to the exclusion of the other main party (labour).
4. The accounting profession engages in mystifying the processes

of accounting in order to exercise power. Value positions held by accountants are based on marginal economics and are deficient because of their market basis.

5. Accountants are ignorant of the extent to which the discipline is both socially constructed and socially constructing.

6. Accounting must be changed to take account of social relationships in a much wider manner, perhaps by incorporating a labour theory of value.

7. Accountants, accounting educators and accounting students must appreciate that they have a choice in their social relationships; they must consciously take sides in social conflict.

8. Social accounting as presently advocated by most of the literature is deficient, because it only considers additional disclosures and perhaps externalities, does not envisage a change in the ownership of capital resources, would regulate the market mechanism rather than dispose of the market altogether, is too close to the marginalist economic position, and is based on a modification of the status quo. Social accounting is evolutionary rather than revolutionary, and consequently, when viewed from a radical perspective, is considered inadequate and obstructionist.

If this synthesis is valid it is reasonable to ask what contribution the radical paradigm can make towards social accounting in the form advocated by the mainstream literature.

THE CONTRIBUTION OF THE RADICAL PARADIGM TOWARDS SOCIAL ACCOUNTING

The radical paradigm in accounting does not support current attempts at implementing social accounting as discussed in later chapters of this book. The areas of social permission theory (the social contract and organizational legitimacy) and administrative theory are adjacent to the radical paradigm but do not present the same analyses. The radical paradigm provides an alternative view of the place of corporations in society, together with the accounting discipline which supports and regulates these corporations. It is an important view which can stimulate us to question both our own value system and that of the discipline within which we work.

The problem with the radical approach to social accounting is that the literature attracts those readers already prepared to question the basis of Western-style capitalism. In other words, the radical literature tends to be an example of 'preaching to the coverted' in some ways, and may be ineffective when attempting to convince the majority of accountants and managers of the need for additional accountability. Alternatively, it might provide a worst-case example of a 'future' if corporations do not change some aspects of their organization and embrace notions of a wider accountability. This is particularly appropriate when discussing environmental degradation.

The conventional view of the relationship of accounting to society and social change is that of a service activity, which reacts to change, not that of a policy-making system, which is proactive and initiates changes. Consquently accounting as a discipline evolves and the social accounting area is evolving only slowly, as later chapters will demonstrate. If society indicates, through the political process, a desire for more rapid changes in disclosure practices, the accounting discipline will respond. Until that time progress can only be made slowly by those accountants prepared to work through the existing system.

SOCIAL ACCOUNTING AND THE RADICAL PARADIGM – A SUMMARY

The diagram of the relationship of value theory and accounting, which is adopted from Tinker and shown in Figure 2.3 acknowledges the importance of another source of influence on accounting, namely legal, religious, scientific and other social beliefs. This amounts to a cultural effect which affects disclosure practices. The effect of culture on accounting appears to be considerable and a force for stability and against revolutionary change.

This effect does not mean that change is not desirable but that change is likely to be slow and evolutionary rather than rapid and revolutionary. Accordingly, the radical approach is not thought to be a particularly productive vehicle at the present time for influencing accounting practice, although the contributors offer particularly stimulating insights in the form of alternative views of the world.

Within the context of developing strategies to gain acceptance for social accounting disclosures or justifications for the expenditure of additional discretionary resources, this chapter has identified the radically related arguments. Furthermore, the differences between arguments for disclosures which are based upon notions of the social contract and arguments based upon more radical views of the corporation and its environment have been explored. The author argues for the more evolutionary direction because it is likely to be more advantageous as a strategy leading to the development and adoption of social accounting. This is not to suggest that the radical approach does not have value. However, in terms of interesting practising accountants and others in social accounting, there are considerable philosophical limitations.

These limitations are associated with the mainstream view of the role of the market mechanism, private ownership of property, and the importance of individual over collective actions. The radical view of accounting would seek to de-emphasize or eliminate the use of the market mechanism and is basically opposed to capitalistic modes of production, seeking to use alternatives such as administrative organizational structures.

The radical view of organization and ownership in Western society seems to be a long way from persuading the majority of the population to join in any popular movement for change. Environmentalists would probably argue that as our environment becomes progressively degraded, changes will be forced upon society. This view will be included in Chapter 6.

SUMMARY

The introductory chapter indicated that many writers in the area of social accounting have assumed that the ideas put forward for developments in this field are desirable, justified and fill a demonstrated need. The early literature argued a case for social accounting and non-traditional forms of reporting; later contributions have taken this case to be self-evident. Clearly, to a vast majority of the accounting, managing and investing community, the advantages are not self-evident, otherwise more would have been achieved towards implementing additional accounting disclosures in the last decade. Furthermore, the interests of diffferent groups are no more congruent about social accounting than they are about other aspects of our complex society.

Chapter 2 uses three approaches to associate the attributes of social accounting with the arguments put forward by different parties. The attributes of social accounting associated with a particular user-group may lead to a strategy by which greater acceptance of non-traditional accounting and the attendant use of additional discretionary resources may be achieved.

The first section introduced market-related arguments which may be used to justify social accounting disclosures through the information content of additional disclosures and the effects these may have on corporate income and stock market values. Evidence of information content may be of interest to groups associated with traditional shareholder and management roles. The research connecting additional social responsibility accounting disclosures with share prices and other market related indices is conflicting, although there does appear to be some information content present in these disclosures. Shareholders and creditors may be interested in this information and a justification based upon shareholder-usefulness could be a partial strategy to obtain additional information in the form of social accounting disclosures.

The socially related arguments discussed in the second section may be used to develop the notion of a social contract between productive organizations and other groups. The moral agency of the corporation may be established and, through the notion of a social contract with business, other groups such as employees, customers and the general public are entitled to additional information. The strategy to achieve a greater demand for social accounting by those who are sympathetic to additional disclosures might be to stress the complementary rights and obligations of the corporation through moral agency and not by a radical attack upon the basic system. This approach leads logically to an emphasis on organizational legitimacy as the pragmatic expression of social permission theory. Managers who are unable to accept the moral imperative of the social contract arguments may be prepared to consider the amoral position of the organizational legitimacy approach.

The Corporate Report (ASSC, 1975) referred to the information needs of a wider group of users including employees and the general public: all those with 'reasonable rights' to the information. Despite the far-reaching and apparently radical nature of the accounting recommendations contained in *The Corporate Report*, there do not appear to be any radical political or organizational considerations. The recently constructed Australian conceptual framework also provides a basis for a wider view of accounting. Other conceptual frameworks may do so when they are revised.

The market-related and socially related approaches are different means of looking at the world without envisaging radical changes in society. The strength of these approaches is that they view the world in a similar way to most shareholders, creditors, managers, customers, employees and the general public. These groups may be socially conditioned, nevertheless, such that their reactions are predictable and in favour of evolution rather than revolution. The effect of culture on accounting sub-cultures, which was briefly introduced, may have a bearing on this condition of relative stability. The later chapters base the structure of a more socially responsible accounting on the social contract rather than on the radical paradigm because of a concern with implementation. Strategies for implementation are best provided for shareholders and creditors through market-related studies and for other groups through the social contract and organizational legitimacy positions. The evolutionary process of accounting will lead to a decrease in the emphasis placed on the market studies and to a corresponding increase in the emphasis placed on the other arguments. Both public- and private-sector organizational activities are included in the arguments advanced.

The radical approach, and the associated literature discussed in the last section of the chapter, offers a most interesting field for discussion.

The radical paradigm is offered as an alternative to the social permission theory, the social contract and theories about organizational legitimacy. The economic nature of the corporation is seen as a part of the whole society to be considered along with social, moral and quality of life factors which cannot be processed through the market-place. The motives and interactions of individuals and collectives are seen as problematic. A particular problem is the extent to which organizations can manipulate the regulatory environment within which they operate, including the regulation exercised over the disclosures in annual reports. This is believed to apply with financial disclosures and, therefore, thought to be applicable to other forms of reporting.

The radical literature is, by definition, unsympathetic to the shareholder/creditor groups, and impatient with the evolutionary nature of the reforms/changes contained in the socially related arguments. Perhaps the research of the radical paradigm should be directed towards large-scale public-sector developments in the areas categorized by the author as socio-economic and social-indicators accounting; but the majority of radical theorists are concerned with private-sector organizations. A radical strategy is unlikely to generate the climate in which a majority of managers, investors and accountants will be inclined to favour the development of social accounting.

The classification of social accounting: an introduction 3

INTRODUCTION

Normative-deductive accounting research is not currently fashionable. However, there should be some interest in developments of the kind which this part of the book sets out to explain, particularly since the use of additional resources has been justified in Chapter 2. McDonald (1975) classified theories of accounting as descriptive (theories *of* accounting) and normative (theories *for* accounting). Furthermore, after Lindblom (1959), he associated the two alternatives with different methods of arriving at the policies shown in Table 3.1.

The rational-comprehensive approach is associated with a normative view leading to a theory for accounting. The successive limited comparisons approach corresponds more with the evolution of accounting. Goals are required in both cases; however, they are arrived at in different ways. In the descriptive approach goals are deduced from observing actions, decisions and policies, whilst in the normative approach:

> goals are stated *a priori*, and decisions, actions, and polices are evaluated or judged in terms of established goals. Thus, goals, their nature and scope, must be of concern in any discussion of accounting or any other discipline. (Lindblom, 1959, reprinted in McDonald, 1975, pp. 15–16)

The remaining chapters are frequently concerned with normative accounting and have the goal of explicating the confused area of research often referred to as social accounting, by reference to a framework or classification which may lead towards a more socially responsible accounting. The issue of what constitutes social accounting is addressed first, followed by a discussion of measurement problems. Later chapters deal with each of the component parts into which the author has divided the field to permit easier examination; this is the

Table 3.1 Alternative approaches to policy formation (adapted from McDonald, 1972)

Rational comprehensive (root)		Successive limited comparisons (branch)	
1a	Clarification of values or objectives distinct from and usually prerequisite to empirical analysis of alternative policies	1b	Selection of value goals and empirical analysis of the needed action are not distinct from one another but are closely intertwined
2a	Policy formulation is therefore approached through means–end analysis: first the ends are isolated, then the means to achieve them are sought	2b	Since means and ends are not distinct, means–end analysis is often inappropriate or limited
3a	The test of a 'good' policy is that it can be shown to be the most appropriate means to desired ends	3b	The test of a 'good' policy is typically that various analysts find themselves directly agreeing that it is the most appropriate means to an agreed objective
4a	Analysis is comprehensive; every important relevant factor is taken into account	4b	Analysis is drastically limited: (1) important possible outcomes are neglected; (2) important alternative potential policies are neglected; (3) important values are affected.
5a	Theory is often heavily relied upon	5b	A succession of comparisons greatly reduces or eliminates reliance on theory

Source: Lindblom (1959).

suggested organization for social accounting research. The philosophical justification for this field of study, which was discussed in Chapter 2, is then set into the context in which it most frequently appears: the consideration of social responsibility and total impact accounting. Finally, the separate areas are reintegrated to form a system of accounting which is more socially responsible, thus demonstrating the usefulness of the classification system.

References to social accounting may be found in company reports, press releases, the news media and, occasionally, political speeches. The frequency of these references would suggest that social accounting might be increasingly important in the future, as the discipline of accounting is extended to include a variety of items which are not disclosed at present. However, the development of alternative disclosures is particularly subject to social and economic conditions. Consequently it can not be claimed that development will be continuous or without periods of regression. As discussed in Chapter 2, a number of alternative approaches may be used to justify a concern with this form of reporting.

However, the argument for an increase in socially relevant accounting information cannot be made simply by justifying the basic notion, and a closely argued case must be clearly established for the implementation of the disclosures. The case for an extension of social accounting measurements and disclosures is affected by confusion and problems with measurement and evaluation. The confusion arises partly because the term 'social accounting' is used in different ways, by different groups of people and the measurement difficulties are always present in any new area (they are what accounting is all about). The disagreements about how far accountants should go in their measurement and reporting activities are traceable to fundamental differences in philosophies about disclosure and reporting. Indeed, some of the works considered in the section dealing with the radical critique would suggest that the issues are much more complex than simply disclosure and reporting, but extend deeply into the social fabric of the host society.

A study of the social accounting literature suggested the need for a framework within which social accounting research could be fitted. Such a framework might be of assistance in formulating empirical research, in analysing the existing literature or in developing teaching programmes. Furthermore, the fit between current disclosure practices and desired disclosures may be examined through the use of a suitable framework.

THE BASIC OUTLINE: CONFUSION AND STRUCTURE

Those who are interested in the area of social accounting often experience some difficulty in explaining their work to other accountants. The use of 'social' in conjunction with accounting does not seem to work as well as the addition of 'financial', 'management' or 'tax'. These words add a large measure of explanation and precision to 'accounting' that 'social' does not. Perhaps one difficulty, not encountered by the descriptions given above, is the range of total activity which may be included under the heading social accounting. In this book the term is used to cover the following activities.

SOCIAL RESPONSIBILITY ACCOUNTING (SRA)

Social responsibility accounting refers to disclosures of financial and non-financial, quantitative and qualitative information about the activities of an enterprise. This area also includes employee reports (ER), human resource accounting (HRA), and accounting and industrial democracy issues. Alternative terms in common use are social responsibility disclosures and corporate social reporting. This is the most frequently occurring form of social disclosure but perhaps lacks the depth of philosophical concern which is present in the next category.

TOTAL IMPACT ACCOUNTING (TIA)

This term is used to refer to the aggregate effect of the organization on the environment. To establish this effect it is necessary to measure both private and public costs (externalities). Because of the origins of this area it is often referred to as cost-benefit analysis (CBA) or social accounting (thereby confusing the use of that term) and sometimes as social audit. This area has now been expanded to include the subject matter of accounting for sustainable development.

SOCIO-ECONOMIC ACCOUNTING (SEA)

Socio-economic accounting is the process of evaluating publicly funded activities, using both financial and non-financial measures. The entire activity should be evaluated, with a view to making judgements about the value of the expenditure involved in relation to the outcomes achieved. Socio-economic accounting would encompass the value-for-money (VFM) audit functions and auditing of operations and performance.

SOCIAL INDICATORS ACCOUNTING (SIA)

The term social indicators accounting is used to describe the measurement of macro-social events, in terms of setting objectives and assessing the extent to which these are attained over the longer term. The outcomes of this analysis should be of interest to national policy makers and other participants in national and regional political processes.

SOCIETAL ACCOUNTING

Societal accounting is the term used by some writers in this area to suggest a form of accounting that integrates all other forms into an overarching or meta-theory. The discussion of societal accounting is conceptual since implementation at this level is not envisaged or even possible to achieve.

Each of these component parts of the social accounting framework will be considered in turn. However, the characteristics of each type are clearly seen in a comparative format: Table 3.2 shows the basic divisions or components of the framework. The dimensions are based upon a division between the private and public sectors, the time-scale involved and the types of measurement used. The area of social responsibility accounting is predominantly a private-sector, short-term reporting system, using mainly non-financial quantitative and qualitative data. The second category concerns the difficult problem of the identification, measurement, valuation and disclosure of externalities, with particular reference to the environmental effects of entities. Together social responsibility accounting and total impact accounting make up what most of the literature refers to as social accounting.

In contrast, the third division, socio-economic accounting, is a public-sector activity, using qualitative and quantitative data (of both financial and non-financial types) to evaluate short- and medium-term programmes. Social indicators accounting is the macro-level activity which complements the micro-level socio-economic accounting activity. Taken together, these activities are intended to improve the performance and accountability of public-sector activities. Societal accounting conceptualizes all accounting as interrelated. The basic issue of measurement is addressed next.

MEASUREMENT

The American Accounting Association (1975), in the report of the Committee on Social Costs, suggested that three levels of measurement may be involved in the development of social accounting. These are:

Level I   where the activity is identified and described. Examples might be the identification of polluting materials which are being discharged into the environment.

Level II where the activity is measured using non-monetary units. The polluting materials are measured in terms of rate of discharge, the timing of flows, and compliance with existing standards formulated in physical terms such as parts per million (ppm).

Level III where attempts are made to value the effects of discharges. The measurements are converted to financial estimates of costs and benefits to all stakeholders, ranging from shareholders to the general public.

Table 3.2 The characteristics of the various component parts of social accounting

	Division	Purpose	Area of main use	Time-scale	Measurements used**	Associated areas
1.	Social responsibility accounting (SRA)	Disclosure of individual items having a social impact	Private sector	Short term*	Mainly non-financial and qualitative	Employee reports; human resource accounting; industrial democracy
2.	Total impact accounting (TIA)	Measures the total cost (both public and private) of running an organization	Private sector	Medium and long term	Financial AAA Level III	Strategic planning; cost–benefit analysis
3.	Socio-economic accounting (BEA)	Evaluation of publicly funded projects involving both financial and non-financial data	Public sector	Short and medium term	Financial, non-financial Levels II and III	Cost-benefit analysis; planned programmed budgeting systems; zero-based budgeting; institutional performance indicators; value for money audit
4.	Social indicators accounting (SIA)	Long-term non-financial quantification of societal statistics	Public sector	Long term	Non-financial Quantitative AAA Level II	National income accounts; consensus statistics
5.	Societal accounting (SA)	Attempts to portray accounting in global terms – overarching theories	Both All-embracing	All	Financial aggregates	Systems theory; mega accountancy trends

Notes:
* Normally short term to fit annual reporting patterns.
** Refer to section 3.30.

The three levels of measurement may be illustrated by reference to sulphur dioxide gas, which is a common cause of pollution. If sulphur dioxide is discharged into the atmosphere it will soon be detected by its odour, and elementary analysis will confirm that the odour is caused by sulphur dioxide. This is a Level I measurement. The volume of discharge measured over a period of time in physical units, such as parts per million (ppm) will provide a Level II measurement. A Level III measurement is made when we convert the effect of the discharge into financial terms by measuring the financial effects of damage to property and health.

The last type of measurement is the most difficult, because it involves valuation and the assignment of costs to events which are external to the organization. Examples might be: damage to the paintwork of neighbouring housing areas; the destruction of parks and gardens; and the creation of health problems. These valuation problems may be difficult to overcome and the values assigned to the effects of pollution will be open to dispute. The discounting to present value of the cost of future events, such as repairs or replacements, or the payment of damages, is obviously problematic. These measurements are made, however, in calculating compensation for injury, loss of earnings or death from accidents. Even if the local pollution measurement and valuation issues can be resolved, difficulties will arise where the damage is remote from the source in terms of time and distance. To continue the sulphur dioxide example, the effects of low levels of atmospheric sulphur dioxide over long periods of time may be more damaging to health than is currently recognized. This development (because it is currently undetermined) cannot be allowed for in our valuation. Similarly, if sulphur dioxide discharged in one country leads to acid rainfall in another, many miles away, this event cannot be measured and valued in any meaningful way at the present time. However, this position may change as the result of recent environmental problems, which are discussed in Chapter 6.

There is a political dimension to the valuation of externalities because both individual and group value positions are involved. This was especially clear in the section dealing with the radical critique of current accounting systems in Chapter 2. These issues are explored in the philosophical discussion on externalities in Chapter 6 that deals with total impact accounting.

The five categories of social accounting outlined in this chapter are not exhaustive, and further sub-division and classification may result from the development of the sub-discipline of social accounting. Indeed, this may be predicted on the basis of past trends in the development of the accounting discipline. An example of a specific area of attention might be energy accounting which would currently be regarded as a part of general social responsibility accounting disclosure, but which might become a separate concern in the event of another energy crisis. There is also an extensive literature devoted to employee-related accounting disclosures.

The attention paid to practical social accounting seems to be rather patchy. There are SRA disclosures in the private sector, probably due to SRA being short term and identifiable in the normal annual reporting procedure. TIA is beginning to develop as environmental accounting, although so far there is little evidence of practical application. Interest in environmental issues and sustainable development may encourage attention in this area. Public-sector attention is confined to VFM audits.

SUMMARY

This chapter has provided an outline of the proposed classification of social accounting which is advanced in this book, as an aid to under-standing the literature of the subject area and to making further advances through individual contributions and practical applications. The classification covers public- and private-sector activities, long-medium- and short-term time periods, and the use of monetary and non-monetary quantification as well as qualitative statements. The measurement classfication of Levels I, II and III put forward by the AAA report has been incorporated into the schema.

SRA is discussed in Chapters 4 and 5; TIA is the subject of Chapter 6, SEA and SIA are covered in Chapters 7 and 8. The remaining classification of societal accounting is the subject of Chapter 9 and the concluding chapter attempts an overall assessment of the extent to which accounting can be made socially responsible.

Social responsibility accounting

4

A GENERAL INTRODUCTION TO SRA DISCLOSURES

The objective of the next two chapters is to introduce social responsibility accounting, both as a theoretical and as a practical form of socially responsible accounting. In terms of current research and reporting, this area of non-traditional accounting disclosures has received the most attention. A suitable definition for social responsibility accounting (SRA) is:

Voluntary disclosures of information, both qualitative and quantitative, made by organizations to inform or influence a range of audiences. The quantitative disclosures may be in financial or non-financial terms.

SRA usually applies to private-sector organizations and involves a wide variety of information, most of which is non-financial in nature and of potential interest to employees and the general public as well as to shareholders and creditors. Although organizational management may have a target audience in mind, this is usually unspecified, and any disclosure policy may be an implicit rather than an explicit aspect of their strategy. Reports of government-funded activities may contain elements of SRA and these will be dealt with in Chapter 7. Other terms used to describe this area include social responsibility disclosures and corporate social responsibility. The pattern of development of SRA has been to include small amounts of data, in qualitative and non-monetary terms, as part of the annual report to shareholders. These disclosures are voluntary, unaudited and unregulated. SRA may be seen as an extension of the stewardship role, aimed at maintaining or improving the corporate image. Indeed, these two aspects, stewardship and corporate image, may be in conflict where disclosures are voluntary and unaudited. In terms of justification, the organizational legitimacy arguments may be the strongest motivator for these disclosures.

The earliest documentary analysis of published social responsibility accounting is usually credited to Ernst and Ernst (1972–8). This survey of *Fortune 500* corporation annual reports was started in 1972 (1971 reports) and continued until 1978 (1977 reports). Ernst and Ernst were aiming to inform their readership about what organizations were reporting, and not to develop any theory, perform any detailed analysis, or adopt a normative approach; although the categories adopted by the study may have influenced accountants in developing reporting systems. No attempt was made to establish a connection between social responsibility disclosures and share price movements or to prescribe in a normative manner what should be disclosed. The reporting of certain social data has been criticized for a lack of accuracy and objectivity (Wiseman, 1982), but to date, most attention has been devoted to observing and recording rather than to a critical analysis of what has been recorded.

The growing interest in general social responsibility accounting disclosures extends throughout the English-speaking accounting environment. The overall impression provided by these studies is of a limited amount of information about employee- and product-related matters, which is disclosed through mainly qualitative statements. There are a number of aspects of this research which are questionable and are discussed in Chapter 5, which examines SRA in practice.

Although SRA appears to be becoming more acceptable to larger companies, it is necessary to maintain a sense of perspective. Guthrie (1982) reported an average disclosure of 0.2 pages per company report devoted to SRA, and this would appear to be a reasonable estimate, in line with the later Ernst and Ernst studies. However, there was no consideration given to the number of pages in the complete report and consequently no proportions could be calculated.

Surveys of accountants in Australia and New Zealand have shown support for the basic principle of voluntarily disclosing social responsibility data in sections of the annual report (Anderson, 1980; Mathews and Heazlewood, 1983). This support does not extend to compulsory disclosure, and most accountants would not want to be involved in an audit of this information at the present time. Similar surveys carried out among members of the American Institute of Certified Public Accountants (Benjamin, Stanga and Strawser, 1977; Stiner, 1978) and the National Association of Accountants (Barnett and Caldwell, 1974) have also shown some support for voluntary disclosure of social responsibility information. However, there is some evidence that lower levels of support accompany the more difficult economic conditions experienced at the present time.

Mathews and Gordon (1984) found that the degree of acceptance of social accounting as a concept varied according to the professional body to whom the respondent belonged. Management accountants tended to be more favourably inclined towards SRA than those in public practice.

CONCEPTUAL AND OPERATIONAL MODELS FOR SRA

A large part of this chapter is devoted to an examination of the SRA literature. For convenience the models are divided into two groups; conceptual and operational.

The reporting of social responsibility information and accountants' support for this activity must be viewed against the limited conceptual and operational frameworks available for guidance and evaluation. In the discussion that follows a number of examples will be examined in two groups: conceptual models and operational models. The two groups are differentiated by the extent to which the proposed models offer specific detail of the disclosures which are advocated.

CONCEPTUAL MODELS RELATING TO SOCIAL RESPONSIBILITY ACCOUNTING

In this section the following models will be discussed: Ramanathan (1976); Burke (1984); Wartick and Cochran (1985); Logsdon (1985); Brooks (1986); and Gray, Owen and Maunders (1987). The variety of possible approaches is evident from these chosen examples.

Ramanathan (1976)

Ramanathan provided a conceptual framework for the development of social accounting. The main objective and concept definitions have been extracted from the article and grouped together in Table 4.1.

Ramanathan was concerned with all aspects of the social performance of an organization. His framework is wider than others included in this chapter because no separation is acknowledged between SRA and total impact accounting (TIA). Objective 1 is clearly aimed at measuring the total impact of enterprise activities through the net social contribution. Objective 3 is closer to the normally accepted goal of SRA, that is, to provide relevant information about the firm that is appropriate for the needs of the different social constituents. The second objective may be related to either SRA or TIA.

This conceptual model is considered a seminal work in the development of conceptual social accounting, but of limited assistance in determining what should be included in social accounting reports.

Table 4.1   Proposed objectives and concepts for social accounting

Objective 1
An objective of corporate social accounting is to identify and measure the periodic net social contribution of an individual firm, which includes not only the costs and benefits internalized to the firm, but also those arising from externalities affecting different social segments.

Objective 2
An objective of corporate social accounting is to help determine whether an individual firm's strategies and practices which directly affect the relative resource and power status of individuals, communities, social segments and generations are consistent with widely shared social priorities, on the one hand, and individuals' legitimate aspirations, on the other.

Objective 3
An objective of corporate social accounting is to make available in an optimal manner, to all social constituents, relevant information on a firm's goals, policies, programmes, performances and contributions to social goals. Relevant information is that which provides for public accountability and also facilitates public decision-making regarding social choices and social resource allocation. Optimality implies a cost/benefit effective reporting strategy which also optimally balances potential information conflicts among the various social constituents of a firm.

Concept 1
A 'social transaction' represents a firm's utilization or delivery of a socio-environmental resource which affects the absolute or relative interests of the firm's various social constituents and which is not processed through the market place.

Concept 2
'Social overheads (returns)' represent the sacrifice (benefit) to society from those resources consumed (added) by a firm as a result of its social transactions. In other words, social overhead is the measured value of a firm's negative externalities, and social return is the measured value of its positive externalities.

Concept 3
'Social income' represents the periodic net social contribution of a firm. It is computed as the algebraic sum of the firm's traditionally measured net income, its aggregate social overheads and its aggregate social returns.

Concept 4
'Social constituents' are the different distinct social groups (implied in the second objective and expressed in the third objective of social accounting) with whom a firm is presumed to have a social contract.

Concept 5
'Social equity' is a measure of its aggregate changes in the claims which each social constituent is presumed to have in the firm.

Concept 6
'Net social assets' of a firm is a measure of its aggregate non-market contribution to the society's well-being less its non-market contribution to the society's well-being less its non-market depletion of the society's resources during the life of the firm.

Source: Ramanathan (1976, p. 527).

Burke (1984)

Burke has provided a conceptual model of a social accounting information system (SAIS) which is intended to assist decision-makers (the designated users in this case) to select from amongst programmes with explicitly stated social objectives. There are five basic guidelines for developing the SAIS, including the following reference to social information:

> A precise definition of what constitutes social information should be avoided. The social domain has no natural boundaries. It is preferable, therefore, that social information loosely specified as consisting of that set of information not traditionally regarded as economic, or technological in nature, that deals with people's values, relationship (e.g., laws), behaviour and concerns, that could have an important effect (financial and otherwise) on an organisation's performance and the achievement of its goals. (Burke, 1984, p. 100)

Although concerned with the internal decision-making function of the organization, the model put forward by Burke would produce SRA disclosures to society in order to signal that environmental and social concerns have been internalized. The model is illustrated in Figures 4.1 to 4.3. Figure 4.1 details the four primary functions of the SAIS: to survey the environment; to provide information on social goals; to provide inputs to specific decisions; and to evaluate the overall effectiveness of the system.

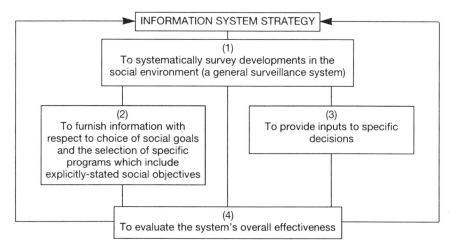

Figure 4.1 The four primary functions of a social accounting information system. Source: Burke (1984, p. 100).

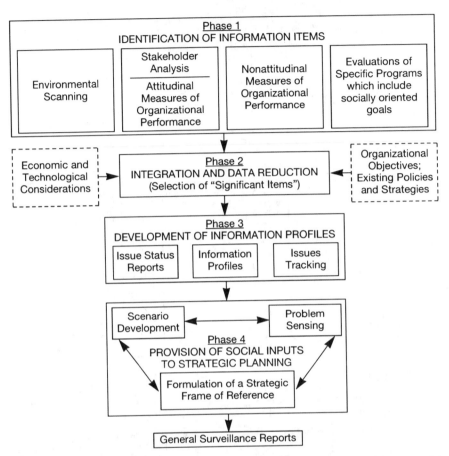

Figure 4.2 Activities comprising the general surveillance component of a social accounting information system. Source: Burke (1984, p. 102).

Figure 4.2 provides a detailed breakdown of the general surveillance component of a SAIS, which is of relevance to the present discussion because one aspect of the surveillance is described as: 'An overall evaluation of corporate social performance including progress reports on company progress' (Burke, 1984, p. 107).

Finally, Figure 4.3 shows the full model with the SAIS related to external factors. Ample opportunities exist for the generation of SRA through the general surveillance system and the internal and external assessment process.

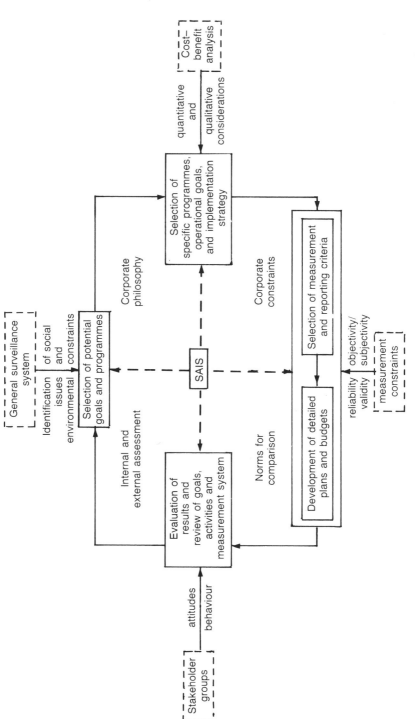

Figure 4.3 A framework for contemplating programmes which include explicit social objectives. Source: Burke (1984, p. 109).

Wartick and Cochran (1985)

Wartick and Cochran argue that there are three challenges to be faced in developing a model for corporate social performance (CSP). These are economic responsibility, public responsibility and social responsiveness. However, even when these challenges have been met a further development is needed; this is termed social issues management. The model is described as follows and illustrated in Table 4.2:

Social responsibility – the first dimension – has been an extremely resilient concept. It has assimilated much of the criticism that has been levied against it. Yet, the two fundamental premises of social responsibility – the social contract and moral agency – remain as the ethical component of social responsibility. Social responsiveness – the second dimension – provides the approach to realising social responsibility. It has become the general means to the ends of satisfying corporate social obligations. Social issues management – the third dimension – is now being developed as the method of operationalizing social responsiveness. (Wartick and Cochran, 1985, p. 767)

Wartick and Cochran did not include specific references to SRA. But management will require information and a medium through which their concern with principles (the philosophical orientation) may be demonstrated. Traditionally the accounting function has specialized in providing information to both management and outside parties. The

Table 4.2   The corporate social performance model

Principles	Processes	Policies
Corporate social responsibilities (1) Economic (2) Legal (e) Ethical (4) Discretionary	Corporate social responsiveness (1) Reactive (2) Defensive (3) Accommodative (4) Proactive	Social issues management (1) Issues identification (2) Issues analysis (3) Response development
Directed at: (1) The social contract of business (2) Business as a moral agent	Directed at: (1) The capacity to respond to changing societal conditions (2) Managerial approaches to developing response	Directed at: (1) Minimizing 'surprises' (2) Determining effective corporate social policies
Philosophical orientation	Institutional orientation	Organizational orientation

Source: Wartick and Cochran (1985, p. 767).

model provided here is consistent with the use of SRA in order to demonstrate the development of corporate social performance and the management of social issues.

Logsdon (1985)

Logsdon examined organizational responses to environmental issues, particularly the example of air pollution from US oil-refining companies. However, the conceptual model she used is introduced here because it illustrates the way in which SRA disclosures may be an important part of the strategies employed by organizations. When confronted by social issues, organizational management may react by resisting or accepting behaviour at any of three stages of development of the issue: emergence, legislation and regulation. The resulting matrix of responses is presented in Table 4.3. SRA may be involved in these activities, but only in a peripheral manner.

In examining the behaviour of firms in the oil-refining industry over a period of 35 years, Logsdon developed a measure of responsiveness. The responses of corporations (resisting and accepting behaviour) were based upon the aggregation of four components: statements about air pollution by top management; changes in organizational structure to assign responsibility for the issue; technical actions to reduce refinery

Table 4.3   Stages in the evolution of a social issue integrated with the generic response categories

Evolution of a social issue	Continuum of responsiveness	
	Resisting	Accepting
Stage 1: Emergence of the issue	Complete resistance by ignoring the issue, discrediting the issue and its proponents, and shifting responsibility to other parties	Development of corporate policy and voluntary activities to achieve the social goal
Stage 2: Legislative phase	Compromise by offering positive and negative inducements in bargaining for weak legislation	Technical and administrative learning by specialists and line managers
Stage 3: Regulatory phase	Reluctant capitulation by compliance with the minimum requirements as late as possible to avoid heavy fines and close-downs, using litigation to delay enforcement	Institutionalization by incorporating achievement of the social goal into incentive structures of line managers and into capital investment decision-making

Source: Logsdon (1985, p. 48).

Table 4.4 Accepting response patterns

Component	Stage 1	Stage 2	Stage 3
Management statements	Acknowledgement of air pollution and voluntary activities to reduce emissions in annual reports First corporate policy	Expand reference to air pollution in annual reports and support some form of federal involvement	Publicize firm's good record in annual reports in pollution control without criticizing legislation and regulations
Structural actions	Assign responsibility for air pollution control at all major facilities and at headquarters to monitor corporate environmental activities	Create full-time environmental affairs units at the corporate level with both external and internal responsibilities	Increase environmental staffs at all levels. Develop reporting systems to evaluate environmental performance
Technical actions	Modest amount of voluntary air pollution control activities. Support industry research efforts and begin R&D projects	More substantial voluntary air pollution control activities and environmental research programmes	Allocate funds for speedy compliance with new regulations. Co-operate with agencies on technical studies to improve standards and equipment
Political/legal actions	Support formation of state and local regulatory agencies	Support some form of federal involvement in air pollution within API. Make its support public in Congressional hearings and advertising	Publicize support for federal regulations and refuse to join litigation and coalitions to limit regulators. Co-operate with agencies and challenge violations only with good cause

Source: Logsdon (1985, p. 57).

air pollution; and political and legal actions related to air pollution (Logsdon, 1985, p. 56).

Propositions were developed relating the components to the predicted responses in both accepting and resisting patterns. The accepting patterns are shown in Table 4.4. The relevance of this conceptual model for SRA lies in the propositions for the accepting responses shown in the table. Logsdon envisaged the use of annual reports to publicize the record of the firm (management statements, stage 3) and the development of reporting systems to evaluate environmental performance (structural actions, stage 3).

When a corporation adopts a resisting pattern there is unlikely to be a place for SRA disclosures, except where they are required by legislation or as part of the measurement process when determining the cost of non- or partial compliance. Once management decides to adopt an accepting response pattern the way is clear for the development of appropriate information systems and two-way interaction with the environment. This process will include accounting reports and is part of the generation of a more socially responsible accounting.

Brooks (1986)

Brooks provided a comprehensive study of SRA in a Canadian setting including a conceptual model which envisaged the production of regular reports as part of the process of developing, monitoring and controlling corporate social performance (the term used by Brooks). The model for managing corporate performance is shown in Figure 4.4,

Figure 4.4 A model for the management of corporate social performance: overall framework established by the board of directors. Source: Brooks (1986, p. 157).

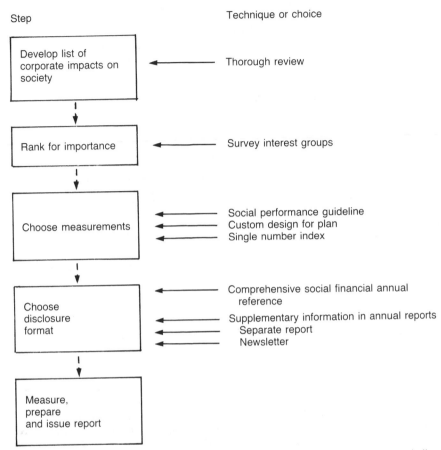

Figure 4.5 Implementation steps for a social accounting measurement and disclosure system. Source: Brooks (1986, p. 245).

whilst Figure 4.5 illustrates the steps by which the social accounting measurement and disclosure system might be implemented.

Figure 4.5 provides a framework for socially responsible corporate activity developed under the direct control of the board of directors. Social goals are identified and operationalized, and social performance is measured, monitored and controlled. Social responsibility accounting would be involved in the measuring, monitoring and controlling stages. The measurement and disclosure process is a most important part of the entire operation and involves the accounting function in a permanent and organized relationship, and not in an incomplete and *ad hoc* manner as is often currently the case.

Brooks provided more detail of the information that would be needed in Figure 4.6. There is not enough detail for this to be considered as an

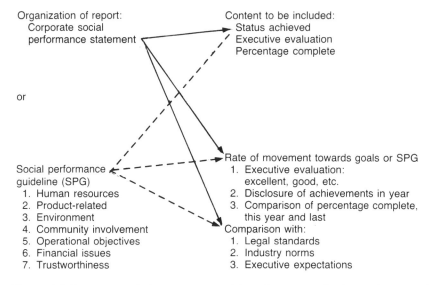

Figure 4.6 Recommended corporate social performance disclosure framework. Source: Brooks (1986, p. 242).

operational model, but the disclosure framework gives some idea of the basic categories involved. There are quite clear indications that Brooks would expect corporations to set goals and measure the degree to which these are achieved, whether against an external standard or an internally determined target. Categories in which social performance disclosures may be expected are also included. The three figures demonstrate a coherent structure which provides for the development of SRA.

Gray, Owen and Maunders (1987)

Gray, Owen and Maunders have provided two forms of conceptual model. The first is concerned with the required characteristics of a social report and is developed from a value position of accountability: the accountability of organizations for their impact on society. The required characteristics are:

1. The report must be accompanied by a full statement of the intended general objectives of the report. The statement should also allow the reader to assess: (a) what selectivity of data has been made and why; and (b) why that particular presentation has been chosen.
2. The objective of a social report should be to inform society about the extent to which actions for which an organisation is held responsible have been fulfilled.

3. The report, its choice of data, emphasis, method of presentation, and availability, should provide information directly relevant to its objectives and in particular to the objectives it holds for the interest groups to whom it is directed.
4. The report should present direct raw (un-manipulated) data that can be understood by a non-expert undertaking a careful and intelligent reading of the report. The report should be audited.   (Gray, Owen and Maunders, 1987, pp. 82–3, 85)

Although important as an initial statement, the set of characteristics does not provide any direction or detail about what should be included (other than general indications). There is a second conceptual model which gives an indication of primary-level influences and relationships between the organization and the environment (Figure 4.7).

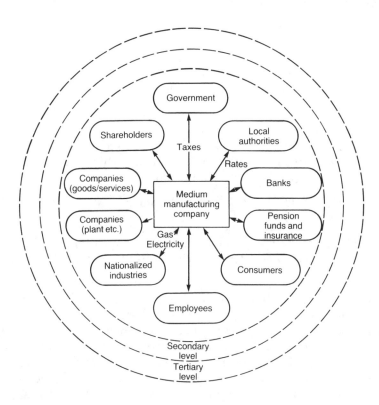

Figure 4.7 Primary-level influences of organizational activity. Source: Gray, Owen and Maunders (1987, p. 77).

OPERATIONAL MODELS RELATING TO SOCIAL RESPONSIBILITY
ACCOUNTING

This section describes a number of models which indicate in more detail
what should be disclosed in a social responsibility accounting report.
These models are designated as operational because of the added detail
provided.

In chronological order, the models covered are the Corporate Report
(ASCC, 1975); UK Government Green Paper (HMSO, 1977); Cheng
(1976); the French *Bilan Social* (Ray, 1978); Jackman (1982); and the UEC
recommendations (1983). A number of other detailed models have been
excluded from this section because they are considered to be more
concerned with TIA than SRA. They will be discussed in Chapter 5.

The Corporate Report (ASSC, 1975)

The Corporate Report has already been described as having a social-
contract perspective. The recommendations did not include social
accounting. The reason appears to be that *The Corporate Report* defines
social accounting in a manner that corresponds to total impact accounting in this book. Social accounting is defined as:

> the reporting of those costs and benefits, which may or may not
> be quantifiable in money terms, arising from economic activities
> and substantially borne or received by the community at large or
> particular groups not holding a direct relationship with the report-
> ing entity . . . (ASSC, 1975, para. 6.46)

and as such should be not be required until:

> acceptable, objective and verifiable techniques have been
> developed which will reveal an unbiased view of the positive and
> negative impact of economic activities.   (Ibid., para. 6.47)

Other recommendations for action in *The Corporate Report* include a
number of areas which are regarded as part of the social responsibility
accounting field, including value added statements, employment
reports, statements of future prospects, statements of corporate objectives and segmental reporting. These recommendations, which follow
discussions about the need for accountability and the rights of
additional parties to information, indicate that *The Corporate Report* provided a conceptual model for at least some aspects of SRA. The append-
ices to the report contain a detailed example of an employment report
and an indication of what might go into a statement of corporate objectives. The impact of *The Corporate Report* will be referred to in the
sections on employee reporting and value added statements. After some

hesitation, it has been decided to classify *The Corporate Report* as operational.

The UK government Green Paper (HMSO, 1977)

The UK Government Green Paper referred to social accounting as:

> a term which covers a range of ideas, many of which are at a very early stage of development. At its simplest it involves reporting, largely on an ad hoc basis, on individual items such as anti-pollution or health and safety measures which may be of greater importance for their social impact than for their financial effects on the company.   (HMSO, 1977, p. 16)

This statement, when added to the suggested content of various reports which are given as separate sections, provides a general indication of SRA content. The Green Paper followed many of the ideas put forward in *The Corporate Report*, including a statement of added value, an employment statement and references to disaggregation, a statement of future prospects and disclosures of energy usage. Only in the case of the employment report does the Green Paper appear to be operationalized in any way. The Green Paper was a limited operational model of what SRA disclosure should include.

Cheng (1976)

Cheng argued for a 'statement of socio-economic operations', the purpose of which was expressed as follows:

> The essential concept of the statement of socio-economic operations is to include what a business organisation has given to or held back from society. The statement is a tabulation of these expenditures made voluntarily and involuntarily by a business aimed at improving the welfare of employees, or public safety of the product, or conditions of the environment. Offset against these expenditures would be negative charges for social action that is not taken but should have been taken.   (Cheng, 1976, pp. 290–1)

The Cheng statement of socio-economic operations would be divided into three parts: internal activities in domestic operations; external relations in domestic operations; and socio-ethical considerations of international operations. The section on internal activities in domestic operations referred to activities in areas like job training programmes, employee safety and health improvements, improvements to working conditions and efforts to conserve energy. The external relations in domestic operations section would include contributions to charity, the installation of pollution control devices, public-education programmes, loans to students, recycling of materials and measures of consumer satisfaction.

In his statement on socio-ethical considerations of international operations, Cheng included the development of human resources, the provision of technical assistance, attempts to improve agricultural productivity and raise living standards in certain regions, as well as statements on corporate morality and realistic sales and profit goals. Many of the ideas contained in the Cheng framework can be used in SRA, although a limited number would appear to be more appropriate to total impact accounting because they involve the valuation of externalities.

The *Bilan Social* (1977)

The *Bilan Social* dates from 1977, although Gray, Owen and Maunders (1987) note that its origins may well have been in the 1968 social unrest in Europe. Legislation required companies with more than 750 employees to publish social balance sheets from 1979. Subsequent amendments meant that, starting in 1982, companies with more than 300 employees had to make a report. Over 7000 French companies are now covered by this legislation.

Gray, Owen and Maunders (1987, p. 28) noted that:

French social balance sheets are exclusively concerned with employment related issues. Information has to be provided under the following seven headings:

> number employed
> wage and fringe benefits
> health and safety conditions
> other working conditions
> education and training
> industrial relations
> other matters relating to the quality of working life to cover the current year and two preceding years.

The amount of information to be disclosed varies according to the size of the company and other factors; some reports may be quite large, but they are not audited.

Jackman (1982)

Jackman produced a very large volume of detail in establishing his framework for disclosure. It was suggested that businesses may take

Table 4.5 UEC's recommended form of social reporting

1.	**A summarized statement.** An outline of the most significant aspects of the social performance of the enterprise over the year together with a statement of principal objectives and review of prospects for the following year.
2.	**A social report.** To be composed solely of quantitative indicators, the precise nature of which is not specified, in the following nine areas:

2. **A social report.** To be composed solely of quantitative indicators, the precise nature of which is not specified, in the following nine areas:

(a) employment levels
(b) working conditions
(c) health and safety   The relationship
(d) education and training   between the enterprise
(e) industrial relations   and the workforce
(f) wages and other employee benefits
(g) distribution of value added
(h) impact on the environment
(i) the enterprise and external parties   The relationship
     (shareholders and other providers of   between the
     capital, local and national government,   enterprise and society
     customers, and suppliers)

3. **Notes to the accounts.** Explaining where necessary the methods and principles used in calculating the figures appearing in the social report, giving full information on any changes of method and indicating the effect of the change on the results shown, and defining terminology used.

Source: Gray, Owen and Maunders (1987, p. 22).

action to improve their reporting to society in the following areas: economic growth and efficiency; education; employment and training; civil rights and equal opportunities; urban renewal and development; pollution abatement; conservation and recreation; culture and the arts; medical care and government. Reporting should follow a social audit check list.

UEC recommendations (1983)

The Union Européenne des Experts Comptables, Economiques et Financiers (UEC) established a working party to make recommendations on the content of social reporting. This is given above in Table 4.5. The formal structure was intentional in that the UEC desired to bring the rigour of traditional financial statement preparation, including the external audit, to social accounting statements.

A REVIEW OF THE MODELS PRESENTED

The conceptual frameworks or models examined here are very diverse and it is difficult to obtain a common pattern from them, other than a concern for accountability to society in a wider sense than is practised at present. Ramanathan (1976) was concerned to define the terms employed in considering social reporting. Burke (1984) provided one of the more involved models in that he attempted to cater to both external users and internal decision-makers. He recognized that ultimately the two groups are connected, in that users need to be reassured that, in the long run, the decision-makers are taking cognizance of social issues in making decisions.

The Wartick and Cochran (1985) approach, which was not reported in the accounting literature, traced the development of the area that they call corporate social performance. The significance of this work for SRA lies in the way in which the development of social responsibilities, social responsiveness and social issues (as perceived by management) generate opportunities for the corresponding information and reporting systems. Logsdon (1985) also contributed to the management rather than the accounting literature, but her paper demonstrated the extent to which the stance taken by management will extend or limit the opportunities which accountants may have to extend their range of reporting services to management for decision-making purposes, or to the public, in the form of accountability statements.

Brooks (1986) provided a comprehensive model which moved from an overall framework developed by the board of directors, through implementation steps for a social accounting measurement and disclosure system, to a recommended disclosure framework. Finally, Gray, Owen and Maunders (1987) offered guidelines for developing social reports.

In terms of the content of operational models, it appears that some or all of the following topics might be included: employee-related information; pollution and environmental protection data; product safety; energy usage; research and development activity; productivity statistics; and community projects and relationships.

Employee-related information may appear in the form of employee reports; or human resource accounting, or, in the case of some European countries, reports to works councils. Employee reports and human resource accounting are discussed later in the chapter. General social responsibility disclosures might include details of the workforce, such as age, location and workplace, sex, average pay scales, and trade union membership. In addition, fringe benefits might be given, together with opportunities for training and advancement within the organization. Details of the safety performance of the organization would also be appropriate.

Pollution and environmental protection data are included in some models, particularly where an organization is part of what has been generally regarded as a polluting industry. Where a firm does not volunteer the environmentally related information, it may be provided by an outside body. The data required is that corresponding to the AAA Levels I and II discussed previously, thus providing details of pollutant or potential pollutant discharge in parts per million or in pounds or gallons or some other physical measure. These details may be in absolute terms or for comparison with government standards or organizational performance in previous periods. After the collection of suitable information, comparison may be made with long-term organization performance or with industry averages.

Organizations are encouraged in some instances to refer to improvements in product safety. However, this is an area where it is difficult to separate information-reporting from forms of self-congratulation or institutional advertising.

Energy usage might also be disclosed, in both monetary and non-monetary terms: monetary disclosures as part of the regular accounts, and non-monetary measurements as SRA. The information could also be reorganized to demonstrate savings, in the case of a production operation, by means of units of output per unit of energy used. This approach is represented in the literature of Roth (1981), Scudiere (1980), and Gartenberg (1980). One argument in favour of disclosing non-financial measurements of energy usage is that it avoids the problem of energy pricing and valuation. It is impossible to make monetary comparisons between periods without using an index. In the absence of a general agreement on indexed financial reporting, the use of non-financial measures would appear to be appropriate.

The disclosure of organizational activity in the field of research and development is often regarded as one of the most sensitive areas and, for obvious reasons of confidentiality, does not appear very often. Non-monetary information about a firm's research and development activities could include the number of projects in the research stage, projects in the development phase, the number of patents held and applied for, the numbers and types of personnel engaged on various projects, and new products or services coming on-stream in the next accounting period. Some form of social accounting standard or even legislation may be necessary if widespread disclosure is to be achieved in this area.

The productivity performance of an organization could be of considerable interest to a wide variety of readers without being too destructive of confidentiality. The issue of productivity in Western economies, compared with that obtained in some of the newer industrialized nations, is topical and likely to remain so for some time. The organization could develop measures of productivity which are free of bias or confidential information. These might be units of production per man-hour worked, tonnes of material mined or converted per man-shift or per machine-hour. It would be important to use meaningful figures that included the desired output of the organization related to a limiting factor involved in producing the goods and service or to the capital employed. An example of the latter type would be units of output per $1000 of capital invested. Many measures could be developed for specific industries or organizations.

Measures of community welfare and good neighbourliness are often high on any list of social responsibility accounting disclosures discussed in the literature. Items such as contributions to charity, local rates and taxes paid, training programmes for local employees, recycling of waste products, and contributions to sporting and educational organizations would be good examples. Many US corporations produce social reports to publicize these activities.

However, it must be recognized that disclosures under this heading would have to be full and frank, rather than biased towards only the 'good news'. Disclosure of social responsibility should be practised fully or not at all. Furthermore, the public reaction to particular biased information may not be what the organization wants or perhaps expects. This aspect has not been investigated, as far as the author is aware. Wiseman (1982) provided examples of reports which were not full disclosures and which may have been misleading. She concluded:

> The findings indicated that the voluntary environmental disclosures were incomplete, providing inadequate disclosures for most of the environmental performance items included in the index. Further, it was demonstrated that no relationship existed between the measured contents of the firms' environmental disclosures and the firms' environmental performance.   (Wiseman, 1982, p. 62)

There is clearly a role for a social auditor, despite the reluctance of accountants to become involved in this area. The concept of the social audit is included in Chapter 6.

THE ROLE OF MANAGEMENT ACCOUNTING IN THE PREPARATION OF SOCIAL RESPONSIBILITY DISCLOSURES

A majority of the models included in the above discussion clearly relate to the external reporting of social responsibility disclosures by corporations. One attempt at formulating a model in terms of the contribution of management accounting is reviewed below (Schafer and Mathews, 1984). The discussion recognizes that some models do indicate an awareness of the importance of management accounting and social responsibility, even though the main thrust is directed towards external reporting.

A number of studies have indicated the need for a management accounting input to the development of social responsibility disclosures. Ramanathan (1976, p. 516) commented that: 'To the extent that a firm's social impacts are not subjected to formal measurement process, these aspects are not likely to enter into the firm's planning decisions or performance evaluation.'

Epstein, Flamholtz and McDonough (1976, p. 28) argued that a larger number of reports are produced for internal use than the public is aware of, because many are not issued for external consumption. The public is left with an impression that corporations only use social responsibility accounting for external purposes.

Although these references suggest that the authors have a firm basis for their statement about the relative emphasis of internal and external reporting, in conclusion they say:

> We need to know more about:
> (4)   the extent to which corporations are using accounting for social performance for decision making and performance evaluation at different levels in the organization, including the evaluation of (a) individuals, (b) divisions and (c) the corporation as a whole.   (Ibid., p. 35)

It will be argued in this section that management accountants need to be involved in social responsibility disclosures, whether they are intended for internal or external consumption. This is especially the case where, as Preston (1981, p. 262) noted:

> (1)   the value of a corporate social reporting activity depends upon its usefulness to management
>
> and
> (2)   there are available techniques for developing social perform-ance information that will have continuing managerial useful-ness over time.

SRA is concerned with the internal reporting of social responsibility data as well as external reporting. One approach is given in the following sections.

STRATEGIC AND OPERATIONAL PLANNING PROCEDURES

Senior management should be responsible for major and far-reaching actions in respect of strategic planning. Objectives which may be adopted at this level are translated into strategic plans of a broad nature, examples might be to 'move into international marketing', to 'retrench plant X' or to 'cease manufacture of product Z'. Once the strategic decision has been taken, the operational planning procedures will fill in the details and operationalize the strategic decision. The models presented by both Brooks (1986) and Burke (1984) introduce the social dimension to the decision-making activity.

Table 4.6 The relationship between strategic and operational planning for social disclosure (partial only)

I.	Objectives
	1. organizational survival
	2. maximization of long-term returns to shareholders
	3. satisfying returns to all parties involved in the enterprise
	converted by top management into
II.	Strategic planning – by senior management (examples)
	1. to improve our safety record
	2. to operate with less environmental impact
	3. to generate a better relationship within our community
	reduced to targets (for example)
III.	Operational planning – by lower levels of management
	1. to develop areas and measures through which safety performance may be improved; these include records, education performance charts, and departmental measures

The same procedure should be adopted in respect of social responsibility disclosures, whether destined for ultimate consumption outside the organization or for use as an internal report. Examples of strategic decisions applied to social responsibility matters might be expressed as 'to improve our accident record' or 'to have a particular change in the hiring record for minorities' or 'to have a less damaging effect on the environment'. In any event, it is extremely important that senior management should be seen to have instigated the process. This will ensure that policies on SRA disclosures have an opportunity to proceed to the operational phase. This process is shown in Table 4.6.

To operationalize a decision to utilize social responsibility disclosures will require management to set general areas within which to operate. Subsequently, specific planning measures must be generated within these areas. The areas and measures listed in Table 4.7 are only a sample of those from which operational management might choose a final programme. Each organization would have to develop specific, as well as general, planning measures, to deal with problems within identified areas. The sequence of strategic planning decisions, followed by operational planning and action, leads naturally to the use of these measures for control purposes.

CONTROL SYSTEMS

The use of budgetary control systems must be acknowledged as a most important characteristic of the modern organization and these principles may be applied to social responsibility measures. The operational

Table 4.7 The relationship of reporting areas and planning measures

Areas	Planning Measures
1. Environmental	(a) Liquid, solid, gaseous discharge in physical measures such as lb. and gals. (b) Specific measures of particular materials in parts per million (ppm) of toxic gases, for example
2. Product utility reliability	(a) Number of complaints from customers (b) Reactions from consumer bodies (c) Reports from independent consultants
3. Energy efficiency	(a) Cost of energy used (b) Specific measures of energy used in physical terms for particular areas (c) Cost of energy per unit of output (d) Energy used to output ratio in specific plants and cost centres
4. Productivity per unit of individual employee or plant time	(a) Physical output in terms of process time (b) Physical output in terms of employee time
5. Employee/employer relations (unions where applicable)	(a) Official disputes as a proportion of normal working time (b) Unofficial disputes as a proportion of normal working time (c) Use of agreed grievance procedures by employees
6. Employee conditions/ safety management	(a) Lost-time accidents involving serious injury (b) Lost-time through minor accidents, analysed by plant, division, etc.
7. Research and development	(a) Number of patents held (b) Number of active researchers (c) Number of projects at varous specified stages of development
8. Community activity	(a) Specific measures of community service: scholarships, loans, provision of equipment and personnel, sponsorship, etc.
9. Minority employment	(a) Employment at different levels within the organization (b) Comparison with previous employment records and those of other organizations

planning process outlined above would be applied to divisions, departments and sections, and leads logically to the development of budgets for social measures as well as for physical and financial quantities. It is possible to budget for an accident record or a particular level of injuries in much the same way as for any other operational input relationship. Another example might be a budgeted improvement in environmental impact by reducing the discharge of a particular pollutant, even where the present output is below required (or statutory) levels.

Budgets may be flexed in the usual way to allow for activity levels above or below those originally envisaged. Furthermore, using a system of planning budgets will ensure that an appropriate recording system is established and maintained, since operational management will need to show compliance with the budget. Once the fixed (planning) budget is adjusted for actual activity (flexed), a comparison of budgeted and actual results is possible. The variances developed as a result of this comparison have the same strengths and weaknesses as control devices as those developed from the physical and monetary measurements. The variances from budgeted safety or environmental impact performance must be investigated if outside significant limits. The development of variances may have a particular importance for the measurement of divisional performance.

DIVISIONAL PERFORMANCE MANAGEMENT

The measurement of divisional performance and the subsequent control of divisional management from a central position are difficult problems. Divisional management has been assessed in the past by means of highly condensed financial aggregates such as return on capital employed (ROCE) and to some extent this system continues in operation. Undue reliance upon this type of measure can lead to dysfunctional actions in terms of overall corporate performance. A number of undesirable practices may result, including a reduction in the level of maintenance and research and development, the sale of currently unused assets, and sometimes managerial decisions which lead to higher output in the short term. These actions may produce a disaffected workforce and industrial disputes in the longer term.

The use of social responsibility accounting measures in divisional performance measurement may help to overcome the limitations of ROCE (or similar financial measures such as return on investment (ROI)). The package developed might include measures of employee morale (turnover of personnel) as well as of research and development, safety, and environmental impact (measures of pollutants). These SRA measures would be disclosed in addition to the more traditional financially based measures. The evaluation of divisional performance would then be seen by the management concerned as balanced and aimed at the longer term, in which case many of the dysfunctional consequences of unidimensional measures may be avoided. The usefulness of social responsibility accounting systems designed and operated by management accountants, for control and performance evaluation, is probably a sufficient reason for their introduction.

SUMMARY

This section has examined the issue of SRA from the management accounting perspective. This contrasts with the usual financial accounting perspective, and a number of authorities within the SRA literature have indicated the importance of management accounting to the development of the area. However, there is some doubt about how much SRA is performed for the use of management and not disclosed in accounting reports.

Management accountants should take an active role in developing objectives, strategic and operational policies and standards for SRA. This would enable budgetary control systems and variance analysis to be used to ensure adherence to previously agreed standards in the areas normally included in SRA, in particular those connected with employees, safety, product improvement, community relationships, energy usage and environmental impact. An additional benefit could come from a more balanced system of divisional performance evaluation for use with segregated management structures.

A discussion of SRA would be incomplete without consideration of four areas which are frequently treated independently, although probably belonging under this general heading. These are employee reports, human resource accounting, accounting for industrial democracy and value added statements.

EMPLOYEE REPORTS

Employee reports form part of the SRA field as defined in this book. However, the gain in popularity in Australia and the United Kingdom has led to a specialized literature for this sub-group. Despite an increase in popularity, employee reports are voluntary, unregulated and unaudited disclosures. Consequently, quality varies and there is no uniformity of use within different industries. The approach taken by the French *Bilan Social* and other European countries is based upon legislation, and is quite different from that of Anglo-American accounting.

Many of the items that Cheng (1976) included in his first statement (internal activities in domestic operations) are to be found in employee reports or employment statements (Taylor, Webb and McGinley, 1979).

The UK Government Green Paper included a section on employee statements, separate from the entry on social accounting. In the case of the employment statement:

> What is proposed is that companies should publish an employment statement which sets out information about its workforce and employment policies which are relevant not only to employees themselves but to shareholders and others concerned with the company. The aim is to provide sufficient information about the workforce and about the way in which the employment resources are managed to give an indication of the effectiveness of management in this crucial area of the company's activities . . .
> (HMSO, 1977, p. 9)

Examples of suitable information include: numbers of employees joining and leaving the organization; employment and training policies; matters relating to trade unions and participation in decision-making; the number of man-days lost as a result of industrial disputes; pension and sick-pay arrangements; and employment opportunities for the disabled.

The Green Paper does not distinguish between employment reports, which are *about* employees and a part of the annual report to shareholders, and employee reports, which are made *to* employees. Both may be considered part of the SRA disclosures. Although much of the information would be common to both reports, they have different objectives. The employee report is usually designed to present employees with a number of items of information not otherwise available to them. The employment report is a part of the annual report to shareholders and could be used where no employee report is used.

The incidence and content of employee reports have been discussed in the accounting literature in Australia, New Zealand and the UK. Published work includes examples of current practice, the attitude of employers, employees and trade unions towards employee reports and some attempts at a normative framework for employee reports.

In Australia, Taylor, Webb and McGinley (1979) and Webb and Taylor (1980) reported on the information given in company reports. They referred to a lack of uniformity and quality in the disclosures. Hussey and Craig (1979) and Craig and Hussey (1981) conducted surveys of employees and employers respectively. The information sought from employers was designed to obtain a profile of current reporting practices. In the survey employees were asked what they would like to see in employee reports, and the extent to which they understood the material given in actual examples. Follow-up interviews found that many employees did not understand the material provided as well as they had indicated in their responses to the questionnaire.

The problem of readability of employee reports, an important part of the report's understandability, was investigated by Pound (1980). The results were interesting and also disturbing, since it found that many employee reports were written in a way which would render them incomprehensible to a large proportion of the target audience. The basis of this type of research was extended through work by Lewis, Parker, Pound and Sutcliffe (1983).

It has been observed in respect of general SRA disclosures that most of the literature is devoted to descriptive analysis and empirical studies, with correspondingly little attention to providing a normative framework. The same general comment can be applied to employee reporting. Jackman (1982) provided for employee reports as part of his social audit. The most important information excluded from his extensive list of data is simplified financial information, which frequently provides the basis for employee reports. Financial information would probably include value added statements, which are included in Jackman's paper, but not as a part of the social audit check list. Lewis, Parker and Sutcliffe (1982) have suggested a framework which would provide a better foundation for research into financial reporting to employees. The authors indicate dissatisfaction with much of the work previously carried out. The research framework was designed to assist future efforts in the area by providing several critical propositions, which they argue must be examined in order to make any meaningful progress. They are: employees do not require employee reports; employees do not require employee reports for any decision-making purposes; certain specific employee decision types; employees do not require information for 'other' (non-decision making) purposes; employees are not familiar with the concept of employee reports; employee reports received by employees are perceived as management propaganda vehicles; and employee reports have in the past supplied employees with the particular types of information which they require.

Little work of this nature has been carried out in New Zealand. Chye (1982) provided a review of the literature and a limited number of examples of company employee reports from 1980 annual reports. Smith and Firth (1986) surveyed employees and found that most of the respondents welcomed the reports and thought that they understood them, but wanted more future-orientated and non-financial quantitative information.

In the UK Purdy (1981) examined the provision of financial information to employees with a particular emphasis on the environmental and organizational pressures which may induce companies to produce employee reports. Purdy included in his study a reference to the style of management and the degree to which management attempted to obtain feedback from the production of employee reports and the disclosure of financial information.

Hussey (1979) considered several aspects of UK employee reporting, including the perception of employee reports by employees. Jackson-Cox *et al.* (1984) examined the place of information disclosure so far as it impinges on the industrial relations strategies of corporations and trade unions and the development of a code of practice for the disclosure of information.

Employee reports are difficult to classify. Do they belong to the field of financial reporting, or to that of social responsibility accounting, or both? There is usually a large financial component made up of a value added statement and simplified financial statements. There is often a large non-financial component, including a diagrammatic representation of the financial material (division of the value added as a pie-chart, for example) and statistics about the organization and workforce. A quantity of qualitative material will often be present such as 'a message from the Chairman'. There is some evidence that employees are more concerned about their own place of work than about the group of companies to which their own employing company belongs, whereas financial accounting reports are consolidated.

On balance, the author considers that most employee reports should be treated as potentially SRA disclosures. Employee reporting (or reporting to employees) is predominantly a Level I and II measurement exercise, except where financial data are reproduced from the regular annual accounts. The Level III measurements of employee activity have been separated off in the form of human resource accounting. This is discussed later in this chapter.

ACCOUNTING AND INDUSTRIAL DEMOCRACY

An extension of the employee reporting literature has been concerned with industrial democracy. This term is used to refer to the involvement of labour in decision-making and may be formal, as envisaged by the Bullock Report (Department of Trade, 1977), or less formal, as in providing trade union negotiators with additional information for use in collective bargaining or negotiation over plant closures and redundancy (Gray, Owen and Maunders, 1987, ch. 9). Major contributions have been made by critical theorists, concerned that trade union negotiators should be sufficiently well-versed in financial matters that they can understand and critique the accounting data provided by management (Bougen and Ogden, 1985). Radical researchers have also explored the logical extension of industrial democracy in the form of feasible socialism (Tomlinson, 1985) and worker co-operatives (Jefferis and Thomas, 1985).

Many of the models used in accounting and industrial democracy have been criticized for viewing the costs and benefits of alternative actions from a management perspective and not taking into account workers' separate costs and benefits (Bougen and Ogden, 1985). An explanation for this phenomenon could be that employee representatives are concerned with mastering the financial accounting data and have not yet come to appreciate the resources available in the form of non-traditional accounting. Although individual firms are unlikely to be swayed by the costs of unemployment following a decision to close a plant, government may be encouraged to intervene if presented with a statement of total costs and benefits to all parties.

The majority of Anglo-American SRA models do not deal with the topic of accounting and industrial democracy, although the provision of information to works councils and other employee groups is provided for in continental Europe. There are historical and cultural reasons for these differences (Mathews and Perera, 1991).

HUMAN RESOURCE ACCOUNTING

Human resource accounting (HRA) was once an important area of theoretical discussion and may become topical again, although at the moment there is little being written in this area. HRA has not led to widespread modification of reporting practice and it is difficult to know exactly where HRA would fit into the framework of social accounting proposed herein. The valuation arrived at is a monetary amount, frequently derived from data which are not cost-based. It must, therefore, be a Level III measurement (under the system proposed by the AAA) of the data which could be produced as a general SRA disclosure or as part of an employee report. The following examination proceeds on the basis that it is the logical framework of reporting socially useful information that we are describing, and not possible reporting practices in the near future.

The purpose of HRA is to place a value on the human capital employed by the firm in a manner similar to the valuation of other assets. A section of the literature favours putting these values on the balance sheet in a similar form to that of a capitalized lease. Other writers think that it would be sufficient for the capitalized figures to be included with other social responsibility disclosures. The valuation for HRA would be based on the number of each type of employee within the organization. Average and total value of employees would be expected to alter in line with changes in staffing, the amount of training undertaken, and the increase or decrease in employee morale. The value of the human resource may be determined according to one or more of the following approaches: conventional accounting; replacement cost; discounting of future salaries; and economic value (Unruh and Mathews, 1992).

The conventional accounting approach would be to capitalize expenditures related to recruiting, training and developing personnel. These amounts would then be amortized over the useful life of the asset. There are obvious difficulties in accumulating this data, and furthermore, what constitutes a useful life for an employee? Not only do employees retire or die, they often move from position to position and employer to employer. Finally, how does an organization value a new employee who arrives with a variety of skills acquired elsewhere? A partial response may be found in the literature dealing with accounting for pension schemes, but this does not address the problem of the uncertainty surrounding continued employment.

A replacement cost approach may be used in an attempt to value the human resources of an organization. The replacement cost is a measure of the costs which would be incurred in replacing the existing personnel, including recruiting, hiring, training and developing personnel to their existing levels of competence. Presumably, under this system of valuation, those employees thought incompetent would have a low, zero or even negative value, since they could leave without being replaced. The total value under this approach could be quite different from the accumulated cost approach. Both methods of valuation could be adjusted for price-level changes.

A third approach would be to value employees at the capitalized value of their discounted future salaries for the expected period of employment. This method requires a number of estimates or assumptions in respect of the period of employment, the career path, the level of salary paid during the career path, and last, but not least, a discount rate with which to obtain the present value.

The last approach to be included here is the measurement of human resources at their economic value. Flamholtz (1974) suggests developing an estimate of future services from each employee and discounting this to get the economic value of that person. The total of individual economic values would be the value of the human resource to the organization.

The difficulties attached to the last two approaches are immediately apparent. Accountants generally do not favour estimates being made of future costs and/or benefits associated with employees, and then discounting the value of these estimates with a rate which may be largely guesswork. The use of an historical-cost or replacement-cost approach might be acceptable to accountants, but would be rejected by other theorists. Early advocates of human resource accounting argued in favour of putting value on the balance sheet along with other assets. There are alternative courses of action which could be taken, such as listing the value of employees as part of the employment report, or in some other socially orientated disclosures.

There are a number of difficulties attached to the development of HRA. These may be categorized as behavioural, methodological and theoretical. Behavioural problems arise when employees and others object to the valuing of human beings, because the 'worth' of the individual is under examination. Whilst the valuation process may be acceptable to senior management, organized labour often has disagreements over historical relativities in pay scales, and the process of valuing individuals or groups is likely to cause further industrial difficulties, including strikes.

The methodological problems are many, and centre about the usual difficulties of measuring inputs and outputs. These problems are compounded in some models by the use of present values of future events, necessitating the development of discount rates. The theoretical difficulties stem from the isolated nature of much of the HRA work. It is not grounded in the reality of other accounting developments. This criticism may also be levelled at later sections of this book; however, HRA purports to measure the value of employees as assets, but the vast majority of the literature is on a level which makes practical accomplishment most unlikely. This is analogous to the situation with plant, which is valued at cost and not the present value of the future cash flows which influenced the acquisition decision, despite many theoretical arguments in favour of the latter.

In a recent return to the HRA issue, Flamholtz (1985) has developed in conjunction with Touche Ross, a stochastic rewards valuation model (SRVM) for use in determining the 'net present value of the average person at each job level'. Flamholtz provided a number of potential users of the system, including personal advancement analysis within the firm and a number of uses on behalf of clients. The author summarized the work as follows:

> Although the system requires significant further refinement and research, this pilot study represents a potentially significant advance in the human resource accounting field. The study is also significant because there are, at present, relatively few examples of actual organizations which have developed human resource accounting systems.   (Flamholtz, 1985)

VALUE ADDED STATEMENTS

Value added statements have a place in the SRA literature, although they are composed of financial data that is derived, for the most part, from conventional financial accounts. Value added statements were advocated in *The Corporate Report* (ASSC, 1975) and the UK Government Green Paper (HMSO, 1977). They have also been examined by commentators on behalf of the principal accounting bodies in the UK (Renshall, Allan and Nicholson, 1979; Gray and Maunders, 1980). Consideration has been given to technical particulars, such as whether value added should be calculated on a production or sales basis, and whether it should be shown as a gross or net figure before distribution.

Burchell, Clubb and Hopwood (1985) have charted the rise and fall of value added statements in the UK and associated their use with accounting in a social context in which the discipline responds (or is induced to respond) to particular social factors. Value added has been used in parts of Europe (Dierkes, 1979), but statements are reported to be almost non-existent in the US (Choi and Mueller, 1984). The important factor at work appears to be the use to which the information is to be put, rather than the type of information. Value added statements, which reflect the production and distribution of value added, are perceived by many to demonstrate the team approach to generating value added. They are therefore part of social responsibility accounting.

SUMMARY

This chapter has considered a number of conceptual and operational models for SRA, the involvement of management accountants in developing both internal and external disclosures, employee reports and accounting for industrial democracy, human resource accounting and value added statements. A number of conceptual models were examined and found to range from philosophical positions and definitional statements, to historically generated categories of response by accountants and managers, to given changes in the social and legislative environment. Several models emphasized the interrelationship of the entity and the surrounding environment, whilst others were more concerned with the development of a further (social) dimension as an aid to decision-making, which was also sensitive to the needs of outside parties.

Several operational models were considered (the difference between conceptual and operational being defined in terms of details of what should be disclosed) and found to be couched in terms of employee reports, product information, energy reports, community involvement and environmental impact. A number of specialized areas were also included, such as SRA and management accounting, accounting and industrial democracy, human resource accounting and value added statements. It was noted that historically continental European models were devoted almost exclusively to employee matters.

Social responsibility accounting in practice   5

INTRODUCTION

Social responsibility accounting captures a variety of information that organizations want to disclose. A number of studies designed to find out what is disclosed are reviewed below. They are followed by a brief examination of some of the problems inherent in this type of research. The studies are grouped according to the country of origin and are intended to be illustrative of the disclosures in each. The chapter concludes with a partial explanation of differences by reference to studies on culture and accounting.

A REVIEW OF SRA STUDIES FROM AROUND THE WORLD

AUSTRALIA

Studies carried out in Australia between 1979 and 1984 included Trotman (1979), Kelly (1979), Trotman and Bradley, (1981), Pang (1982), Guthrie (1982) and Gul, Andrew and Teoh (1984). There have been no major studies since the mid 1980s.

Trotman (1979)

Trotman used a sample consisting of the accounts of the largest 100 companies listed on the Sydney Stock Exchange. Disclosures were analysed under the headings of environment, energy, human resources, products, community involvement and 'other'. Trotman found an increased incidence of disclosure, from 28 companies in 1967, to 48 in 1972 and 69 in 1977, with 'the environment' and 'human resources' as the most frequently included categories in 1977. Disclosures were categorized into monetary quantification, non-monetary quantification and qualitative disclosures. About half of all disclosures were found to be qualitative. The proportion of social accounting material in the annual reports was measured in terms of 'average pages per company report': 0.08 in 1967, 0.30 in 1972 and 0.57 in 1977. It is the quantification of disclosures which makes this study particularly important in the Australian context. Unfortunately, Trotman did not reveal the decision mechanism by which particular disclosures were judged to be eligible for inclusion.

Kelly (1979)

Kelly used selected social responsibility disclosures from the annual reports of 50 selected Australian corporations over the period 1969–78. The results confirmed Trotman's findings of increased disclosure over the time period and drew attention to differential aspects of reporting. Kelly found that large corporations tended to disclose more environmental and product information than did smaller organizations, whilst companies in the primary and secondary sectors of the economy tended to disclose more environmental and energy-related information than corporations engaged in tertiary activities. The opposite was true in the case of information about the interaction of the firm and its local community.

This study was important in the context of Australian social responsibility accounting research, because it established statistically significant relationships between types and sizes of industries and various social responsibility disclosures. However, the sample size was quite small (50 companies) and this limits the ability to generalize from the results.

Trotman and Bradley (1981)

The study by Trotman and Bradley was designed to test a number of specific hypotheses concerned with volumes of disclosures and (1) the size of companies; (2) their systematic risk; (3) social constraints as perceived by management and (4) the long-term effects of decisions. The sample comprised 207 companies listed on the Australian Associated Stock Exchange. The annual reports of the companies selected (all volunteers arrived at by process of elimination) were examined for social responsibility disclosures in the area of environment energy, human resources, products, community involvement and 'other'. The number of companies producing suitable disclosures was 40% of the sample selected (83 reports). The extent of social responsibility disclosures was measured through a line-by-line examination of the report, which produced a proportion of the total discussion of all issues.

The size of companies was measured in terms of both total assets and total sales at the 1978 balance sheet date. Systematic risk was defined as the contribution of the individual security to portfolio risks, using beta measurements supplied by the Australian Graduate School of Management. Measurement of the social pressures perceived by companies and management's decision horizon were taken from a previous survey by Bradley. Statistically significant relationships were found in the following areas:

1. Company size (total assets and total sales) was associated with social responsibility. Larger organizations tended to provide more disclosures.
2. A positive correlation was found between the volume of social responsibility data disclosed and the extent of the social constraints faced by companies.

Positive relationships of lesser significance were found between systematic risk (beta) and the volume of social responsibility data provided, and the disclosures and emphasis on long-term developments within the organization. The Trotman and Bradley study was important because of the direction it gave to social responsibility disclosure research in Australia and the increased sophistication of its analysis.

Pang (1982)

Pang modelled her study on that of Trotman (1979) and examined the social responsibility disclosures of a sample of 100 companies listed on the Sydney Stock Exchange in 1980. The 100 companies included the 70 largest companies (based on market capitalization) and 30 companies selected at random. The reports were analysed in terms of community involvement, environment, energy, human resources and products and consumer issues. The results showed that in 1980, 79 companies made some form of social responsibility disclosure, the larger companies disclosing socially related material more frequently than the smaller companies. Disclosure rates ranged from 92% for those with a market capitalization above $A500m to 73% for those less than $A100m.

The location of the social responsibility information was also considered. Alternative formats included: a separate report (4); a separate section of the annual report (25); separate headings in various reports (18); and coverage as part of other major topics in the annual report (32). Larger companies tended to provide separate disclosure of social activities, whereas smaller companies tended to disclose these activities in conjunction with other matters in the annual report.

Guthrie (1982 and 1984)

Guthrie (1982) examined the annual reports of the top 150 listed Australian companies for 1980. The study was aimed at showing trends in SRA disclosures and analysing the extent and type of disclosure activity. Content analysis was used to place information within four dimensions: theme; evidence; amount; and location. 'Theme' was based on categories such as environment, energy, human resources, products, community involvement and others. 'Evidence' described the form of disclosure: monetary, non-monetary, declarative (qualitative) and none. 'Amount' was the familiar measure by the proportion of pages devoted to social responsibility matters; and 'location' referred to a choice between management reviews, a separate social disclosures section, parts of other sections of the annual report and a separate booklet on social responsibility.

The results showed that 42% of the companies surveyed included some form of social responsibility disclosure, with the different themes having the following relative importance: human resources 43%; environment 21%; community involvement 14%; energy 9%; products 5%; and 'others' 8%. The evidence section showed that 60% of all disclosures were declarative (that is, non-quantitative), whilst 24% gave some non-monetary quantification. The reports giving both monetary and non-monetary quantification were limited to 12% of those making some disclosure, and only 4% gave monetary disclosures alone.

The most popular places for locating social responsibility disclosures were the director's report (50%), or a non-specific section of the annual report (40%); and only 10% used a specific section of the annual report devoted to social responsibility disclosures. No company issued a separate booklet on socially related matters. The amount of disclosures was a mean of 0.68 pages; however, 11% disclosed more than one page, whilst 40% reported less than 0.25 pages. The overall results tended to confirm previous studies. The important dimensions added by Guthrie are content analysis, which incorporated checks on validity and reliability, and the addition of variability to the average figure for disclosure.

Guthrie (as reported in Guthrie and Mathews, 1985) continued this analysis with a further study in 1984 using 1983 Annual Reports. Because the analyst conducted both studies using the same instrument for measurement, it was possible to tabulate comparative data for certain features for 1980 and 1983. These comparisons related to the top 50 companies on the Sydney Stock Exchange, as measured by market capitalization.

In both 1980 and 1983 annual reports 56% of the sample companies made some form of social responsibility accounting disclosure. Of the

Table 5.1   Types of social responsibility accounting disclosure

| | 1980 | | 1983 | |
	Companies reporting	% of total	Companies reporting	% of total
Environment	15	30	6	12
Energy	4	8	1	2
Human resources	22	44	26	52
Products	1	2	0	0
Community involvement	8	16	8	16
Others	4	8	5	10
Total	54	100	46	100

Note: Some companies reported more than one theme.

Table 5.2   Type and quantification of social responsibility accounting disclosures

| | 1980 | | | | 1983 | | | |
| | Quantitative monetary | | Disclosure non-monetary | | Quantitative monetary | | Disclosure non-monetary | |
	No.	%	No.	%	No.	%	No.	%
Environment	1	2	1	2	2	4	1	2
Energy	2	4	3	6	0	0	0	0
Human resources	1	2	12	24	3	6	19	38
Products	0	0	0	0	1	2	0	0
Community involvement	1	2	0	0	1	2	1	2
Others	0	0	0	0	1	2	0	0
Totals	5	10	16	32	8	16	21	42

Note: Many corporations made more than one disclosure.

various possible SRA themes, in 1980 it was found that human resources accounted for 22 disclosures, the next highest number was environment (15) and community involvement (8). Of lesser importance was energy (4), others (4) and products (1), from a total of 54 reporting companies. In 1983 there were considerably fewer disclosures for environment (6) and only one related to energy. These results are reported in Table 5.1.

Of the 54 disclosures identified it was found that only 21 were expressed in quantified terms, either monetary or non-monetary. This represents approximately 44% of the total disclosures. The results shown in Table 5.2 indicated that human resources had the highest incidence of quantified disclosure with 13 disclosures, followed by energy, community involvement and environment. There were no entries for community involvement and products. In 1983 the only

Table 5.3 Quantification of social responsibility accounting disclosures

| | 1980 | | 1983 | |
	No.	%	No.	%
Both monetary and non-monetary quantification	3	10	8	29
Monetary quantification	2	6	1	3
Non-monetary quantification	11	40	14	50
Declarative	12	44	5	18
Total	28	100	28	100

Table 5.4 Location of social responsibility accounting disclosures

	1980	1983
Director's report	12	9
Separate section of annual report devoted to SRA	0	1
Other section	16	18
Separate booklet	0	0

Table 5.5 Number of pages devoted to social responsibility accounting disclosures

Pages	1980	1983
0.01–0.25	11	6
0.26–0.50	8	10
0.51–0.75	2	6
0.76–1.00	3	1
1.01 or more	4	3

significant change was the increase in quantification of disclosures related to human resources.

Table 5.3 outlines the results for the degree of quantification. In 1980 16 of the 28 companies quantified their disclosures, but only five companies (16%) had some form of monetary quantification and 12 companies (40%) had no quantification whatever in the identified SRA disclosures. In 1983 there appeared to be an increase in the number of disclosing companies which were willing to quantify disclosures, from 56% in 1980 to 82% in 1983.

Table 5.4 indicates that SRA disclosures were located throughout the annual reports with 12 appearing in the Chairman's report (45% of disclosing companies). However, the majority of companies disclosed this information in the general body of the report, and no company provided a separate SRA booklet. In 1983 there was little change in these disclosure patterns.

Table 5.5 indicates that in 1980 there were approximately 42.25 pages of social responsibility accounting disclosure identified. The average number of pages devoted to SRA information, per disclosing company, was 0.68 of a page. There were only seven (11%) of the companies with more than one page of the annual report devoted to SRA whilst 25 companies (40%) of disclosing companies devoted less than 0.25 of a page to SRA. Similar results were obtained for 1983 with the average being 0.70 of a page.

In the 1983 annual report review, a new category was introduced into the recording instrument, that of the issuing of bad or negative news about any one of the themes. The main reason for the 11 disclosures on human resources was the reduction of staff employed because of retrenchments and reorganization of the corporation.

There are obvious advantages in having the same analyst examine the annual reports using a 'proven' instrument. A greater degree of comparability should result. It can be seen that, on the whole, there were few changes in SRA in Australia between 1980 and 1983 as evidenced by the annual reports of the top 50 companies on the Sydney Stock Exchange.

Gul, Andrew and Teoh (1984)

Gul, Andrew and Teoh used the instrument developed by Guthrie on a random sample of 136 annual reports of Australian companies. The results they obtained differed to some extent from those reported in the previous section, probably as a result of the random sample used in place of the sample of larger companies adopted by Guthrie. Results showed that 30% of the companies sampled made SRA disclosures. These included 42% of the companies in the construction industry and 32% of the companies in the manufacturing industry. The information disclosed consisted of 36% relating to the human resource, 32% relating to community involvement and 10% relative to the environment. It was found that large companies made more disclosures about employees, but disclosures about community involvement was spread across firms of all sizes. The largest proportion of monetary quantification was concerned with community involvement, and the majority of disclosures were in the directors' report.

The authors concluded that a reasonable proportion (30%) of companies surveyed included SRA disclosures, and for foreign-owned companies the proportion was 50%. There are limitations associated with the study in terms of the use of a relatively small sample and only one year's reports.

NEW ZEALAND

Robertson (1977)

In a 1977 New Zealand study Robertson reported on a survey under-taken to assess the extent and kind of corporate social reporting in published annual reports. This was achieved by using the annual reports of the largest 100 companies, (based on paid-up capital) as at September 1975. The analysis found that for 54 companies there were 79 qualitative, 17 quantitative and 34 monetary disclosures. However, any references to 'social' matters were included, no matter how trivial, and 24 of the monetary disclosures referred to housing assistance for personnel. Although a useful beginning, the study lacked quantifi-cation. For example, the extent of disclosure is not quantified, in con-trast to the work of Trotman and the other studies discussed previously.

Davey (1985)

Two New Zealand studies provide an insight into the problems associ-ated with this type of research. Davey examined the annual accounts of a 15% random sample of firms listed on the New Zealand Stock Exchange at 31 March 1982. This gave a sample of 32 firms which were classified as primary, heavy industrial, manufacturing or service industries. The accounts were analysed for the type of disclosure tax-onomy used (all were found to use an inventory approach), differing measurement levels, any form of attest relationship, and the volume of each type of disclosure as measured by six-character 'words'.

It was found that social responsibility disclosures had increased con-siderably since Robertson's 1977 study, but that most were generalized qualitative statements without any attempt at attestation, and with a low score on the scale of quality used. Approximately 60% of the sample made disclosures exceeding 100 'words' in length. There was no con-firmation of the relationship between size of organization (as measured by total assets) and the volume of social responsibility disclosures. This is contrary to the Australian studies of Trotman, Trotman and Bradley, and Kelly, and may have been the result of the small sample size.

Davey constructed a 'corporate social responsibility worksheet' which allowed for disclosure under the headings of employment, corporate objectives, product, philanthropy, environment, energy and 'other'. Guidelines were provided for the calculation of 'words', the determi-nation of the type of disclosure (inventory approach, cost approach, programme management approach, benefit/cost approach), the quality of disclosure (on a seven-point scale) and any evidence of independent audit or attestation. An example of the worksheet is given in Figure 5.1.

It is evident that much of the analysis is subjective. However, it may be hypothesized that the total of 'words' and the percentage of total wordage attributed to a particular form of disclosure (for example, product) could be expected to remain reasonably constant between observers.

Ng (1985)

The reproducibility hypothesis was tested by Ng, who used the same test instrument with the same sample of companies but for three years (1981, 1982 and 1983). She found that even a careful attempt to replicate the word-count (for 1982 reports) did not yield the same results, because of the impossibility of different observers reacting in the same way to some of the statements. The extent of the differences are detailed below.

In Table 5.6 a comparison of the percentage of the sample reporting SRA shows a consistent upward bias by Ng compared with Davey. That is, Ng discarded fewer disclosures as unworthy of inclusion because they were of a self-serving or public-relations nature. The only category where Davey recorded a higher number of words was 'other' because Ng seems to have gone to greater lengths to categorize some of the difficult entries which Davey had assigned to this category. A forced-nature choice may have been employed by Ng to avoid the 'other' category, and this may reflect the individual characteristics of the researcher.

Table 5.7 provides comparative data on each category of disclosure. The results presented in this table indicate the subjective effect of using different observers. Ng had a different reaction to marginally subjective statements than Davey and this had an aggregate effect of increasing her word count by 32%.

Table 5.6 Percentage of sample corporations reporting SRA

	Davey %	Ng %
Total companies reporting disclosures	84	100
Percentage of companies reporting:		
employment	66	88
corporate objectives	38	41
product	3	28
community support/philanthropy	16	19
environment	6	13
energy	0	3
other	13	3

Company name _____   Balance date _____

| | 1981 | | | | 1982 | | | | 1983 | | |
	W	%	T	Q	A	W	%	T	Q	A	W	%	T	Q	A
(1) Employment															
minority															
safety															
training															
assistance/benefits															
remuneration															
profiles															
share-purchase scheme															
morale															
industrial relations															
other															
(2) Corporate objectives/															
policies															
(3) Product															
development															
safety															
quality															
(4) Community support/															
philanthropy															
(5) Environment															
pollution															
aesthetics															
other															
(6) Energy															
(7) Other															

W = words of social disclosure
% = percentage of words and social disclosure
T = type of social disclosure
Q = quality of disclosure
A = whether the disclosures have been audited.

Figure 5.1 Corporate social responsibility worksheet. Source: Davey (1985).

Table 5.7   Comparative data on each category of social disclosure

Category of disclosure	Davey Words	%	Rank	Ng Words	%	Rank
Employment	4449	57.6	1	6155	60.3	1
Corporate objectives	2497	32.3	2	1536	15.0	2
Community support/ philanthropy	297	3.8	3	593	5.8	4
Environment	177	2.3	5	364	3.6	5
Product	28	0.4	6	1313	12.9	3
Energy	0	–	7	212	2.1	6
Other	281	3.6	4	33	0.3	7

Like Davey, Ng did not find the association between the level of disclosure of SRA and industry size or characteristics that the Australian studies have reported. This was the case for both individual years and average results over the three years.

UNITED STATES

Buzby (1974)

Buzby examined 38 items of information, both financial and non-financial, to determine the extent to which they were included in annual reports. These items were ranked using a panel of financial analysts. The analysts' ranking, plus a literature search, was used to construct a set of weighted criteria for each item which was then applied to a sample of 88 company reports from small and medium-sized organizations. The measures were intended to determine the extent of disclosure, the average extent of the relationship between importance and disclosure, and the average extent of the overall disclosures. Listed items of a non-financial nature were number of employees, plant and warehouse sizes, locations and ages, and indications of employee morale. Buzby concluded that many items were inadequately disclosed in the sample, and that correlations between the relative importance of items and the extent of their disclosure were low.

Ingram (1978)

In a study of the information content of firms' voluntary social responsibility disclosures, Ingram found that information content depended to a large extent on the market segment. This study was referred to in greater detail in Chapter 2.

Ernst and Ernst (1972–8)

Probably the most well known studies in this area were those carried out by Ernst and Ernst between 1972 and 1978. The 1978 report was very comprehensive and, like all the studies in the series, it was based upon annual reports of the *Fortune 500* companies. The survey showed a small decline in the number of companies which made social responsibility disclosures (from 91.2% to 89.2%), the first reduction recorded in the series. The average number of pages devoted to social responsibility disclosures was 0.56, an increase from 0.43 in the previous year. There was a small decrease in the number of companies quantifying their disclosures (from 60% to 59%). One notable feature of the 1978 Ernst and Ernst report was the considerable attention given to examples of disclosures and to the method employed in the survey. The authors were aware of the subjective nature of these studies:

> The identification and categorisation of SRA information is a subjective task because there is no widely accepted definition of 'social responsibility', or agreement as to what constitutes a corporate socially responsible activity.   (Ernst and Ernst, 1978, p. 30)

The authors attempted to reduce the degree of subjectivity and bias and stated:

> If anything, the amount of disclosure reported in the survey is understated because of the selective approach employed in identifying and categorizing disclosures and the possibility of human error. (Ibid., p. 31)

The incidence and types of SRA disclosures found in the 1977 *Fortune 500* annual reports are shown in Table 5.8.

CANADA

Burke (1980)

In a study published in 1980 Burke compared the SRA disclosure (called social measurement disclosures (SMD)) and material social measurement disclosures (MSMD) for US and Canadian company reports. The results of the study are revealing in that the difference between the two categories of disclosure was designed to overcome the problems which have been apparent in other studies. The definitions used were: SMD, 'any disclosure about an area of social concern not traditionally reported upon'; MSMD, an SMD that provided a reasonably *comprehensive* profile of a company's activities in such an area. Apart from breadth of cover-

Table 5.8   CSR information *ex* Ernst and Ernst (1978)

		No. of companies disclosing
A.	Environment	
	1. pollution control	222
	2. prevention or repair of environmental damage	25
	3. conservation of natural resources	65
	4. other environmental disclosures	76
B.	Energy	
	5. conservation	210
	6. energy efficiency of products	75
	7. other energy-related disclosures	48
C.	Fair-business practices	
	8. employment of minorities	87
	9. advancement of minorities	78
	10. employment of women	81
	11. advancement of women	237
	12. employment of other special-interest groups	30
	13. support for minority businesses	30
	14. socially responsible practices abroad	71
	15. other statements on fair-business practices	173
D.	Human resources	
	16. employee health and safety	115
	17. employee training	133
	18. other human resource disclosures	54
E.	Community involvement	
	19. community activities	93
	20. health related activities	59
	21. education and the arts	116
	22. other community activity disclosures	93
F.	Products	
	23. safety	70
	24. reducing pollution from product use	37
	25. other product related disclosures	77
G.	Other social responsibility disclosures	
	26. other disclosures	94
	27. additional information	26

age, meeting the MSMD test required specific data in quantitative form (Burke, 1980, p. 21).

The differences were reported in a series of tables detailing the number of companies in each country that reported disclosures at both levels for a range of categories. The relationship of size of corporation to extent of disclosure was explored, and it was found that larger companies were more likely to provide meaningful social measurement disclosures. It is clear from this study that there were important differences between Canadian and US companies at that time.

Demers and Wayland (1982a and b)

Demers and Wayland examined the annual reports of major Canadian companies which have taken the initiative in the SRA field. The information gleaned from the reports was reported in narrative form and may be summarized as follows:

General Foods (1977 report): annual seminar on nutrition; sponsorship of awards to journalists; employment of blind tasters in quality control area; the programmes continued in 1978; a five-year energy conservation plan was launched in 1978.

Canadian Industries (1978 report): installed new system for evaluating occupational accidents, including comparisons between company's record and the rest of the chemical industry. Figures given for rate of accidents for company employees for both 1977 and 1978. Company-owned collection of contemporary Canadian art touring the country.

Imperial Oil (1977 report): devoted four pages of the annual report to community relations; SRA items included: formation of teams to deal with oil spills; petroleum industry participation in environmental protection groups; existence of 86 employee–management consultative groups; a survey of employees on their expectations and attitudes towards the company; employee health programmes; job safety programmes which produced a dramatic reduction in the number of hours lost due to accidents; continued support for higher education, reduction of energy costs.

Fina (Petro Canada) (1976 report): concentrates social actions in area of environmental protection; detailed involvement, including donating time of employees; improvement in quality of refinery waste water; donations to 215 agencies in the field of industrial relations; enlarged company newspapers; 25 university scholarships for the children of company employees.

John Labatt (1979 report): indicated a substantial increase in contributions to social programmes (from $648,000 to $778,000) for use mainly in local communities; also summer jobs for students in community programmes; social responsibility committee within the board of directors; and an exchange programme for children of Labatt employees in different parts of Canada.

Imasco (1977 report): sponsorship of sporting events; scholarships to assist performing artists; contributed $840,000 to non-profit agencies.

Gas Metropolitan (1978 report): opened a training centre to instruct firefighters in the control of natural gas leaks; free medical examinations for employees; retirement preparation courses.

Bombardier (1978–9 report): social involvement through foundation; installation of park, construction of a cultural centre; donations to Canadian universities; donations to charities, both local and international.

Brooks (1986)

In a very comprehensive examination of corporate social performance in Canada, Brooks analysed the SRA component of company annual reports for 22 matched pairs for the years 1974 and 1980. He was particularly interested in changes to reports over this period and concluded that:

> there has been relatively little change in the percentages of space allocated to social responsibility disclosures between 1974 and 1980 . . . according to the nonparametric sign test for matched pairs . . . the only changes in disclosure which are significant . . . are those for Human Resources – Pictures.   (Brooks, 1986, p. 73)

It is noteworthy that Brooks recognized the need to separate pictures and script in his analysis. This is a problem with many SRA disclosures, and few analysts appear to state their approach with the same clarity.

Brooks provided examples of the SRA disclosures of US and Canadian corporations and an international comparison of SRA studies, which is considered in a later section of this chapter.

UNITED KINGDOM

There appear to have been relatively few comprehensive analyses of UK company reports to determine the type and volume of SRA disclosures. However, there are a number of studies dealing with specific aspects of the SRA field, such as value added statements or employee reports, and reference has been made to these in other parts of this book. Gray, Owen and Maunders (1987, p. 56) state that: 'In terms of systematic publications, CSR can be grouped under four headings: value added statements, employment reports, employee reports, and 'other' social reporting.'

Gray, Owen and Maunders (1987, p. 57) and Burchell, Clubb and Hopwood (1985, p. 386) have referred to the pattern of development and decline which appears to have affected value added statements in

Table 5.9 Value added statements in annual reports

Year	1975–6	1976–7	1977–8	1978–9	1979–80	1980–1	1981–2	1982–3
No.	14	42	67	84	90	88	77	64
%	5	14	22	28	30	29	26	21

UK company reports during the 1970s and 1980s. The data from these studies, originating with the Institute of Chartered Accountants in England and Wales *Survey of Published Accounts* are given in Table 5.9. Although the use of value added statements is not increasing, there appears to be a substantial minority of companies making use of this form of disclosure.

The same authors' comment on the incidence of employment reports (information about the work force) within the annual report. They state the percentages of companies providing employment statements to be: 1975–6, two; 1976–7, five; 1977–8, six; 1978–9, four; 1979–80, five; 1980–1, six; 1981–2, five; and 1982–3, three.

The legislative framework which influences the disclosures of companies on employee-related matters has been changing in recent years, particularly the Companies Acts 1981 and 1985. However, the survey of company reports of 300 large companies shows that they are still providing disclosures in excess of the requirements of the Companies Acts. The details of these disclosures for 1982–3 are given in Table 5.10.

The third form of SRA disclosure referred to by Gray, Owen and Maunders is the employee report. Lyall (1982) analysed 60 employee reports received from a random sample of companies chosen from *The Times 1000* largest UK companies. He found that the most frequent disclosures were profitability (57 companies), value added (43 companies), divisional information (29 companies), financial resources (21 companies), and capital investment (21 companies).

Marsh and Hussey (1979) analysed 302 employee reports and found that the most commonly included information was a financial highlights

Table 5.10 Human resource information disclosure in excess of Companies Act

Type of information	No. of companies (n=300)
Health and safety	46
Training	53
Employee communication/participation/policy etc.	65
Pensioners	16

Note: The number of companies disclosing at least one item was 120.
Source: Gray, Owen and Maunders (1987, p. 59).

statement (77.2%), a value added statement (40.7%) and a balance sheet (38.7%).

As indicated previously, comprehensive analysis of annual reports of UK companies covering all categories does not seem to be very common. Gray, Owen and Maunders (1987) offer such an analysis in the form of a comparison with the results of the last of the Ernst and Ernst studies. This is shown in Table 5.11.

CONTINENTAL EUROPE

The literature relating to SRA disclosures in continental Europe is dealt with in this section. Although they are not of prime concern to this book, which is of necessity directed towards developing socially related accounting within Anglo-American influenced accounting systems, these reports enable a comparison to be drawn between continental European and Anglo-American SRA disclosures.

Belgium

Theunesse (1979) described the legal obligations which apply to Belgian enterprises and reported upon an empirical examination of annual reports of Belgian companies for the year 1977. Thirty-four reports were examined (from the 50 largest limited companies) and the results are summarized in Table 5.12. Theunesse noted that the reports were designed to give a good image of the company and that no audit provision existed in respect of the information provided. The cost of strikes was given prominence in annual reports.

Delmot (1982) reported on social reporting in Belgian enterprises; in particular a sample of 58 companies in 1980. Of the 58 companies, 32 published social information within their annual reports (in addition to that which they are required by law to give to works councils). It was stated that 27 reports provided descriptive information, eight produced a value added statement, 15 used non-monetary social indicators, and 12 used ratios to impart the information. The contents of the social information section of the annual reports are given in Table 5.13. The most common size of report was between two and four pages, a position reported by 41% of the companies survey; 28% reported more than four pages and 19% between one and two pages. The motivation for reporting was stated by some companies to be the French Bilan Social.

France

The Bilan Social requires details of numbers employed, wages and fringe benefits, health and safety conditions, other working conditions,

Table 5.11   Frequency of publication of CSR information

		UK 1982–3	USA 1978
A.	Environment		
	1. pollution control	10	133
	2. prevention or repair of environmental damage	7	15
	3. conservation of natural resources	–	39
	4. other environmental disclosures	–	46
B.	Energy		
	5. conservation	16	126
	6. energy efficiency of products	10	45
	7. other energy related disclosures	2	29
C.	Firm business practices		
	8. employment of minorities	1	52
	9. advancement of minorities	26	47
	10. employment of women	6	49
	11. advancement of women	–	142
	12. employment of other special interest groups	11	18
	13. support for minority businesses	–	18
	14. socially responsible practices abroad	15	43
	15. other statements on fair-business practices	1	104
D.	Human resources		
	16. employee health and safety	46	69
	17. employee training	53	80
	18. other human resource disclosures	75	32
E.	Community involvement		
	19. community activities	13	56
	20. health and related activities	5	35
	21. education and the arts	11	70
	22. other community activity disclosures	7	56
F.	Products		
	23. safety	11	42
	24. reducing pollution from product use	–	22
	25. other product related disclosures	14	46
G.	Other social responsibilities disclosed		
	26. other disclosures	11	56
	27. additional information	49	16

Notes:
UK data: analysis of sample of 300 reports used for financial reporting, 1983–4.
USA data: Ernst and Ernst (1978) adjusted from sample size of 500 pro rata to 300 to provide comparison with UK.
Source: Gray, Owen and Maunders (1987, p. 60).

education and training, industrial relations, and other matters relating to the quality of working life for the current year and two preceding years. There would appear to be little additional disclosure of a voluntary nature.

Table 5.12   Contents of annual reports of Belgian companies, 1977

Contents	% of reports
Value added statement	3
Number of employees	74
Labour turnover	56
Remuneration	47
Training possibilities	47
Age structure of workforce	29
Working conditions	26
Composition of workforce	24
Accidents	21
Social conflicts	18
Relations with other groups	15
Future staffing policy	29
Contact procedure between staff and management	44
Consumer-related data	26
Data related to the environment	35

Source: Theunisse (1979, pp. 19–21).

Table 5.13   Contents of social information in annual financial reports

Item	%
Size and distribution of workforce	88
Labour turnover	78
Working hours	72
Remuneration and social charges	66
Training possibilities	63
Absenteeism	59
Hygiene and job security	59
Relations with social partners	59
Social works	44

Source: Delmot (1982, p. 15).

Germany

Gray, Owen and Maunders (1987, pp. 29–30) reviewed the work on SRA disclosure in Germany and noted that three approaches towards the production of social reports may be distinguished. These were:

1. a broadly based and partially integrated social cost-benefit reporting system;
2. an extension of the traditional employee-orientated report;
3. corporate goal accounting and reporting in which quantitative indicators are used wherever possible to describe the attainments of corporate objectives in areas of social performance (such as consumer and employee relations) and promotion of the general public welfare.

Brockhoff (1979) examined the reports of 300 German companies issued between 1 December 1973 and 30 November 1974; 205 published a social report during that period. A variety of information was disclosed:

1. Two companies explicitly stated that social activities had been made part of the objective function of the firm.
2. 256 reports published the total number of employees.
3. Reports contained information on a wide variety of social benefits provided to employees, including: sports and leisure activities; supplementary health insurance; company medical services; profit-sharing and capital formation; training (not including apprenticeship programmes); security of the workplace; employee housing; apprenticeship programmes; pensions and retirement benefits.
4. Reporting on research and development.
5. Reporting on environmental protection.

Brockhoff noted that there were very wide differences in reporting practices between industry segments.

Dierkes (1979, p. 97) reported the results of a detailed analysis of the social reports of 14 companies. The analysis addressed the following questions:

1. Which concept of reporting has been used, referring to the recommendation of the study group on practical aspects of social reporting?
2. To whom is the social report directed?
3. Which functional group in the company has the ultimate responsibility in combining the report?
4. Was the report certified by a certified public accountant?
5. Which are the important sections of such a report, and which areas are still neglected?
6. What indicators are used?
7. How intensive is the reporting with respect to giving specific data on expenditures or achievements?
8. Does it provide the reader with comparative information from previous performance periods or is it based on other companies' activities?
9. Is the report just narrative or does it give detailed technical information?
10. Are goals, measures and plans mentioned in relatively specific terms or in very selective general statements?

Schreuder (1979) explained the complexities of social reporting in Germany where several conceptual frameworks are in use, leading to correspondingly different reporting practices. A number of examples are given in his article, including the reports of Steag AG and Deutsche Shell AG which have been widely quoted as examples of different forms of social report. Schreuder (1979, p. 121) concluded:

> The overview presented in this paper suggests that the German developments in the field of corporate social reporting are noteworthy in at least the following respects: (1) the variety of conceptual models proposed in the literature; (2) the actual course of developments in practice; and (3) the evolving debate between the corporations and the trade unions. As such these developments would seem to be of interest to students of corporate social reporting in many other countries.

The Deutsche Shell report has been commented on by Van den Bergh (1976) and Most (1977). Van den Bergh comments that – 'employees are the most strongly emphasised group in all the [German] social reports'; whilst for Most, 'the 1975 annual report of Deutsche Shell A.G. is a portent of things to come'. The contents page of the Deutsche Shell AG report is shown in Figure 5.2.

Holland

Dekker and van Hoorn (1982) have commented on the scarcity of empirical research on social reporting in Holland. They cite four studies:

1. Van Ommeren (1974), who analysed 21 social or personnel annual reports for 1973 with regard to 29 elements related to the social policies of companies.
2. Feenstra and Bowma (1975) investigated the annual reports of 40 Dutch companies for the period 1970–3. They described aspects of the reports from which may be deduced the concern shown for company personnel and the environment. Many of the elements examined were common with those used by Van Ommeren.
3. Bakker (1975) examined 12 annual reports from 1973 on 13 elements of social policy.
4. De Gier (1976) studied seven 1975 social annual reports on 18 elements related to the social policy of companies.

Dekker and van Hoorn (1977) investigated 64 1975 social annual reports of Dutch companies to determine the contents. Table 5.14 shows the information provided which was not related to employees. It is clear that, like many of the continental European reports examined in this section, most of the information provided relates to employees and their interests.

Table of contents

1. Introduction
2. The framework of Shell's policy; general developments in the energy market
   - 2.1 The policy of the OPEC countries
   - 2.2 The impact of the German mineral oil market
   - 2.3 The Federal government's energy programme
   - 2.4 Obligation to maintain minimum stock levels
   - 2.5 Structural and business activity problems of the mineral oil industry
   - 2.6 Special levies on domestic oil and natural gas production
   - 2.7 Long-term aspects
3. The goals of Shell's corporate policy
4. The performance of Deutsche Shell AG
   - 4.1 Supplying the consumer on conditions determined by the market
   - 4.2 Development of new application techniques and products
   - 4.3 Achieving a reasonable return on investment
   - 4.4 Taking account of our employees' interests
   - 4.5 Paying regard to the general public welfare
5. Explanations pertaining to the German Shareholders' Act
   - 5.1 Explanations of the balance sheet
   - 5.2 Explanations of the profit and loss account
6. Tables
   - 6.1 Social accounts
   - 6.2 Relations with investors
   - 6.3 Account of performance
   - 6.4 Balance sheet
   - 6.5 Profit and loss statement

Figure 5.2 The concept of goal accounting – social reporting: the example of Deutsche Shell AG. Excerpt from Deutche Shell AG. Annual Report, p. 4. Unauthorized translation by Dierkes and Coppock (1977), cited in Schreuder (1979, p. 117).

Table 5.14 Non-employee-related data reported in Dutch social annual reports, 1975

Type of data	No.
Financial/economic expectations as to the future	27
Its consequences for the (internal) social policy	18
Ergonomics	4
Employees' participation in decision-making	2
Suggestions box	22
Cost c.q. savings aspects of these suggestions	9
Impact on milieu of the environment	13
Costs of these measures	0
Benefits of these measures	0
Contacts with local government	8
Contacts with action groups	0
Actions of action groups	0

Source: Dekker and van Hoorn (1977, p. 27).

Sweden

Gray, Owen and Maunders (1987) suggest that Sweden provides examples of internal rather than external social reporting and cite a study by Jonson *et al.* (1978) which calculated the financial savings resulting from a reduction in absenteeism. In a different type of study, Gröjer and Stark (1977) developed a goal-orientated social accounting report, with the different constituencies receiving explicit consideration. Although employees featured prominently in the report, environmental factors were also included.

OTHER COUNTRIES

Research into SRA disclosures is being carried out in several other locations, in addition to those reviewed here. However, these appear to be isolated events and not part of any concentrated research effort.

Teoh and Thong (1984) have reported on SRA disclosures in Malaysia, and Low, Koh and Yeo (1985) on disclosures in Singapore. An Indian report is cited by Gray, Owen and Maunders (1987, p. 26) and, although described as an 'outlier', it is also thought to be important as a public-sector development which may set an example for the private sector in that country. Tokutani and Kawano (1978) have provided an extensive note on the Japanese social accounting literature, some of which corresponds to SRA disclosures.

LIMITATIONS OF THESE STUDIES

SUBJECTIVE ANALYSIS

It is evident from the comparative works of Davey (1985) and Ng (1985) and the concern with replication expressed by Guthrie (1982), Ernst and Ernst (1978) and Burke (1984), that some researchers are aware of the subjective nature of this type of investigation. There seems to be very little difference between qualitative data which is aimed at conveying information and statements which are designed for advertising purposes. Whether a self-congratulatory message imparts information depends upon the perceptions of the reader. Many studies do not report any methodological safeguards or even acknowledge that there might be a problem at all. This is not to argue against this type of research. However, researchers have to guard against the inherent subjectivity of the analysis through publication of the instruments used and attempts at replication by the same and other analysts. Ernst and Ernst (1978) have addressed this issue but concluded that the data is an understatement in the final analysis. This is only a partial solution to the difficulties presented by subjectivity.

The surveys reported here suggest that replication studies are urgently needed since, although Guthrie has found his own instrument to be reliable, other research has produced conflicting results when used on the same material by a second researcher. Other studies have been reported as single studies, often without all the details.

The subjective nature of many of the qualitative SRA material makes analysis extremely problematic. Consequently, until studies are commonly replicated, all those interested in the area must be wary of accepting published results too readily. A further issue is to what extent disclosures can be compared between different accounting systems because of the different cultural values involved.

THE INTERRELATIONSHIP OF CULTURE AND ACCOUNTING

A further difficulty arises because of cultural and other influences at work in different accounting environments. This issue is considered in depth since it provides a possible explanation for many of the differences in reporting practices which were illustrated in the earlier part of the chapter. The discussion follows that of Perera and Mathews (1990) and Mathews and Perera (1991).

It has been demonstrated (Gray, 1985) that the effects of culture may be used to group countries together in order to study their accounting systems. Although a relatively recent area of study, the culture-accounting interrelationship has provided some interesting ideas. This section attempts to apply some of these ideas and developments to the social accounting field (Perera and Mathews, 1990).

Research on national systems of accounting has focused particularly on the Anglo-American countries (that is, USA, Canada, UK, Australia and New Zealand) and continental Europe (Lafferty, 1975; Benston, 1982a, 1982b; Oldham, 1981; Nobes and Parker, 1981; Holzer, 1984). As national differences in accounting systems and practices became increasingly evident, attempts were made to identify international patterns and to classify countries on the basis of those patterns. Two alternative approaches have been taken; the first involves the identification of relevant environmental factors and links them to national accounting practices (Mueller, 1967, 1968; Zeff, 1973; Radebaugh, 1975; Nobes, 1983, 1984). The second involves the classification of accounting practices by using statistical analysis and then attempting to explain the patterns discovered by reference to environmental factors (Frank 1979; Nair and Frank, 1980; Da Costa et al., 1978; Goodrich, 1982; Belkaoui, 1983).

Accounting and culture

Recently there has been an increasing interest in applying behavioural ideas to accounting. This has, no doubt, enriched the field and contributed significantly to changing the status of accounting from being a purely technical discipline. Research in this area has ranged from a consideration of the psychological factors which influence the preparers of accounting statements, to a socio-political consideration of the role of accounting in organizations and societies.

The most recent set of ideas emanating from the established social science areas to be applied to accounting comes from cultural anthropology. Culture has featured prominently in more recent discussions of the factors influencing the accounting development of a country (Nobes and Parker, 1981; Bromwich and Hopwood, 1983; Choi and Mueller, 1984; Arpan and Radebaugh, 1985; Perera, 1985; Riahi-Belkaoni et al., 1991). It has also been argued that the lack of consensus across different countries on what represents proper accounting methods is because their purpose is cultural, not technical. The content of reports depends on local history and convention (Hofstede, 1985). This is probably why the product of accounting, that is, financial statements and reports, sometimes has a shareholder orientation, at other times a creditor orientation, and occasionally it serves the interests of national planners or public administrators (Mueller, 1985). It is clear that cross-cultural behavioural research in accounting is likely to provide some explanation about why there are differences in accounting techniques and practices between countries, and to answer questions about whether the findings of researchers in one culture can be transformed without modification for effective use in another culture.

In the field of management, Hofstede (1983a) has sought to analyse differences in work-related values across cultures. His study was based upon data collected through an employee attitude survey in a multinational corporation. The survey took place twice between 1968 and 1973, and involved different subsidiaries in 64 countries and 116,000 questionnaires in 20 languages.

Culture-based societal value dimensions

In an attempt to develop a commonly acceptable, well-defined and empirically based terminology to describe cultures, Hofstede identified four distinct dimensions which he considered reflected the cultural orientation of a country. These were (a) individualism versus collectivism; (2) large versus small power distance; (3) strong versus weak uncertainty avoidance; and (4) masculinity versus femininity. The application of these items to accounting has been discussed in detail by Gray (1985) and Perera and Mathews (1990).

Different cultural environments: Anglo-American versus continental European

It may be reiterated here that the ideas developed in any society are a product of the socio-political-economic environment. Therefore, a proper understanding of that environment is a precondition for any considered explanation of why the participants behave in a particular way, because human behaviour is usually reflective of some pattern of thinking. This can be illustrated by a number of specific examples. The growth of economic activity in the UK took place in an atmosphere of classical liberalism with a broadly *laissez-faire* approach to government. This was also true of the economic growth that began to gain momentum in the US in the middle of the ninteenth century. In such a highly individualistic atmosphere, the promotion of investment by trying to interest people with uncommitted funds in various investment projects became an important activity. Once prospective investors began to assess investment opportunities on the basis of their expected earnings, financial statements that included some kind of earnings figure became a necessity for the functioning of the entire system (Abel, 1971). This was the background for the development of capital market activity which is the main source of funds for investment in both countries. The activities of these markets have resulted in continuous pressure being exerted for the provision of financial information for investors, making investors the most important recipients of accounting reports from companies. The pressure for disclosure had a significant effect on the development of accounting principles and practices in these countries, and the requirements of the capital markets became a major factor influencing their disclosure patterns. Furthermore, financial reporting and capital market activity were so closely related that they became interdependent (Barrett, 1977). Similar developments took place in other Anglo-American accounting countries, such as Australia, Canada and New Zealand. It was assumed that these developments should be implemented by accountants, independent of legal direction or government intervention.

The position in much of continental Europe is quite different. In both France and Germany there has been a tradition of state intervention in economic affairs. Unlike the position in the UK and USA, the influence of the classical economists was far more limited in continental Europe. Instead, there has been a succession of economic theories with a common thread of anti-individualism. Financial accounting in France is generally influenced by legislation, due mainly to the determination of the French government to obtain data for macro-accounting purposes. The 1947 *Plan Comptable Général*, which has been adopted by virtually all enterprises in the country, contains a detailed chart of accounts and a series of model financial and statistical reports which are considered necessary for micro- and macro-accounting purposes. The French plan makes it clear that amongst its objectives in seeking data on an enterprise are (1) the promotion of more reliable national economic policies; (2) the minimization of social misunderstandings; (3) to ensure the availability of data for government studies of market trends, and (4) assistance to the government authorities in exercising control over the economy. Furthermore, French companies have traditionally relied much less upon an active new issue market as a source of long-term funds than have UK and US companies. This has resulted in a lesser emphasis being given to the provision of investor-orientated corporate financial reporting and to the audit function as a safeguard for investors. Therefore, the primary influence upon the development of accounting principles and practices in France has been the General Accounting Plan, rather than the pronouncements of the accounting profession. Similarly, in Germany, as demand for industrial capital increased during the second half of the nineteenth century, strong banks, rather than individuals organized by a promotor, emerged as suppliers of a significant portion of that capital.

The environmental differences described above are reflected in the different approaches taken in those countries with regard to accounting issues. For example, it is widely held that accounting reports should be orientated towards the user's needs on the assumption that the public interest will be best served by a user-orientation. In industrialized countries the public interest is taken to be synonymous with the interest of the main group that provides capital. However, this group varies from one country to another; for instance, in the US it is the private investors (Nobes and Parker, 1981), in the UK it is the institutional investors such as pension funds and building societies (Lee and Tweedie, 1977), in France it is the family holdings and the state, and in Germany it is the banks (Hopwood and Schreuder, 1984). The social and cultural differences between these countries can also be seen in the paths they have taken towards the development of social reporting.

Social reporting: international pressures for more disclosure and national disclosure patterns

There has been considerable pressure at an international level, particularly from the UN and the EC, for greater disclosure with special reference to information which is relevant to employee interests. The 1977 UN proposals highlighted the need to extend the scope of required disclosures beyond purely financial reporting. These proposals, although not specifically recommended, favoured the production of separate social reports. Areas identified for disclosure were: labour and employment; production; investment programmes; organizational structure; and environmental measures.

The fifth EC directive on employee information and consultation, and the Vredeling proposals for giving information rights to employees of 'large' companies (issued in 1980 and revised in 1983) are even more extensive in scope. The directive requires the disclosure of information relating to corporate organizational structure, employment, the economic and financial situation, probable developments in production, sales and employment, production and investment programmes, rationalization plans, and plans for new working methods or other methods that could have 'a substantial effect' on employee interests. The OECD (1980) statement also required the disclosure of the average number of people employed, categorized by function, together with employment costs showing social security costs and pensions. However, despite these pressures at an international level for a well-chosen programme for promoting greater disclosure in social reporting, the extent of regulation at national level tends to be minimal (Gray *et al.*, 1984), with the notable exception of France, where employee reports are required by law. In France, since 1977 large corporations have been required by law to publish a separate social report (*Bilan Social*). In that report detailed information must be disclosed about a wide range of matters including: employment; wages, salaries and social security payments; hygiene and safety; conditions of work; training; and trade union activities. The emphasis here is on the impact of the corporation on employees. The extent of voluntary disclosure is significant and growing in other European countries, such as Germany, The Netherlands and Sweden, where additional special employee reports are often provided (Schoenfeld, 1978; Schreuder, 1979). Disclosure of information relating to employees is also required from US and UK companies, but on a much smaller scale.

Some specific examples of differences in reporting practices

Employee reporting. The continental European countries seem to be much more advanced in regard to 'social' or 'employee' reporting, at both institutional and practical levels, than the Anglo-American countries. This can be explained to some extent in terms of their different cultural environments because systems usually develop unique characteristicts as a result of both internal and external pressures. Pressure groups and institutional influences which are active in developing social disclosures in industrialized countries generally include employees and trade unions, shareholders, community leaders, environmentalists, con-sumerists, idealists and moralists, professional guidelines and pro-nouncements, and legislation and regulation. In a given country some of these groups will be more prominent than the others, and the emerg-ence of such pressure groups is likely to be influenced by the cultural background. As clearly demonstrated elsewhere by historical develop-ment and also Hofstede's analysis of culture, the UK and US are both orientated towards individualism, whereas France and Germany are relatively less individualist- and more collectivist-orientated. It is interesting to see how the pressures for social disclosures have varied between these two groups of countries. Employees have been a power-ful force in France and Germany, whereas consumerists and environ-mentalists have been more influential in the US and to a lesser extent the UK.

Industrial democracy. In the collectivist-orientated cultures of continen-tal Europe, industrial democracy or worker representation has provided a co-determination framework for corporate performance and disclos-ures. As a result, employees have been a powerful force. By contrast, in more individualist cultures, the relationship between the employer and the employee is a business relationship based on the assumption of mutual advantage. Either party can terminate the relationship in favour of a better deal elsewhere. In classical economic theory, which was largely responsible for moulding the individualist cultural thinking, employees are 'labour', a 'factor of production' and 'part of a labour market'. They are not regarded as important contributors to decision-making by the management. This is why employee and union pressure in North America has been relatively insignificant. For example, when top-ranking officials of each of the 20 largest Canadian unions were surveyed in 1984 about industrial democracy, they did not agree that workers should be represented on boards of directors and doubted that this would become widespread by 1994 (Brooks, 1986). Therefore, contrary to the European experience, social disclosures in the US and Canada have developed from other forces, such as environmentalists, consumerists and idealists. Also, in the UK the issue of expanded social reporting has not met with rapid acceptance, partly due to the current value accounting debate which tended to retain the forefront of disclos-ure proposals for many years.

Environmental disclosures. In contrast to the position on employee reporting there is some evidence of a greater concern on environmental matters in North America. Tinker (1985) has referred to the Love Canal scandal; Wiseman (1982) and Rockness (1985) have examined the ver-acity of corporate disclosures on environmental matters; and the Ernst and Ernst studies (1972–8) of disclosures by *Fortune 500* companies showed that considerable attention was given to environmental matters, as was demonstrated in a summary of the 1978 survey earlier in the chapter (Table 5.8). The table also incorporates similar data from UK studies. The categories provided are in contrast with continental European reports which emphasize employee matters almost exclusively. Brooks (1986, p. 213) has provided a useful analysis of the issues addressed in corporate social reports. Table 5.15 shows the different emphases which have already been noted.

A number of attempts have been made to link the provision of environmental information, whether supplied by the reporting organizations or an outside body such as the Council for Economic Priorities (CEP), with changes in the market price of shares. This work, which has already been discussed in Chapter 2, follows the general trend of the individualist, market-related, cultural features already referred to.

Conversely, the discussion of the measurement and valuation of externalities has been contested by several academics on the grounds that shareholders would be forced to pay for additional information which they would not want. The same view would be put forward in relation to other social disclosures (Benston, 1982a, 1984).

Concluding comments

This section of the chapter has explored the implications that recent work on the effects of culture on accounting may have for social accounting, as a developing area within the accounting discipline. The study of the impact of culture on accounting has a relatively short history and has not yet been extended to the developing area of social accounting. No attempt has been made at this stage to consider differences within the major groups such as those between the US and Canada and the extent to which the UK approach is moving towards that of continental Europe as a result of that country's membership of the EC.

The application of the work of Hofstede and others to the field of international accounting differences is worthy of a further extension to the social accounting field and should not be ignored by social accountants working in both empirical and normative-deductive domains.

SUMMARY

This chapter has examined a number of studies which detail actual SRA disclosures in several countries. These disclosures vary in content, but most are of qualitative or non-financial quantitative information provided by private-sector organizations, except for financial data in value added statements. The reports may be voluntary or compulsory, depending upon the country concerned. In most of the Anglo-American

Table 5.15 Issues addressed in corporate social reports

	West Germany n=16×2	Austria n=6×2	Switzerland n=9×2	Japan n=29	US Monetary n=500	US Non n=89	Australia n=50
	Two-year period				One-year period		
Human resources							
General person, policy	12	4	14	3	30	89	26
Size of workforce, distribution, changes	10	5	7	2			
Employment of foreigners	3	1	2	2			
Labour costs	11	6	6	2			
Working conditions	10	1	2	2			
Training and development	15	6	12	1			
Fringe benefits – general	19	10	10				
Employee health services	9		1				
Company pension plans	8	5	4	1			
Company housing	9	2	3				
Employee ownership of property	4		1				
Labour representation	5		2	2			
Communication with employees	7		3				
Communication involvement	NA	NA	NA	NA	54	71	8
Environment	19	1	10	10	161	61	6
Energy	NA	NA	NA	NA	39	107	1
Product-related matters	NA	NA	NA	10	1	7	0
Research and development	9	4	7	NA	NA*	NA*	
Miscellaneous	7	2	8	12	1	1	5
Stockholder relations	6			4	NA	NA	
Fair-business practice	NA	NA	NA	NA	19	70	

Notes: Sources as per Table 8.4 US statistics do not include 180 companies with only non-monetary, verbal disclosures.
* subsequent to the survey date, the FASB required research and development disclosure.

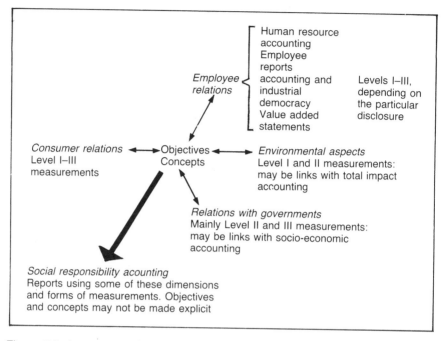

Figure 5.3 A summary of social responsibility accounting components.

accounting systems (US, Canada, UK, Australia, New Zealand) SRA disclosures are voluntary. In most of the continental European countries examined (France, Germany, Belgium, Holland, Sweden) there are systems of legislative and customary differences, mainly dealing with reporting to employees, which impact on the disclosures made by corporations. In addition to legislative and customary differences in the volume and type of disclosures, there appear to be differences in their nature, with North American and Australian disclosures comprehending a wider variety of information (environment, product, energy, as well as employment) and the continental European corporations concentrating on those matters which affect employees. UK disclosures appear to occupy a point between the other two groups.

The various aspects of SRA disclosures are brought together in Figure 5.3, which uses the four dimensions of social responsibility disclosures suggested by Jackman (1982), at different levels of measurement. The diagram illustrates the various links which may be made between the different dimensions. It also indicates where there may be links with other forms of social accounting measurement and reporting which have not yet been discussed in detail.

However, progress in the area of SRA disclosure is not uniform. Although some aspects, for example employee reports, have attained a measure of uniformity and acceptance of content and style, there are still considerable variations in other disclosures. This applies particularly to product- and environment-related disclosures, and those attempting to record community activity. The more esoteric areas of SRA such as human resource accounting and matters related to industrial democracy have not made much progress at all.

The chapter concluded with an examination of some of the difficulties involved in analysing SRA disclosures. The first main problem is one of subjectivity. The reports do not lend themselves to consistent analysis even where the same instrument is involved. Comparability of reports over time and between different countries of origin is obviously hindered by subjectivity and the lack of a standarized approach. However, an attempt to standardize approaches to SRA disclosures will encounter the second difficulty which is referred to in this chapter: the influence of culture upon accounting in general and forms of social accounting in particular. Recent research has indicated strong societal pressures towards particular forms of accounting and reporting which are likely to prevent widespread conformity or comparability between the products of differing cultural backgrounds.

It seems clear that SRA is an important growth area in accounting disclosure. However, it is likely that some aspects will show more growth than others, developing a stronger literature at the same time. A survey of the social accounting literature shows an overwhelming concern with SRA as the archetypal social accounting. The next chapter considers total impact accounting, which promises to take over SRA as the front-runner of social accounting development.

Total impact accounting (TIA)

6

INTRODUCTION

The objective of this chapter is to introduce the second category of social accounting in the framework aimed towards a more socially responsible accounting. Total impact accounting is defined as follows:

> The term total impact accounting (TIA) refers to attempts at measuring, in monetary terms, the total cost of running an organization in its existing form. The total cost of running an organization may be divided between private and public costs.

Unfortunately, confusion persists with the use of the term 'social accounting' because many writers refer to SRA material as 'social accounting' whilst economists use the term for macro-level national accounting. The distinction between the two areas is made clearer in this book by the descriptions given in Table 3.2.

This chapter consists of an introduction, a consideration of the philosophical issues which are generated by proposals to account for externalities, an examination of a number of the better-known models for achieving disclosure, reference to the concept of the social audit, and an account of the recent developments within environmental accounting.

The total cost of running an organization may be divided between private and public costs. Private costs, also called internal costs, are already recorded and measured by the accounting system, as the individual costs of material, labour and overheads. After accumulation, these costs are used in the preparation of intermediate and final accounts, many of which are published under statutory requirements and form the traditional disclosures to the shareholders. Internal costs are also used in the preparation of product costs and for the valuation of inventory. Public costs, also called external costs or externalities, currently must be borne by the community as a whole. The classic examples of externalities leading to public costs are those of pollution by fumes, smell, noise and waste discharge. Others are plant-induced traffic congestion or excessive demands on medical and social services which result from the operation of a particular plant.

The difficulties faced by proponents of total impact accounting are related to the identification, measurement and valuation of externalities prior to their possible disclosure in accounting reports. Although the identification of many potential social costs is not difficult, measurement and valuation is not easy. It is possible to see smoke or dust pollution leaving factory premises and to smell gaseous contaminants polluting the atmosphere, but how can a value be attached to the **effects** of these phenomena? The process of valuation has the two aspects of occurrence and measurable effect, both of which are problematic.

The American Accounting Association Committee on Social Costs (1975) suggested that three levels of measurement could be involved in any case of social accounting. These levels were discussed in a previous chapter. Level III measurements require that non-financial quantification be converted to a financial estimate of costs and benefits. In the case of pollution, the cost of emissions above an acceptable limit may be internalized as a private cost, through fines or even closure, or through the award of damages to individuals. The cost to the community will possibly involve damage to buildings, increased maintenance costs and loss of amenities or poor community health. Estimates of the public cost may serve as the basis for fines or damage awards.

Two measurement difficulties which have not been addressed by the Levels I-III disclosure hierarchy are time and distance. How much time can be expected to elapse between the event (for example, the sulphur dioxide discharge) and the resulting effect (damage to something or someone)? Although a social cost undoubtedly exists, if discharges which were considered harmless are subsequently found to be cumulative and eventually harmful it is difficult to see how the organization can be made to bear the cost. However, once the knowledge is made public, a different set of rules may be applied. Examples which come to mind are expectant mothers and thalidomide, miners and pneumoconiosis, and the effects of asbestos. In the area of cumulative pollution, we can refer to the poisoning of soil around plants processing arsenic, cadmium and other heavy metals.

When considering the physical distances from effluent discharge and the resulting effects, what geographic limits should be placed on the measurement of social costs? It has been asserted that the improved local effects of passing sulphur dioxide into the atmosphere via tall chimneys in the UK has resulted in acid rainfall in Scandinavia; and the effects of atmospheric pollution from the US are felt in parts of Canada. The fallout from the Chernobyl nuclear power-plant is a prime example of the problems of time and distance which would remain even if there was any intention to compensate losing parties.

How does TIA deal with time and distance problems? One approach would be to look at the costs and benefits of organizations over their entire life and get away from conventional accounting periods and short-term matching principles. It is difficult to do this with changing knowledge and technology, and there may still be costs which could not equitably be charged to an organization, because of new developments and knowledge, although some form of insurance policy might be developed. In respect of distance, the matter is complicated by national boundaries. If an organization discharges material inside one country, it does not matter whether the effect is felt next door or at the other end of the land, since only one jurisdiction is involved. However, where international pollution is involved, the jurisdiction issue is likely to be more difficult to deal with.

The consideration of pollution, its measurement and valuation, is not new. Estes (1973) has cited one of the oldest and most famous calculations of social cost: that of the estimate of smoke damage in Pittsburgh. This 1993 study produced a cost which, in 1959 terms and if extended to the entire United States, would have been $11 billion annually. The 1993 cost could be much higher. Taylor (1975) has referred to the work of the Programme Analysis Unit in Britain and described some of the difficulties experienced in determining the social costs of pollution in that country; in particular, who is responsible for the costs. Beams and Fertig (1971) have indicated that accountants need to take action to convert social costs into private costs in order to protect the environment.

Once the identification of externalities and their effects has been achieved and the measurement systems developed and deployed, it will be possible to turn to evaluation. The evaluation stage requires conversion of the measured outcomes of externalities into a financial quantity for disclosure in either internal or external accounting reports. Because the effects of externalities may be spread over several time-periods, aggregation and discounting will be required and consequently a discount rate must be determined for use in this process. The varied nature of externalities will ensure that the procedures required for measurement and evaluation will also be varied. For example, the valuation of an externality such as a pollutant, which is of nuisance value, will differ from that accorded to one which is likely to damage property. Both will be different from that where a health hazard already exists. The discount rate could also vary from one class of externality to another.

Clearly, the field of disclosing externalities is technically complex.

However, the decision to attempt the identification, measurement and valuation is the starting point.

THE PHILOSOPHICAL PROBLEM

For some accountants the major difficulty with the valuation of externalities is not in knowing that they exist, or even in their identification and measurement, but in recognizing that there is an **accounting** problem at all. The philosophical nature of the question of measuring and valuing externalities in accounting may be illustrated by reference to the work of Ramanathan and Schreuder and of Benston.

The conceptual framework for social accounting put forward in Ramanathan (1976) appears to have been designed for the private-enterprise organization. It was also noted in Chapter 4 that the framework is inclusive of both SRA and TIA. Indeed, the major impact may well be on the valuation of externalities rather than on general SRA disclosures. A later paper by Ramanathan and Schreuder (1982) developed the arguments in favour of the valuation of externalities, in the quest for a more realistic development of private sector costs. As they have commented (p. 15):

> The ultimate aim of CSAR is not to weaken the corporate and/or market system, as many opponents of its development seem to think, but to strengthen these systems by making them more inclusive.

They suggest that this would be achieved by using a macro approach. A large proportion of government expenditure, raised through general taxation, is devoted to neutralizing the externalities resulting from private-sector activities and, therefore, the private sector costs of the firms concerned are currently lower than they should be because of the public costs created through externalities. There is a large difference, in some cases, between enterprise costs and the total impact of the enterprise on society. The payment of corporation tax may offset some of the private costs which are put on to the public purse as externalities; however, any equality of tax payments and clean-up costs (or other public expenditures) would be coincidental.

Ramanathan and Schreuder argue that a system of linked macro and micro indicators could result in the total cost to society of neutralizing externalities (government costs) being allocated to the firms responsible for the externalities in the first place. This policy would have a number of effects. First, general taxation could be lowered as a result of specific recoveries, and the use of specific charges or taxes would force the organization to internalize costs through the regular accounting system. The cost structure would then be comparable to that of an organization that did not produce externalities. Second, in some industries there would be a general rise in the cost structure leading to higher prices and reduced demand. Third, the viability of some industries might be reduced and others increased. The weakness in this approach lies in the operational phase, that is, getting macro and micro indicators which may be linked together to provide a framework for specific charges or taxes. This is admitted by the authors:

> Finally, we may point toward one area of agreement between proponents and opponents of CSAR, namely the finding that the current state-of-the-art has not yet moved sufficiently from the phase of initial individual experiments to the stage of operationalization and testing of more general frameworks. We feel the social indicators approach which integrates micro and macro perspectives is a promising avenue of research to pursue for this purpose, and we shall direct our future research efforts accordingly.
> (Ramanathan and Schreuder, 1982, p. 29)

Underlying the work of Ramanathan and Schreuder is a philosophical position which was classified by Den Uyl (Chapter 2) as social permission theory, which takes into account a number of theories such as the social contract and, perhaps, organization legitimacy. This philosophical position leads to an acceptance of new types and forms of disclosure and, inevitably, to an evolutionary perspective on accounting as a discipline.

Benston (1982a) has taken a different philosophical position in respect of social accounting, social responsibility issues and the valuation of externalities. He introduces his argument on the issue of to whom is the corporation responsible? The options suggested are to shareholders, to stakeholders or to society in general. All three sectors are affected by the assumption (explicit or implicit) that corporation managers may misuse shareholders' resources. Benston attempts to undermine this assumption by considering four types of limitation: the market for goods and services; the market for finance and for corporate control; the market for managerial services; and internal and external monitoring systems (Benston, 1982a, p. 89).

The limitation on managerial freedom, exercised by the market for goods and services, is provided by an appeal to the free-market philosophy. This enabled Benston to conclude: 'Hence, most (if not all) of the expenditure on social responsibility is borne by the shareholders or managers'; and: 'The considerable extent to which enterprises change products, merge, and go bankrupt supports the conclusion that producers are severely constrained by consumers' preferences for price and quality' (Benston, 1982a, p. 90).

The belief in the concern for shareholder wealth by managers was maintained in the face of arguments by Williamson (1964) and Marris (1964) that managers are only interested in 'satisfactory', rather than maximum, profits and shareholder wealth. These arguments are rejected in part because many managers earn more from their involvement as shareholders through share option schemes than from their salaries. The second limitation is that of markets for finance and corporate control, which are believed to be efficient and to penalize inefficient management by charging higher rates of interest. The evidence from takeover research leads Benston to 'support the conclusion that there is, in fact, little dysfunctional managerial discretion' (ibid., p. 91).

The market for managerial services works to reduce managerial discretion since managers are engaged in a competitive market for their services. Benston uses the results of a study to argue that there is a significant positive relationship between executive changeover and a poor market performance of company stock (ibid., p. 92).

Finally, management misuse of shareholder funds is prevented by the internal and external monitoring systems. This leads Benston to argue that, although some social responsibility disclosures may benefit shareholders, most would not do so:

> The principal implication of the analysis for corporate social responsibility is that if concern for shareholders is the motivating factor behind this accounting, there is no reason to require its inclusion in public reports. To do so would impose costs on shareholders for the benefit of those who contract with it (e.g., employees) or would support the values of some group in society (e.g., advocates of programs that they say are socially responsible) over others (shareholders, customers and employees).   (Ibid., p. 93)

Benston next considered (p. 94) externalities which are examined on a net basis (that is, positive externalities and negative externalities must be offset): the cost to society as a whole is the difference between these aggregate costs and benefits. This approach may lead to an apparently inflexible mechanistic and possibly immoral view of externalities as indicated in the following passage in relation to pollution costs:

> Thus if all the area residents are associated with the factory (say as employees or suppliers), the disability from breathing polluted air is a cost of dealing with the factory and will be reflected in the wages or prices for goods paid by the factory owners. Therefore, there is no externality.   (Ibid.)

Benston conceded that negative externalities such as pollution will not be self-controlled, and by implication regulation may be necessary. He further argued that the measurement of externalities is so difficult that social responsibility reports will not contribute much to the determination of these costs. He analysed the contributions of Abt (1977), Estes (1976) and others, before concluding that an ideal system can never be attained. Lesser systems based upon indicators and supplementary reports are then examined. They are found wanting because 'it benefits anyone, including the owners of corporations, to impose negative externalities on non-contracting parties and to report on social matters only when the result is likely to be beneficial to the owners' (ibid., p. 98).

Benston concluded that social responsibility accounting (by which he meant both the reporting of voluntary non-financial and financial data as well as attempts to value externalities) is not a viable proposition:

> the analysis presented above concludes that shareholders are likely to be well served in the accounting procedures voluntarily adopted by corporate managers and directors. Similarly, employees, customers, creditors and others who have contractual relationships with corporations are likely to be well served. The remaining area to which external reports of social responsibility might be directed, the imposition of negative externalities on the general public is not likely to be self-regulating. But the inherent problems of measuring externalities places resolution of the problem outside the scope of accounting. (Ibid., p. 102)

A similar, though shorter paper, presents the same analysis in respect of corporate governance and social responsibility (Benston, 1982b).

Benston has concluded that social responsibility accounting (by which he means both the voluntary reporting of non-financial data as well as attempts to value externalities) is not a viable proposition. In taking a classical free-market position Benston is ignoring trends towards a greater questioning of organizational legitimacy by the public. These issues were ignored completely by Benston. Furthermore, by rejecting organizational attempts at social responsibility, Benston may have encouraged the conditions under which legislation is eventually inevitable, to the ultimate disadvantage of the shareholders whose interests he seeks to protect. The philosophical position underlying this analysis may be identified as the individual agreement theory put forward by Den Uyl.

Schreuder and Ramanathan (1984, p. 411) have provided a critique of Benston which seeks to identify his position as normative, and not positive as he claimed:

> our comments partly provide an internal critique of Benston's argument pointing towards logical inconsistencies, fallacious arguments and unwarranted conclusions. Other comments, however, challenge the very framework set up by Benston, questioning whether this is the only possible mode of analysis, revealing the normative

foundations of this framework and suggesting that the value premises involved are not the only ones possible or acceptable.

The authors conclude that Benston's analysis is limited, and that is the
position taken here. It is argued that it is limited because accounting is
a discipline which evolves as society evolves, and the basic philosophy
of large sections of the population is changing. To account only to
shareholders is to ignore many other groups who, because of choice
or lack of wealth endowments, are not shareholders but employees,
customers, suppliers or members of government bodies.

The purpose of presenting the views of Schreuder and Ramanathan
and Benston was to establish the contrast, which highlights the difficulties imposed by the philosophical underpinning of arguments about the
measurement of externalities. The debate finally emerges as a conflict of
value systems which are normative and untestable.

ISSUES IN THE EVALUATION OF EXTERNALITIES

This section serves to indicate a number of circumstances where the
valuation of externalities might yield interesting results. Consequently
one would expect to encounter models dealing with these areas.

COSTS OF POLLUTION

Pollution is a negative externality which may affect the health and
enjoyment of individuals as well as the value of private and public
property. A secondary effect will be a reduction in the costs of production within the corporation, an improvement in competitive position, more successful marketing and greater sales, all of which will add
to the potential for further pollution. The valuation of pollution is a
major issue addressed by many TIA models.

VALUE OF PROPERTY

The value of real property, particularly that which is owned by individuals or corporations, may be increased or decreased by external
factors. Pollution by noise and odour or an increase in heavy road
traffic, or by some perceived disadvantages may result in a loss of
property values. Similarly, an action taken by one party may enhance
the value of the property of another party. Should some accounting be
made for these particular externalities, and if so, how? This aspect of
externalities does not appear explicitly in the accounting literature and
is a suitable topic for further research.

COSTS OF CONGESTION

A negative externality which may be very difficult to deal with is the cost of congestion, particularly of transport channels. The location of commerce and industry may lead to choked roads and railways and, increasingly, the airways. This problem often requires capital expenditure by a government which may be paid for by the corporation through taxes, but may also be financed by other taxpayers. A similar problem exists with the provision of power to industry, where peak power needs may necessitate the provision of additional equipment which will be used only infrequently. The problem is 'solved' by the imposition of a fixed charge based on maximum demand at the peak time. However, the charge may not cover the provision of the additional capital equipment which is paid for in part by other users.

VALUE OF PUBLIC IMPROVEMENTS

In some cases corporations provide a positive externality by effecting additions to the stock of public goods in the form of roads, railways, harbour facilities and buildings. These are treated as donations or as part of the set-up costs for the enterprise.

These issues, and many others, have to be addressed if externalities are to be valued. Externalities must be included with private costs to determine total impact accounting measures. The position of net positive externalities is often not explored. An assumption is made that in most cases the outcome will be a net negative externality. Clearly, there is considerable work to be done in this area.

VALUATION AND DISCLOSURE MODELS

A number of models, designed to facilitate the identification, measurement and valuation of externalities, can be found within the social accounting literature. Several models are considered here, in order of their date of publication.

Linowes (1972)

One of the earliest attempts to design a model which would account for externalities, and consequently enable the total impact of the organization to be calculated, was provided by Linowes (1972). His socioeconomic operating statement is produced in Table 6.1.

The operating statement divides the impact of the organization into three areas; relations with people; relations with the environment; and relations with product. Sub-totals in each area summarize inprovements

Table 6.1   Socio-economic operating statement

X Corporation
Socio-economic operating statement for the year ending 31 December 1991

I.	**Relations with people**	
	A. Improvements	$
	1. Training programme for handicapped workers	10,000
	2. Contribution to educational institution	4,000
	3. Extra turnover costs because of minority hiring programme	5,000
	4. Cost of nursery school for children of employees voluntarily set up	11,000
	Total improvements	30,000
	B. Less detriments	
	1. Postponed installing new safety devices on cutting machines (cost of the devices)	14,000
	C. Net improvements in people actions for the year	16,000
II.	**Relations with environment**	
	A. Improvements	
	1. Cost of reclaiming and landscaping old dump on company property	70,000
	2. Cost of installing pollution control devices on Plant A smokestacks	4,000
	3. Cost of detoxifying waste from finishing process this year	9,000
	Total improvements	83,000
	B. Less detriments	
	1. Cost that would have been incurred to re-landscape strip-mining site used this year	80,000
	2. Estimated costs of installing purification process to neutralize poisonous liquid being dumped into stream	100,000
		180,000
	C. Net deficit in environment actions for the year	97,000
III.	**Relations with product**	
	A. Improvements	
	1. Salary of vice-president while serving on government Product Safety Commission	25,000
	2. Cost of substituting lead-free paint for previously used poisonous lead paint	9,000
	Total improvements	34,000
	B. Less detriments	
	1. Safety device recommended by Safety Council but not added to product	22,000
	C. Net improvements in product actions for the year	12,000
	Total socio-economic deficit for the year	69,000
	Add: Net cumulative socio-economic improvements as of January 1 19X1	249,000
	Grant Total net socio-economic actions to 31 December 19X1	180,000

Source: Linowes (1972, p. 60).

and net them off against what are termed detriments, to give a net figure.

Although the design of the statement appears logical, the content is not consistent with most of the literature dealing with externalities. There is no estimate of cost or benefit to the environment in the future and consequently no discounted future effect. The costs referred to are current actual or opportunity costs and do not relate to the cost of the activities of the enterprise in the public domain. For example, in the section on relations with the environment, the 'cost of detoxifying waste from finishing process' is shown as an improvement (this is a private and not a public cost), and one of the detriments is the 'estimated costs of installing purification process to neutralize poisonous liquid being dumped into stream'. The latter are not the costs of the externality (the cost to the public) which would be the costs which result from the continued dumping (dead fish, loss of fishing amenities, or reduced value of farm land). This approach does not provide a satisfactory means of valuing or disclosing externalities.

Dilley and Weygandt (1973)

In a frequently quoted study, Dilley and Weygandt presented a statement of funds flow for socially relevant activities in respect of a power utility company, which is reproduced in Table 6.2. The majority of the items listed have an actual or potential effect on the environment; however, in all cases the costs are actual and current. Future costs to the public are not calculated and benefits are not evaluated except in terms of current costs. For example, the benefits of creating less-unsightly plant and equipment in a variety of ways is measured in terms of current costs, which does not measure the future benefit of the expenditure in reducing an externality (in this case unattractive places to work in or pass by). A more complex example is the increased cost of using low-sulphur coal as feedstock for the plants. This cost is correctly stated as incremental, and yet the incremental benefit, in terms of reduced damage, is not valued in the manner suggested in most of the literature on externalities.

The model put forward by Dilley and Weygandt is still deficient, although perhaps of greater utility as a means of disclosure than that used by Linowes.

Ullman (1976)

Ullman put forward a model for the disclosure of environmental impact called the corporate environmental accounting system (CEAS) which employed non-monetary measurement. It has been described as 'partial

Table 6.2

Statement of funds flow for socially relevant activities 1971

	$
Environmental	
Installation of electrostatic precipitators (Note 1)	26,000
Construction of power plants (Note 2)	2,089,000
Construction of transmission lines (Note 3)	35,000
Electrical substation beautification (Note 4)	142,000
Incremental cost of low-sulphur coal (Note 5)	33,670
Conversion of service vehicle to use of propane gas (Note 6)	3,700
Incremental cost of underground electrical	
installations (Note 7)	737,000
Incremental cost of silent jackhammers (Note 8)	100
Environmental research	
Thermal 17,000	
Nuclear 1,955	
Other 38,575	
Subtotal	<u>57,530</u>
Total environmental funds flow	3,124,000
Other benefits	
Charitable contributions	26,940
Employee educational and recreational expenditure (Note 9)	6,000
Total other benefits	<u>32,940</u>
Total 1971 funds flow for socially relevant activities	31,156,940
As a percentage of 1971 operating revenues	7.9%
As a percentage of 1971 advertising expenses	8.50%

Notes to funds statement

1. The company will complete installation of two electrostatic precipitators in 1973. Costs in 1971 totalled $26,000.
2. The company is building power plants which will begin operation in the middle to late 1970s. Incremental cash costs of environmental controls installed in these plants during 1971 totalled $2,089,000.
3. The company is constructing a high-voltage transmission line from another community to the company's service area. Environmental cash costs resulting from wider spacing in line towers totalled $35,000 in 1971.
4. The company constructed a new substation in 1971 with an enclosed structure rather than open exposure of the electric transformers. The cost of this enclosure along with landscaping of existing substations totalled $142,000 in 1971.
5. The company used approximately 150,000 tons of coal during 1971 for electric power generation. Low-sulphur-content coal comprised 8.6% of this coal consumption with the remaining 91.4% being coal of higher sulphur content. The low-sulphur coal cost approximately $2.61/ton more than the high-sulphur coal.
6. Motor vehicles fuelled with propane gas contribute substantially less air pollutants to the atmosphere than gasoline-fuelled vehicles. During 1971 the company converted nine more of its fleet of 115 vehicles to use propane gas. The cost of this conversion was $3,700. Seventeen company vehicles are now operated on propane gas.

Table 6.2   *Continued*

7. Underground installation of electric transmission lines has increased since environmental attention has focused on the aesthetic pollution of poles and wires. During 1971 the company installed underground electric transmission lines, which cost $737,000 more than putting the same lines above ground.
8. Jackhammers used by the company are, with one exception, of the normal, noise-polluting type. One jackhammer purchased during 1971 with noise controls costs $100 more than the regular jackhammers.
9. The company reimburses employees for educational expenditures and provides recreational opportunities such as the annual company picnic. Such expenditure amounted to approximately $6000 in 1971.

Source: Dilley and Weygandt (1973).

non-monetary and output oriented'. A complex calculation is required to develop the input-output relationship which is based on the equivalent factor or EF. This is then used in conjunction with physical measures of environmentally relevant inputs and outputs to arrive at CEAS units. The units are used to prepare a CEAS balance sheet consisting of three sections:

1. environmental effects produced by the production process: materials and energy used, pollution and waste generated and dissipated; plus:
2. impacts due to the use of products sold to customers not subject to CEAS; minus:
3. materials, respectively material content of products sold to customers subject to CEAS (Ullman, 1976, p. 76).

The CEAS model includes a wide range of impacts but does not necessarily measure, even indirectly, the cost to third parties of discharging gaseous matter (his example). Furthermore, the literature on externalities does not normally include the impact of products sold to customers as a cost of operation of the initial producer.

Estes (1976, 1977)

Estes (1976) attempted to model systematically the impact of the organization on the environment from the perspective of the environment. Table 6.3 presents a social impact statement prepared on this basis and divided between social benefits and social costs. The majority of entries are in present cash flows and set off the payments made to society against the payments received from society. However, Estes placed a number of externalities amongst the costs, consisting of a variety of forms of environmental damage. The model put forward by Estes

Table 6.3

	The Progressive Company Social impact statement for the year ended 31 December 19X1		
	$	$	$
Social benefits			
Products and services provided		xxx	
Payments to other elements of society			
Employment provided (salaries and wages)	xxx		
Payments for goods and other services	xxx		
Taxes paid	xxx		
Contributions	xxx		
Dividends and interest paid	xxx		
Loans and other payments	<u>xxx</u>		
		xxx	
Additional direct employee benefits		xxx	
Staff, equipment, and facility services donated	xxx		
Environmental improvements		xxx	
Other benefits		<u>xxx</u>	
Total social benefits			xxx
Social costs			
Goods and materials acquired		xxx	
Buildings and equipment purchased		xxx	
Labour and services used		xxx	
Discrimination		xxx	
In hiring (external)	xxx		
In placement and promotion (internal)	<u>xxx</u>		
		xxx	
Work-related injuries and illness		xxx	
Public services and facilities used		xxx	
Other resources used		xxx	
Environmental damage		xxx	
Terrain damage	xxx		
Air pollution	xxx		
Water pollution	xxx		
Noise pollution	xxx		
Solid waste	xxx		
Visual and aesthetic pollution	xxx		
Other environmental damage	<u>xxx</u>		
		xxx	
Payments from other elements of society			
Payments for goods and services provided	xxx		
Additional capital investment	xxx		
Loans	xxx		
Other payments received	<u>xxx</u>		
		xxx	
Other costs		<u>xxx</u>	
Total social costs			xxx
Social surplus (deficit) for the year			xxx
Accumulated surplus (deficit) 31 December 19X0			<u>xxx</u>
Accumulated surplus (deficit) 31 December 19X1			<u>xxx</u>

Source: Estes (1976, p. 96).

incorporated the cost of environmental damage as determined by surveys, analysis, avoidance costs, restoration costs and surrogate valu-

Table 6.4

	Customers	Employees	Shareholders	Suppliers	Government[+]	Contiguous community	Society at large	Total social impact
XYZ Corporation Social impact statement for the year ended 31 December 1980 (in $ millions)								
Social benefits								
Products and services provided	1.80	0.10	0.10	–	–	–	–	2.00
Cash payments made (purchases, taxes, salaries, dividends, etc.)	–	0.40	0.10	0.60	0.15	0.05	0.10	1.40
Additional employee benefits	–	0.10	–	–	–	–	–	0.10
Environmental improvements	–	0.02	–	–	–	0.03	0.10	0.15
Staff services, facilities, and equipment services donated	0.01	0.01	–	–	0.01	0.02	–	0.05
Other social benefits	–	–	–	–	–	–	0.20	0.20
Total benefits	1.81	0.63	0.20	0.60	0.60	0.60	0.40	3.90
Social costs								
Human services used	–	0.30	–	0.04	–	–	–	0.34
Materials acquired	–	–	–	0.30	–	–	–	0.30
Structures and machinery acquired	–	–	–	0.20	–	–	–	0.20
Discrimination in hiring placement, and purchasing	–	0.02	–	0.01	–	0.03	–	0.06
Cash payments, received	1.60	0.09	0.14	–	0.01	–	–	1.84
Environmental damage air, water, noise, aesthetic pollution; solid waste; terrain damage)	–	0.10	–	–	–	0.15	0.05	0.30
Public services and facilities used	–	–	–	0.25	–	–	–	0.25
Industrial injuries and illness	–	0.10	–	–	–	0.02	–	0.10
Corporate crime (price-fixing, tax fraud, bribery, etc.)	0.05	–	–	0.01	0.02	–	0.02	0.20
Other social costs	–	–	–	–	–	–	0.20	0.20
Total costs	1.65	0.61	0.14	0.56	0.28	0.20	0.27	3.71
Social surplus (deficit)	0.16	0.02	0.06	0.04	(0.12)	0.10	0.13	0.19

Note
[+] Separate columns could be provided for different levels of government – federal, state, and municipal. *Source:* Estes (1977).

ation and shadow pricing, all of which may present measurement problems. The valuation (conversion of physical measurements to financial entries) will necessitate an examination of discount rates, with the two main alternatives being a social time preference rate or the use of a social opportunity cost rate.

In a later paper Estes (1977) subdivided the social impact statement between a number of constituencies, expressing social costs and benefits for each constituency. This development is presented in Table 6.4. Although intended as a refinement, the resulting statement is rather complicated.

The overall approach taken by Estes is similar to the concept of TIA developed by the author; however, TIA is intended to be taken from the organizational perspective in the conventional manner and not from that of the environment.

Dierkes and Preston (1977)

Dierkes and Preston reviewed a number of attempts to deal with the problems of accounting for the physical environment. A number of specific proposals were included, for example that of the Council on Economic Priorities issued in 1975, and the American Accounting Association proposal that social costs be accounted for in terms of the Levels I, II and III hierarchy, both of which are cited with approval. The authors noted that any proposal for an accounting for environmental impacts needs to have a systematic framework but not one which aims at bringing all events to a common valuation:

> The framework outlined here does not suggest the use of a unique performance measurement unit and certainty not a *monetary* measurement unit for all areas of environmental impact. On the contrary, it uses a wide variety of measures appropriately developed for the various specific impact areas. (Dierkes and Preston, 1977, p. 14)

They put forward a model based on inputs and outputs, which assumed that the company has a formal policy statement requiring information about the environmental impact of decision making. The model is illustrated in Table 6.5. Extensive use is made of Levels I and II in the AAA hierarchy, with lesser reliance upon Level III. To this extent the model avoids the issues which Estes was prepared to address.

The social cost figures obtained may be used for three purposes:

1. for government use – is the community willing to tax itself sufficiently to correct the problem?
2. as a basis for negotiation between the parties; and:
3. the 'social costs' may be expressed as 'effluent charges' levied

Table 6.5 Environment

Factor	Description	Input (Commitment) Measure	Further information	Description	Output (Performance) Measure	Further information
Energy	Research and development	D,No., $		Consumption – total	$,$ per sales	
	Savings measures	D,$		oil	$ per unit output	
	Policy and goals	D,No., ($ or %)		gas		
				coal		
				other		
				Re-use waste heat	$,% of total consumption	
Air pollution	Policy and goals	D,No.		Noise level (nearest house)	dB A	Comparison with Standards
Water pollution	Research and development (by pollutant or waste).	D,No. $		Air pollution by pollutant	W,W/P	
Solid waste				Water pollution by pollutant	W	
Noise	Control equipment	$,D.		Water charges	B.o.D.	
	Recycling equipment	% of total investment		Solid/semi-solid dumped	$	
		% increase in production cost	% production costs	Solid/semi-solid sold	$,W	
					$,W	
				New by-products	D,S,$	
				Complaints	No.	
				Lawsuits	No.,$	
Despoliation of landscape	Policy and goals	D,No.		Complaints	No.	
	Rehabilitation (landscaping)	D,$		Lawsuits	No.,$	
	Beautification	D,$ size area despoiled size area reclaimed				

	Policy and goals			
Raw materials*		D,No.	Type	W,%,$
			Waste	W,%,$
			Use of recycled materials	W,%,$
	Research and development: substitution recycling	D,No.		
	Research and development	$		
Packaging		D,No.,$	Returnable	W,%
			Waste	W,%
Transport	Modal policy	D	Energy use	$,W
			Pollution	(as above)

Notes

* Consideration may also be given to the use of scarce non-renewable resources, and the use of renewable but long-term resources, e.g., trees.

No. = Absolute quality. Could mean both staff and beneficiaries.
$ = Cost in applicable currency.
% = Proportion or percentage in terms of applicable denominator.
D = Description of policy, measure, goal, activity.
Fr = Frequency of activity.
T = Length of time applicable to activity.
W = Weight.
S = Sales.
P = Product.
A = Assessment.

Source: Dierkes and Preston (1977, p. 15).

Table 6.6   Societal profit and loss account

Erwebswirtschaftliche Erfolgsrechnung		Gesellschaftsbezogene Erfolgsrechnung	
Costs	Revenues	Social costs	Social benefits
Profit		Net social benefits	

Gesellschaftsbezogene Erfolgsrechnung	
Social costs	Social benefits

I. Producer's surplus for:
  1. labour performances
  2. fixed assets
  3. materials
  4. capital
  5. entrepreneurial performances
  6. bought-in performances
	I. Consumers' surplus for:
	  1. product A
	  2. product B
	  3. product C
	  4. product D

II. Value of negative external effects on:
  1. employees
  2. population
  3. companies
  4. public entities
	II. Value of positive external effects on:
	  1. employees
	  2. population
	  3. companies
	  4. public entities

III. Net social benefits	III. Net social costs

Source: Schreuder (1979, p. 110).

against the course of the pollution. These latter – which, in effect, result in the 'internalization' of previously 'external' cost impacts – then enter the managerial calculations of an individual firm just like any other costs of doing business. (Ibid., p. 2)

This is the approach taken by the author in the concept of TIA.

Eichhorn (1979)

In contrast to the detailed models put forward by Estes and Dierkes and Preston, Eichhorn has offered a societal profit and loss account which is theoretical and conceptual and apparently incapable of implementation. The outline is reproduced Table 6.6. Schreuder has noted that models of this type are useful as a frame of reference against which less-ambitious models may be evaluated.

Gray, Owen and Maunders (1987)

Gray, Owen and Maunders (1987) illustrated the involvement of the organization with its environment at three levels. The first, correspond-

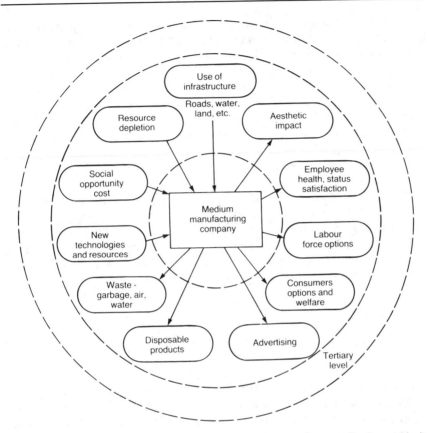

Figure 6.1 Conceptualization of the relationship of the organization with its environment. Source: Gray, Owen and Maunders (1987, p. 78).

ing to conventional accounting, or possibly conventional accounting and SRA, was used in Chapter 4. The second illustration is shown as Figure 6.1 and includes a range of environmental interactions, some of which are similar to, or actually are, externalities. It should be noted that this model is conceptual and does not provide any details of the mechanism which would provide for the measurement and valuation of identifiable events.

MODELS OF EXTERNALITIES: A SUMMARY

The seven models reviewed in this section cover the main types available for consideration until the developments which are discussed in the section on the emergence of environmental economics and accounting. Linowes and Dilley and Weygandt use the historical cost structure to indicate the costs and benefits of preventing externalities and the costs associated with non-prevention. Ullman deals exclusively with non-financial measurement on a macro scale. Estes and Dierkes and Preston offer models which not only use financial measurement for current items but impute the costs of unprevented externalities. However, the approach taken by Estes has been criticized as providing an ideal position which cannot be realized where market-based valuations do not exist. The Dierkes and Preston model is designed to accept both financial and non-financial data. The last two approaches by Eichorn and Gray, Owen and Maunders revert to conceptual models, leaving out any procedures by which the measurement and valuation may be accomplished.

The TIA disclosures envisaged in this book involve the calculation of externalities and then their internalization into the cost structure of the enterprise. In terms of the approaches discussed above, a combination of Estes and Dierkes and Preston would be the closest. It is clear that additional research is required in this area to fulfil the potential which TIA holds for those with a concern for environmental matters.

SOCIAL AUDIT

INTRODUCTION

Modern financial accounting practice associates the preparation and disclosure activities with the checking and attesting function known as auditing. Financial or external auditing has been an important part of accounting for several hundred years, and later variants include internal and operational auditing in the private sector, and value-for-money auditing in the public sector.

Social accounting activities have induced a demand in the literature for social audits, although the term is often used to describe different activities. This section considers the social audit in the context of SRA and TIA; value-for-money audits are dealt with in Chapter 7. The discussion of social audits can be divided between an internal monitoring of social responsibility accounting disclosures, an external audit of SRA and TIA disclosures on behalf of the producers, and an external audit of the performance of the corporation from the perspective of society as a whole.

INTERNAL MONITORING OF SRA DISCLOSURES

Two examples of conceptual SRA models discussed in Chapter 4 (Brooks, 1986; Burke, 1984) were concerned with providing social information to aid managerial decision-making. These models included a feedback provision whereby the effect of the decisions on the environment was monitored and fed back to aid further decision-making. This activity is a form of social audit, although admittedly outside of the normal usage of that term.

EXTERNAL AUDIT OF SRA AND TIA FOR PRODUCERS

The idea being explored here is an audit of SRA and TIA disclosures by appropriately qualified personnel, with an audit report being passed to the management or the shareholders of the organization. There are relatively few examples of this procedure being undertaken, perhaps because SRA disclosures are not produced in sufficient quantity to make an independent audit worthwhile, and TIA has an underdeveloped methodology about which there might be insufficient agreement to permit attestation.

Brooks (1980) documented the use of a particular technique (an attitude survey approach) for use with a social audit. Although described as a survey of internal personnel, the subject was the external relations of the company and, consequently, the contribution fits into this section. Sellers (1981) provided a conceptual model for developing a social audit. The model consisted of four distinct interest groups: the entity, the auditors, the standard-setting bodies, and the constituent (or user) groups. One interesting point was that despite the stage of development of SRA, Sellers referred to the standard-setting bodies in a manner that indicated his belief that newer forms of disclosures will follow the same development pattern as has occurred previously.

Filios (1985) used the term 'social process auditing' in referring to the audit of corporate activities in the social area. The relationship between the organization and the government is not to be neglected since:

The aims of an accounting system for social goals are:
- Determination of the specific goals and objectives to be sought through government intervention and the specific actions to be taken in specific programmes and activities.
- Evaluation of social alternatives and determination of the effectiveness and efficiency of efforts expended to maintain or improve social conditions.   (Filios, 1985, p. 482).

Gray, Owen and Maunders (1987) have given an example of a corporation-inspired audit of SRA disclosure by Atlantic Richfield, which they described as a rare event.

EXTERNAL AUDIT OF CORPORATIONS – A SOCIETAL PERSPECTIVE

Gray, Owen and Maunders (1987) have examined the issue of social audit in some detail. They concluded that very few organizations have an external audit of their SRA or TIA disclosures and that most social audits are undertaken by organizations with consumer or labour groups as their main constituencies. As examples they refer to the work in the UK of Social Audit Limited, Counter Information Services, the work of local authorities, and finally, the work of the government in monitoring social performance.

Social Audit Limited provided educational material on social audits and has in the past provided detailed reports. The general view appears to be that the reports are searching but not deliberately anti-business. Counter Information Services provides anti-reports which are labour-orientated and ideologically informed by Marxism and critical theory. In the UK a number of local authorities have been concerned by the closure of factories in their administrative areas, and have attempted to delay or avoid these changes. Social audits, in this context, are concerned with the costs of shutting down plants, leading to a loss of rating income, unemployment and social problems and the cost to employees compared to the savings and benefits to the organization (Owen and Harte, 1984; Harte and Owen, 1986).

Government monitoring of social performance is carried out in many fields, including race relations, sexual discrimination, air pollution, water pollution, health and safety at work, protection of consumers, rights of employees, the implementation of mental health legislation, and public protection (police). However, government departments frequently attempt to mediate between different groups and do not want to provide wide-ranging information about their own activities. It is clear, however, that one method of enforcing widespread social audits is through legislation in a similar manner to the current statutory audit.

SOCIAL AUDIT – A CONCLUSION

It may be concluded that very little audit of SRA and TIA disclosures takes place at the behest of the corporation, on behalf of management or shareholders. However, management may be provided with internal reports to monitor socially sensitive activities, such as effluent discharge.

The social audits which are normally encountered are those produced by outside parties of consumerists or those looking to criticize the organization from a radical position. There is little momentum to develop social audits at present although some writers imply that the government needs to be involved. The audit issue is re-examined as part of the environmental accounting development.

THE EMERGENCE OF ENVIRONMENT ECONOMICS AND ACCOUNTING

This chapter has outlined the philosophical issues involved in accounting for the total amount of the entity, including private costs and externalities which are translated into public costs. Furthermore, a number of models for total impact accounting and social audit have been presented for consideration. It is not difficult to see that further development is needed before environmental accounting can be applied to the problems of modern Western-style economies.

Recent developments have taken two new approaches. The first is the work of environmental economists such as Siebert and Antal (1979) and Pearce *et al.* (1989), whose work has been important in encouraging others to look at the issues of intergenerational effects and sustainable development. Second, and more important for our purposes, has been the work of Gray (1990, 1991) in developing further measures of environmental accounting and disclosure which, if implemented, would assist in controlling the entities which are endangering the environment. The discussion will be developed by examining the literature in terms of these two approaches, and is based upon Mathews (1991).

ENVIRONMENTAL ECONOMICS

Two publications provide a very good flavour for the environmental economics literature of the past decade, which has in turn provided an opening for the proposals of environmental accountants.

Siebert and Antal (1979) provided a good introduction to some of the problems facing the industralized world in the closing years of the twentieth century; problems which originated with the economics of the nineteenth and have been exacerbated by many factors, including the way in which accounting concentrates on monetary values, private ownership and the determination of value through the market-place.

Mathews (1991, p. 111) noted that this book provided 'an excellent introduction to economic/environmentalist thought, which provided good background information, and a solid basis from which to proceed to more advanced material'. Documented environmental problems are placed clearly before the reader:

Not only is the air we breathe saturated with pollutants from our economic development; our water is also contaminated. Germany's celebrated Rhine transports 24 million tons of poisons and pollutants to the Dutch frontier yearly. Daily, this represents about 3 tons of arsenic, 450 kg. of mercury, 30,000 tons of sodium chloride ions, 16,000 tons of sulfates, 2,200 tons of nitrates, and over 100 tons of phosphates. (Siebert and Antal, 1979, p. 11)

and:

We are now threatening the earth's store of oxygen. The demand for oxygen is constantly rising. Every combustion process requires oxygen. A VW uses as much oxygen in 900 km. as does a person in a year; a jet at takeoff consumes as much as a 17,000-hectare forest produces in a night. (Ibid., p. 37)

Conventional economics are blamed for many problems because the environment has been regarded as a free good, externalities have been ignored, and social problems have often been addressed via economic growth which frequently leads to further problems. The goals of economic growth and environmental quality are conflicting and distorted if one measure, such as GDP, is used as the sole measure of social well-being. The position with regard to the dysfunctional effects of industrialization is well stated:

Social groups must be prepared to calculate into their real income the value of an improved environment, and must be willing to sacrifice income increases in the traditional sense of the term in favor of improvements in environmental quality. (Ibid., p. 134)

The suggested way forward towards an improved quality of environment does not include regulation or tighter emission standards, as might have been expected, but instead relies upon an emission tax:

The authors believe that only taxes, emission standards, and pollution permits should be considered to be key measures. Subsidies, public investments, the concept of a 'basic right' to the environment, and moral suasion are simply insufficient as primary answers to the allocative problem. (Ibid., p. 164)

The rejection of a regulatory approach is characteristic of the environmental economists but not the environmental accountants.

Pearce et al. (1969) authored a report for the UK Department of the Environment, which was well received by the minister and has had some influence with academics in both economics and accounting. Their treatment begins with the concept of sustainable development, a topic which has a number of interpretations. Pearce et al. (1989, pp. 1–2) adopted the position that:

Sustainable development involves devising a social and economic system which ensures that these goals are sustained, i.e., that real incomes rise, that educational standards increase, that the health of the nation improves, that the general quality of life is advanced.

The concept of intergenerational equity was outlined: future generations should not be left worse off by the actions of the present generation:

> What is the justification for ensuring that the next generation has at least as much wealth – man-made and natural – as this one? The intuitive idea underlying this approach to sustainable development is that of *intergenerational equity*. What is being said is that we can meet our obligations to be fair to the next generation by leaving them an inheritance of wealth no less than we inherited.
> (Ibid., pp. 34–5)

The environment should be protected by valuing it, in order to demonstrate that environmental services are not free:

> The fact that we find *positive* values for so many environmental functions means that an economic system which allocates resources according to economic values (i.e., consumer preferences) *must* take account of the economic values for environmental quality.
> (Ibid., p. 81)

It is at this point that Pearce *et al.* demonstrate their adherence to the economics approach to the environmental problem. Their chapter on 'Accounting for the Environment' presents information on a macro (economics-orientated) scale, as for the national accounts, and not in an accounting manner (as for the enterprise). Later chapters compound the problem by arguing in favour of cost-benefit analysis (albeit with allowances for environmental damage) and having concern for sustainable development and aggregate environmental capital. As Mathews (1991, pp. 114–15) notes, the authors have provided a thorough critique of discounting from an environmentalist perspective, which looks at pure time preference, risk and uncertainty, diminishing marginal utility of consumption, and opportunity cost of capital. Despite the strength of these arguments, the authors do not favour adjusted rates (that is, the use of social rates) but market rates in conjunction with better information. This would include the use of improved valuation techniques, the integration of environmental considerations into all economic decisions, and the incorporation of a sustainability constraint into the appraisal of environmental programmes.

The final chapter explains the role that prices and incentives may play in improving the environment. As might be expected, as economists the authors favour price mechanisms based on markets. However, it is well known that there are market inefficiencies which have led to our present environmental crisis. Pearce *et al.* propose to use the market to remove market-based problems, by ensuring that the value of environmental services are included in the prices of goods and services. This regulatory process is called establishing market-based incentives. It is argued that a market-based system of regulation is more efficient than one based on command and control.

The most powerful tool by which to achieve the proper pricing of products and services is the 'polluter pays' principle. The polluter is made to pay:

1. by setting *standards*, the cost of achieving which is initially borne by the producer;
2. by setting *charges* or *taxes* on the polluting product or input;
3. by setting a standard, issuing *pollution permits* in amounts consistent with the standard, and allowing those permits to be *traded* (ibid., p. 158).

Market-based incentives include pollution charges and taxes, such as a carbon tax, and creating markets for pollution permits.

The Pearce report was an extremely important addition to the study of environmental economics and should be consulted by accountants who are interested in the area. The most important features include: the concept of sustainable development; the separation of capital into natural and man-made assets, together with a commitment to intergenerational equity; the description of macro accounts based on both physical and monetary measurements, the arguments over discount rates; and finally, the use of market-based incentives to ensure that the environment is properly valued.

The authors adopted a number of positions with which accountants might disagree, including the emphasis on markets and against regulation, together with the use of only macro accounts. However, these are interdisciplinary differences and should be recognized as such. Accountants are challenged by this book to define a position which will take those parts which are acceptable and produce alternatives to those which are not.

ENVIRONMENTAL ACCOUNTING

Recent work in this area is exemplified by that of Gray (1990, 1991) whose prolific output has provided many new ideas for the study and implementation of environmental disclosures in annual reports. The following material provides only a brief review of these works.

Gray (1990) built on the work of environmental economists, including Pearce *et al.* (1989). Gray does not regard the solutions put forward by the economists as satisfactory because they are still preoccupied with continued economic growth, choose to rely upon market-determined values, ignore ethical perspectives when discussing environmental matters, and do not favour regulation and the enforcement of standards of conduct. Gray favours a systems approach by which he seeks to demonstrate the interrelationship of society and the environment.

Gray (1990) reviewed the current (inadequate) role of accounting in terms of the environment, due in large measure to a view of social reality which is based upon the economist's view of the world. A new approach is needed from accounting if firms are to consider non-traditional users: consumers and employees, resources, products and the ecosphere, and the financial sector. The first is important, because these groups may not wish to be associated with an insensitive organization; the second, because continued enviromental pollution will result in heightened levels of both requirements and penalties. Finally, ethical investment funds are beginning to appear and these have an effect in the capital markets. In addition to the above, governments will eventually have to take action.

In two crucial chapters Gray presents his recommendations dealing with internal accounting and information sytems and the external reporting of green accounting. In Chapter 5, internal accounting and information systems are considered. Most organizations have undisclosed means of collecting information to assist with decision-making. Gray suggests an enhancement of these systems to include data more directly concerned with avoiding environmental damage. The impetus for change must come from the top of the organization in order to be fully successful. Once an organization has decided to implement change, it is suggested that an environmental department be set up. This would be an independent, identifiable part of the organization, with senior management and board representation. Its role would include: monitoring issues and priorities; engaging in strategic questions; and the integration of environmental awareness and sensitivity into organizational life.

Gray (1990) argues that the organization needs to have an environmental policy which is not of the PR variety. This might include: the particular orientation of the organization; the provision of information for employees, customers and suppliers; as well as the statement of parameters of acceptable activities. Setting up an environmental department and developing an environmental policy must be backed up with an information system:

> The selection and design of the information system will therefore be a complex and crucial element in the organisation's environmental response – systems must be selected that can deliver believable information; of an understandable nature; relevant to the actors receiving or reporting the information; they must identify what is happening and what is not happening – selected from the universe

> of all possible activities – and action/non-action identified against
> yardsticks of acceptable action.   (Gray, 1990, p. 79)

The reports suggested include: a compliance report or audit; an ethical
audit; a waste audit; an energy audit; an emerging issues audit; environmental impact assessment/appraisal/analysis; a general environmental
audit; and a financial environmental audit. The purposes of each are
evident from the titles. The compliance report or audit would make
sure that the organization complies with legal requirements in relation
to the environment. The ethical audit refers to above-the-law requirements which management may require. Setting such requirements
would necessitate an open discussion about a large range of issues
within the organization. The waste audit should identify waste, the
costs associated with the treatment and disposal of waste, and that
which may be recycled. A similar modification to the accounting and
management information system would allow energy flows to be audited. The emerging issues audit would act as a reminder that the problems of the environment are ongoing, and that initiatives must be
maintained.

The environmental impact assessment/appraisal/analysis will have
serious effects on organizations, as governments regulate the planning
and location of industry more thoroughly. There are costs associated
with environmental protection which will have to be included in project
costs. The reference to a general environmental audit is an alternative
to the structured approach detailed above, which might be carried out
by an outside consultant as a starting point. The financial environmental
audit is included as a warning against short-term evaluation to determine whether the organization would be 'better off' if it breaks the law.
If the ethical audit has been effective, there should only be one answer
to such a question.

Other suggestions for an expanded reporting system include: the
environmental budget; the environmental investment rate; and environmental asset maintenance. The environmental budget is a title given to
the process of ranking enviromental criteria on a level with other criteria. Once the pollution budget is set for a period, interorganizational
differences could be levelled out by means of pollution permits. The
investment process would have to be overhauled, including the investment rate, to take account of environmental costs. Taxation initiatives,
as discussed by Pearce *et al.*, will become important, as will other
initiatives, including potential and actual legislation. Gray says of the
best practicable environment option (BPEO) and the best available technology not entailing excessive cost (BATNEEC):

> Both concepts are an attempt to articulate the criteria that regulatory
> authorities must apply to organisational assessment and whilst it

is clear that the State believes that environmental criteria must not dominate commercial criteria, the position is now just a little harder and organisations will have to prove that they did in fact choose BPEO and/or BATNEEC and, further, failure to so prove may lead to retrospectively awarded reparation damages. (Gray, 1990, p. 95)

The records of the organization must be capable of distinguishing between natural and man-made capital. Furthermore, some natural capital will be critical and some will be 'other' natural capital. Concepts of ownership and stewardship will have to be revised.

Gray (1990) argues that there are three reasons for organizations to develop environmental reporting: the principle of accountability; a requirement to report will influence actions; information influences perceptions. External social audits are regarded as influential in providing an alternative view of the organization to that which may be projected by in-house literature. Self-reporting, as advocated by some social accountants for many years, has not been particularly successful. Gray suggests that a pragmatic approach is needed, such as that put forward by the United Nations.

The UN initiative on external reporting addresses (United Nations, 1975) the following areas: the definition of environmental expenditure and activity; the question of whether expenditure on environmental issues could be capitalized; contingent liabilities with respect to future environmental costs; and taxation and disclosure. The points about contingent liabilities and capitalized expenditures are very important, and have a place even in conventional financial accounting. Disclosure is central to accounting and, therefore, a compliance-with-standard approach as advocated by the author seems quite appropriate, even though the data are likely to include non-financial material. Finally, the issue of the nature of assets is revisited. Three elements must be considered: their definition and categorization; transfers between categories (to and from man-made capital); and maintenance of the assets in each of the categories.

As stated by Pearce *et al*. (1989), man-made capital should be separated from natural capital. However, Gray (1990) separates natural capital into two groups: critical capital and other natural capital. The transfer between categories questions the rights and obligations inferred by property rights and ownership. In seeking maintenance of the assets within existing categories, the main objective is to eliminate quickly movements between critical capital and other categories and to slow down movements between other natural capital and man-made capital.

The author concludes that the most pragmatic approach to environmental accounting in the short term would be:

(a) to follow the UN initiative within the current framework of financial reporting; (b) require the addition of a compliance-with-standard report in order to capture the current legal framework of pollution regulation; and (c) in order to initiate a reorientation of the accounting from ownership toward stewardship and to enable the implementation of the Pearce proposals on natural and man-made capital, introduce a redefinition of assets and capital maintenance.   (Gray, 1990, p. 128)

Gray (1991) develops the ideas suggested in Gray (1990) in an examination of current accounting orthodoxy:

(a)   the current conventional orthodoxy of accounting – or rather more specifically of financial accounting and reporting – is indefensible – in its own terms, in its failure to acknowledge its widespread social, economic, political and environmental implications as well as in its failure to encompass social and environmental accountings; and

(b)   a different approach in accounting thought is required that will both overcome the lacunae in current approaches and naturally embrace social and environmental accounting and reporting.   (Gray, 1991, p. 3)

The Gray (1991) approach is set out in Figure 6.2, in which the orthodox and the new accounting are compared. The inclusion of externalities and the perceived need to report other than economic events to groups additional to those addressed at present are quite clearly stated.

Figure 6.3 goes one step further in showing that the 'new' accounting is concerned not only with additional reporting from established processes but also with new processes: a concern for the environment, community, democracy and so on, is placed in opposition to a concern for economic and legal values. The overall equation is concerned with accountability in its fullest sense.

The values pursued by conventional accounting are strenuously attacked because they do not lead to accountability in the wider sense, but only to a narrow conception of decision-usefulness for a limited range of users. Because accounting reports are not neutral, the outcome of biased or partial reports is very important, especially if there are environmental consequences of a permanent or long-term nature. Here we have once again the problems which arise from a reliance upon the notion of values, set by the market through the transfer of private owership rights, which cannot include the biosphere. Figure 6.4 shows the systems diagram of the accountant's perception of the world, which may be compared with the systems world-view extended into the social and environmental domains as shown in Figure 6.5.

After discussing some of the reasons for the present condition of

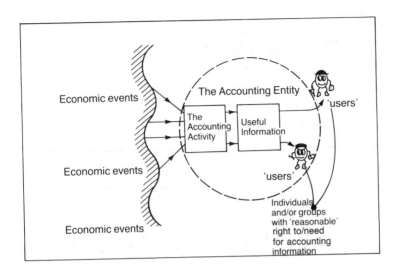

CONVENTIONAL ACCOUNTING	SOCIAL AND ENVIRONMENTAL ACCOUNTING
(1) ORGANIZATIONS Accounting Entity	(1) DEFINE? 'Externalities'?
(2) ECONOMIC EVENTS	(2) OTHER EVENTS e.g. Social Environmental
(3) FINANCIAL DESCRIPTION	(3) OTHER DESCRIPTIONS
(4) USERS Management Investors Bankers Creditors	(4) USERS also Society Labour Community Future generations

Figure 6.2 Conventional accounting and social and environmental accounting. Source: Gray (1991, p. 5).

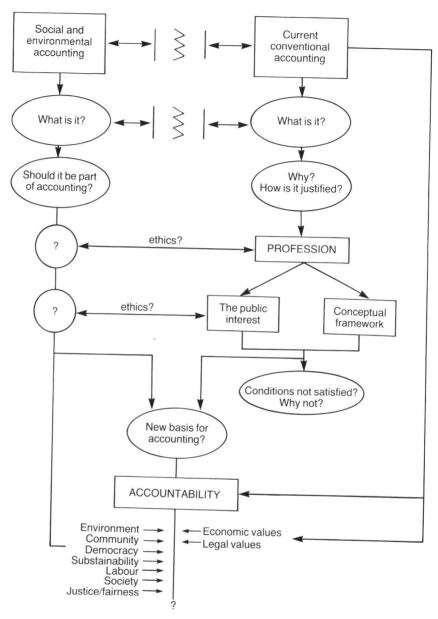

Figure 6.3 Accounting, accountancy profession and environmental crisis. Source: Gray (1991, p. 6).

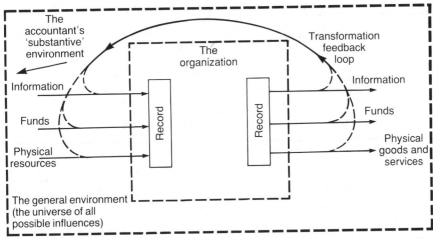

Figure 6.4 A systems view of accounting, organizations and the environment (i).
Source: Adapted from Lowe (1972); Laughlin and Gray (1988), cited in Gray (1991).

accounting and environmental disclosure and the need for accountability based upon the acceptance that additional groups have rights to
information, Gray (1991) provides suggestions for additional disclosures. The first group is taken from a United Nations initiative (Gray,
1991, p. 39):

Financial information:
* disclosure of amount spent on environmental matters (possibly
  enabling capitalisation due to spend impact on EPS), will possibly be split between regulated and voluntary costs;
* disclosure of environmental contingent·· liabilities – most
  especially those arising from remediation costs under 'Super-
  fund' type legislation;
* disclosure of anticipated pattern of future environmental expenditure (possibly split between regulated and voluntary costs).

Non-financial information:
* disclosure of environmental policy for the organisation;
* disclosure of organisational activity in the environmental field,
  including such matters as emissions statements.

The second group (Gray, 1991, p. 41) is much more detailed and is
adapted from Gray (1990):

1. Compliance and ethical audits (meeting legal requirements and
   the organisation's code of conduct).
2. Waste and energy audits (efficient use of inputs).

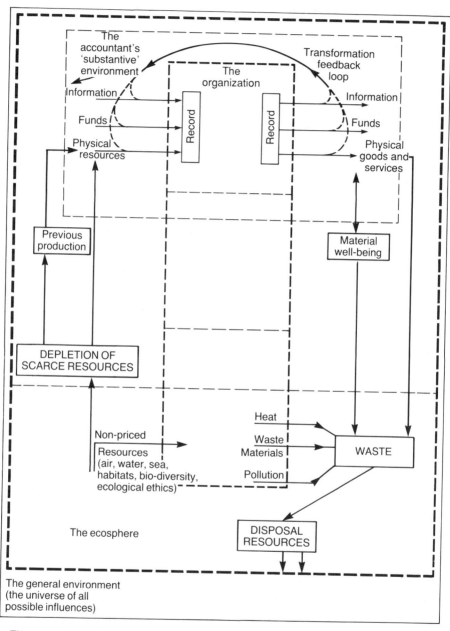

Figure 6.5 A systems view of accounting, organizations and the environment (ii).
Source: Adapted from Lowe (1972); Laughlin and Gray (1988).

3. Environmental budget (financial and non-financial targets and performance appraisal).
4. Environmental impact assessment, environmental hurdle rates, BPEO, BATNEEC, environmental risk assessment (reappraisal of the environmental sensitivity of the organisation's investment policy).
5. Environmental asset accounting and maintenance (accounting for natural assets, accounting for sustainability – the cost in terms of natural resources of the increases in man-made capital).
6. Environmental and social reporting including environmental policy, environmental contingencies, environmental spend, emission statement, compliance-with-standard report. Disclosure of natural and man-made assets plus transfers between the categories.

Gray (1991, p. 43) concluded with an examination of the distinction made by Pearce *et al.* (1989) and others between man-made capital and natural capital. He concluded (after Turner) that natural capital should be divided into critical natural capital and substitutable, renewable natural capital, noting (p. 44):

> The critical capital must, by definition, be immutable in a sustainable world. It is only the 'other' natural capital that can be used for substitution, and then only up to the point where it goes critical.

Clearly, the last word has not been written on environmental or total impact accounting, but there are encouraging signs that many diverse, and potentially conflicting, groups are supportive of the continued development of green reporting.

Owen (1992) provides a timely discussion of environmental accounting issues from several perspectives. The book is divided into four parts, with almost all the papers in two of the sections. The first part consists of a lengthy paper by the editor setting out the implications which 'greenness' would have for the accounting function. Owen concludes that if a reformist (as opposed to a radical) perspective is adopted, then accountants can make contributions in both the internal and external reporting fields. First, by developing management information systems to assist organizations to control micro level responses to macro level initiatives, and secondly, to develop external reporting practices, including the audit function.

However, the world view of many accountants may be an impediment to these developments. Owen notes that a lot of time has elapsed since *The Corporate Report* (ASCC 1975) encouraged developments in the social area. The overall message of the contributions is that the time for action has arrived.

The second part takes up about one-third of the book and is entitled 'The Future of Green Reporting'. The contributions are divided between various interest groups, including industry and commerce (three papers), the trade union movement (three papers), the accounting profession (three papers), green pressure groups (two papers), and the investor (two papers). A number of contributors include suggestions for reporting that are similar in intent (if not in detail); for example, management, trade unions and investors all favour environmental reports and audits. This congruence of views is both encouraging and, frankly, surprising.

The contributions of the representatives of the accounting profession are stated to be personal contributions in two out of three cases. This is unfortunate, since it does make for some confusion on the part of the reader. Are the professional bodies simply being cautious, or are they divided over the issue, or even opposed to disclosure (back to the world view impediment again)? The message given by each of the contributors in this section (apart from institutional advertising) is that there is clearly a role for people with skills similar to those of accountants to design systems that capture and disseminate information, and to audit disclosures. However, in some cases accountants will have to work with members of other disciplines in interdisciplinary teams.

The contributions from the green pressure groups are thoughtful and informative, not controversial. They argue for additional disclosures in many areas, as would be expected, but appear to avoid the more controversial issues, such as the charges that are often made that some multinational corporations ship goods no longer approved for use in their home markets to developing countries for sale there. Avoiding controversies of this nature may be desirable, but this reader was left with the impression that these were rather 'light green' papers.

Approximately one-third of the book is given to part 3, which deals with current trends in green awareness. This part could have been placed before the second part dealing with future trends; however, the order is not particularly important. Part 3 consists of five ungrouped papers dealing with: environmental disclosures in corporate annual reports in Western Europe; current trends in the reporting of green issues in the annual reports of United Kingdom companies; environmental management in practice; the social audit movement; and green investment.

The paper by Roberts concludes that European environmental reporting is voluntary but increasing in volume, with German corporations leading the way. Harte and Owen conclude similarly in respect of disclosures by UK companies. They note in particular the highly selective nature of non-traditional disclosures and the reluctance to disclose bad news. There is a long way to go before a recognizable system of formal accounting for corporate social and environmental impacts is achieved.

The confusion surrounding the function and role of the social audit is brought into focus by the papers dealing with environmental management in practice and with the social audit movement. The political nature of what has been termed the social audit movement is well covered by Geddes. Is this an example of the process of 'regulatory capture' whereby watchdog organizations are subverted by those they set out to watch? Geddes clearly has some concerns about the future of the social audit movement since he concludes that 'we must not expect too much from social audit or place extensive reliance on it'. The final paper in part 3 deals with green investment and the rise of SRI (socially responsible investment) in the US, the UK and Europe.

Part 4 on the further development of green reporting includes only one paper on the practical implications of developing green reporting systems. It covers the problems inherent in dealing with qualitative issues and 'soft data' in general.

SUMMARY

This chapter has considered the development and implementation of TIA. There are definite philosophical difficulties involved in the measurement and valuation of externalities. Many accountants and managers would experience grave concerns about the process of charging back to the entity costs which have 'escaped' into the public arena and may be co-mingled with other similar costs. The same difficulties are not so apparent in the reporting of SRA. However, the considerable difficulties outlined here may provide a spur to the development of measurement and disclosure procedures for TIA. From the difficulties detailed above, the TIA process needs further development before it could become part of a general evaluation of organizational performance. The conventional accounting system within the organization will not recognize externalities or public costs,unless they are converted into private costs by means of fines and/or charges for the release or discharge of noxious material. Of course, such a charge does not remove the nuisance. However, given a reasonably efficient market, the increased cost of production should help to bring about either a reduction in sales (and hence output) as a result of a rise in price, or to draw the attention of management to a worthwhile investment in efficient pollution abatement equipment.

In view of the difficulty of measuring the social cost of externalities in monetary terms, it would appear that the best line of approach, at the present time, is via Levels I and II of the AAA framework. That is, recognizing the sources of possible externalities and measuring them in non-financial terms. This information, if publicly available, would enable the community, via the government, to decide whether a penalty or charge should be imposed. This process forces recognition of the cost as a private cost, and enables accounting systems and management decision-making to function in the usual way. To attempt to measure the cost of externalities after the event, whilst still allowing the discharge (or other action) to take place seems rather shortsighted. Equally, to make an *ex ante* valuation of the externalities over the total life of the programme or project would seem to be very difficult at this stage. To make an *ex post* valuation might be easier, in terms of having more information available, but the firm will have distributed or reinvested the 'excess profits' and be unable to pay the fine when assessed at a later date.

The ultimate aim of TIA is to evaluate private organizational activities in terms of public cost. To do so, TIA must identify actions which are likely to produce social costs or externalities and then obtain both financial and non-financial measures of these externalities. These are then converted into financial measurements. There are many parellels between TIA and cost-benefit analysis (CBA) which is used in the public sector and is discussed in the next chapter. Eventually, the value of some form of TIA may lie in justifying the continued operation of a plant or process. Continued government intervention in the marketplace may result in private organizations taking the lead in using TIA to justify their operations. However, it must be recognized that the degree to which an economy conforms to a free-market model will have a major effect on the development of TIA. At the present time the valuation of externalities in accounting could be best described as having a very low priority with most organizations.

An examination of the models provided by the literature shows that in many instances externalities are not valued at the discounted value of future costs, but at the current historical cost. For example, the cost of environmental damage is valued at the amount which was not expended to stop the discharge and ignores the actual cost of damage to the environment of the discharges themselves.

Social audit was discussed in this chapter in order that disclosures under both SRA and TIA might be included. Very little evidence exists of systematic social audits on a large scale, except in the area of radical critiques of the activities of certain organizations. However, because this form is not sympathetic towards the continued existence of the current economic system it cannot be considered as part of any evolutionary strategy leading towards a more socially responsible accounting.

The recent work by environmental economists and environmental accountants was briefly surveyed. The current concern with sustainable production, and the classifications of natural capital into critical and other categories is clearly important to the future of the accounting discipline. The recommendations put forward by Gray (in particular) would, if accepted, result in additional reports designed to establish conformity with external requirements. These reports would need to be audited and would go a long way to improve the accountability of organizations.

Socio-economic accounting (SEA)   7

INTRODUCTION

Socio-economic accounting (SEA) is concerned with a micro approach to the problems of project selection, operation, control and evaluation in the public sector. The term socio-economic accounting has been defined by Linowes (1968, p. 37) as follows:

> Socio-economic accounting is intended here to mean the application of accounting in the field of social sciences. These include sociology, political science and economics.

Although Linowes was using the term within the private sector, the definition is more appropriate for use within the public sector and has been adopted for this purpose. This chapter establishes more clearly what is meant by SEA, in order to put it into context with other measures of public activities and to provide some idea of appropriate evaluation models.

In order to place SEA (a micro model) in an overall context, we shall first examine cost-benefit analyis (CBA) and planned programmed budgeting systems (PPBS), because these models have a longer-established literature and CBA has been widely used as a planning and decision-making tool for the selection of public projects. CBA and PPBS are alternative models for use in the public sector; however, it will be seen that they are, to a large extent, inadequate.

COST-BENEFIT ANALYSIS (CBA)

CBA attempts to evaluate entire projects using the Level III monetary quantification of costs and benefits relating to a specific project. The process has been used for a number of years, and government agencies justify specific projects on the basis of an analysis which is often very similar to capital budgeting in the private sector. One major difference lies in the discount rate used to bring future costs and benefits to present values. In commercial evaluations a discount rate related to the cost of capital (incorporating a risk factor) is most commonly used, whereas, in publicly funded activities, the rate may be a much lower social time preference rate or social opportunity cost rate. This occurs because commercial and community time-horizons and risk factors are different from those in the private sector.

Prest and Turvey (1965, p. 682) summarized the process of CBA very well:

> Cost Benefit Analysis is a practical way of assessing the desirability of projects, where it is important to take a long view (in the sense of looking at repercussions in the further, as well as the near future) and a wide view (in the sense of allowing for side effects of many kinds on many persons, industries, regions, etc.), i.e., it implies the enumeration and evaluation of all the relevant costs and benefits. This involves drawing on a variety of traditional sections of economic study – welfare economics, public finance, resource economics – and trying to weld these components into a coherent whole.

The importance of CBA to this part of the book is that if a project has been accepted after CBA it will be easier to evaluate the actual performance, by socio-economic accounting or related techniques, because the cost and benefit data will be on record. Many of the benefits will be of a non-financial nature and are difficult to measure, but will be identified during the CBA. For example, if changes are made to an educational programme, as a result of an analysis of objectives, costs and benefits, the costs may be expressed in financial terms, but the benefits may be given in terms of greater teaching effectiveness or a lower dropout rate for students. The articulation of an objective for the programme will aid subsequent measurement and in some cases the routine nature of the post-operative analysis may act to prevent less-viable proposals from being put forward in the future.

The very detailed investigations of social costs in relation to the site of the third London airport (the Roskill Report: Commission on the Third London Airport, 1970) demonstrated some of the difficulties encountered with CBA. These difficulties may be illustrated by reference to three areas of valuation: noise, travelling time, and the value of ancient buildings. In attempting to calculate the cost of noise as a social nuisance the estimate was finally 'based on the maximum loss that the home-owner in the noisier area is able and willing to bear in order to move out of the area' (Estes, 1973, p. 259). Clearly, this is a compromise arrangement or assessment, since individual home-owners will react differently to the loss. Furthermore, potential losses as surveyed by researchers, and actual losses experienced when the property is sold, are not felt in the same way and it is difficult to determine the actual 'zones of noise nuisance' (Mishan, 1972, p. 465).

The valuation of travelling time is also a most interesting and controversial area of social measurement. In the investigation into a third London airport, consideration was given to the distance which aircraft had to fly, and the passengers had to travel on the ground, to get to and from the airport. If a site were further from central Lonon, then it was argued that passengers were inconvenienced by the need to travel onwards from the airport to their destination. The cost of travel was both explicit (fares paid) but also implicit or imputed (less work or less leisure time). The crux of the assessment of this imputed cost was: what is the value of the time taken by a passenger in making the journey from central London to the site of the proposed airport and back? The Roskill Commission did not actually carry out an examination of travelling costs for air passengers, but based its calculations upon other studies which had shown a figure of 25% of income as the average value of travelling time. This figure was incorporated into a model which used an average value for air passengers' income and an estimated increase in business and non-business incomes in real terms over a long period. An adjustment was made for the value of time for accompanying and assisting individuals. The cost of travel for business passengers was calculated as income plus 50% for employers' overhead, and divided by a 40-hour week to give the cost per hour. There has been considerable criticism of the approach taken. Dasgupta and Pearce (1972, p. 230) concluded that: 'research into the value of business and leisure time is not sufficient to support the use of precise figures in a Cost Benefit Analysis relating to air travel'. Mishan (1972, pp. 457–8) noted that the study values business time at ten times that of leisure time, and that the correct measure of business cost is the opportunity cost to the employer. If the employee has to travel in his/her leisure time, then the opportunity cost to the employer is nil and this should be used in the CBA calculation.

The difficulty of assigning values to existing capital goods, which might be altered or removed as a result of present and future developments, such as the building of an airport runway, is dealt with by Churchman (1971). The valuation of an historical structure might vary between an extant fire-insurance valuation as the lower bound, and as the upper level the present value of an investment made many hundred of years earlier compounded at a realistic rate. The present value of the earlier investment forms the upper bound, with a great deal of room for other valuations in between these two outside figures.

CBA can produce problematic decisions because of the combinations of present and future estimates of costs and benefits, the range of possible discount rates, and a need to force non-monetary measurements into the monetary form in order that cash flows may be discounted. Many publicly funded activities, such as health and education, are damaged by being forced in this way. There is always a possibility that cash flows and discount rates may be arranged to obtain the result which is desired on grounds of political expediency. Although CBA may aid the decision process, it does not monitor or audit the project once a decision to proceed has been made. The audit of projects which have been justified by a CBA analysis is almost as important as the original analysis. Poor decisions need to be analysed to find the weak links in the decision process.

PLANNED PROGRAMMED BUDGETING SYSTEMS (PPBS)

An alternative process, for which considerable claims have been made, is the planned programmed budgeting system, which is concerned with the monitoring and control of projects.

Conventional public sector budgets are tied to a particular department for a specified period. They are related to inputs over a defined area, normally on an annual basis. Planned programmed budgeting systems (PPBS) are intended to direct the focus of reporting away from the department and inputs, towards the programme and the output or degree of achievement of the set objectives. The details of the programme and the financial controls may be within the capabilities of the existing accounting systems, but there is a new dimension in the area of output measurement: does the programme achieve the objectives for which it was designed?

Dennison (1979) examines the rise and fall of PPBS in some detail, and the main features of his article are given below. The review begins with an outline of the recent rapid increase in government expenditure and perceived need for a better control of programmes. The author notes the modification of traditional forms of budgeting and the arrival of PPBS:

> In the same way the introduction of a PPBS to aid in resource decision-making could be seen as part of a continuing development, but too often the impression was clearly given that a PPBS approach presented a radical alternative to every other development past or present.   (Dennison, 1979, p. 270)

Thus, the first of Dennison's criticisms is the extreme claims made for PPBS. The second relates to the assumption of rationality for the solutions to problems which were/are generated by PPBS. This assumption means by-passing the political dimension in decision-making and resource allocation:

> Community needs do not allow themselves to be specified as a series of separate and unrelated components; alternative means of satisfying needs are often available but estimating costs and, in particular, benefits, to a sufficient degree of accuracy to demonstrate convincingly that one alternative is better than the other is rarely possible . . . (Ibid., pp 273–4)

The third criticism of the use of PPBS results from the adoption of a defence model in non-defence areas. The PPBS model was developed by the US Defense Department and, because it seemed to satisfy management needs there, it was moved into non-defence departments.

The rise in popularity of PPBS was attributed to the creation of an environment, through the publication of books and articles, which was highly favourable to the model. Its fall in popularity followed from the inherent weaknesses of the model and the earlier over-promotion. The model was not revolutionary but was presented as such; it could not answer the political questions about which programmes should have more support and which should have less, and finally the Defense Department model was inappropriate for wider use. The difficulties likely to be encountered by an education authority in using PPBS are outlined:

> So it was the familiar pattern of a programme structure of activities in pursuit of specified objectives, a multi-year programme and financial plan, and an analysis of programmes (supported where necessary by analyses of alternative means of achieving objectives) which was recommended. (Ibid., p. 279)

Dennison goes on to illustrate the difficulties likely to be encountered in applying tight specifications of objectives to an education system. Despite drawing attention to weaknesses in traditional government budgeting systems, and to the advantages of longer-range plans and more clearly specified objectives, PPBS has declined in relative importance over the last few years.

SOCIO-ECONOMIC ACCOUNTING

Traditional government budgetary control models do not address resource-allocation and decision-making problems in a fully satisfactory manner. The alternative systems considered above – CBA and PPBS – have each claimed advantages and disadvantages. It is probably sufficient for the present purpose to suggest that even if these systems were more widely accepted, they would not address the issues which proponents of SEA are attempting to address. That is, how do we evaluate both input and output in respect of publicly funded projects?

Linowes (1968) favours a different treatment of government and semi-government activities. He argues for the use of accounting techniques and attesting procedures to improve the quality of the data used and the manner in which it is manipulated. This improvement is directed particularly at budgeting, forecasting and project-control activities. Improved measurement techniques are needed because of limited resources and the apparently unlimited demands for greater government involvement in society. Difficult choices need to be made and some programmes must be favoured ahead of others. Although political expediency will always be present, improved quality of information, in the planning, control and post-operational evaluation stages, may eventually lead to better decisions.

Linowes was supported by Mobley (1970) in the development of socio-economic accounting. However, Francis (1973) argues persuasively that many accountants do not have the training or background to deal with complex statistical tools in the social science area. Birnberg and Gandhi (1976) have made useful observations on this issue. Unfortunately, the advocates of SEA have not followed up the early theoretical work with concrete examples of evaluation models. Models of the social audit process have been produced but these are not exclusively designed for use in SEA (Corson and Steiner, 1974). In this chapter an educational evaluation model is discussed in the absence of accounting examples.

Socio-economic accounting models will be necessarily complex since they are required to assist in making decisions about the effectiveness and efficiency of publicly funded activities in the absence of market prices for outputs. Inputs may be valued in financial and non-financial terms, but output will often be limited to non-financial values, for example the number of employable school leavers, reformed prisoners, discharged patients or university graduates.

EVALUATION MODELS

Several models have been generated within the education evaluation literature, including models by Stake (1967), Stufflebeam (1968) and Provus (1971). This borrowing of models has been necessary because of the lack of suitable models in the accounting literature. The Stake model is a judgemental evaluation model, and may offer useful insights into the evaluation of publicly funded programmes by socio-economic accountants. Stufflebeam has provided the CIPP evaluation model which is a scheme for the classification of strategies for evaluating

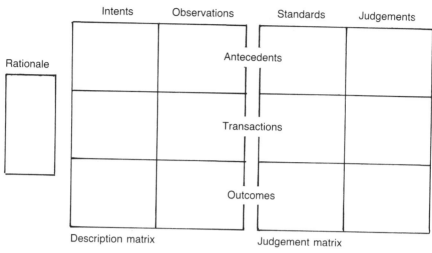

Figure 7.1 The countenance of educational evaluation – the basic matrix design. Source: Stake (1967).

educational change. Provus uses a discrepancy model similar to management accounting budgetary control systems.

THE STAKE MODEL

The Stake model is shown in Figure 7.1. It is a data matrix, providing the evaluator with three kinds of data: antecedent, transactional and outcome. The antecedent data refer to the position which existed at the time the programme was implemented; the transactional data refer to the actual process which is taking place or has taken place as a result of the programme; and the outcome data record the results of the process. These results will include both positive and negative aspects.

In another dimension Stake is concerned with judgement as well as description; that is, an evaluation of actual against planned outcomes from the specific programme. The Stake model is not constrained by setting fixed objectives before beginning the programme, therefore changes of goal may be accommodated. Indeed, both the strengths and weaknesses of this model are to be found in the large amount of data which may be accommodated within the basic framework. The volume of data may be seen as a strength since we are dealing with both financial and non-financial measurements. Conversely, the volume of date makes presentation of a final judgement more difficult because of potential conflict between different aspects of the data. The data itself may be suggestive of the analytical processes to be employed. The

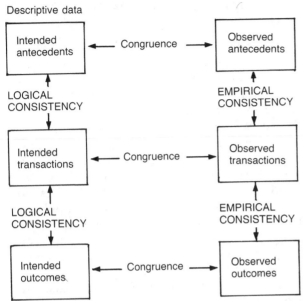

Descriptive data

Figure 7.2 The processing of descriptive data: congruence and logical and empirical consistency. Source: Stake (1967).

model also assists the judgemental function by making clear the criteria which are to be employed in making the judgement.

We have already indicated the role of antecedents, transactions and outcomes and the presence of both descriptive and judgemental aspects. The relationship between intents and observations (both part of the descriptive matrix) is given in Figure 7.2. It will be noted that the comparison between the intended variables and those which are observed in practice will provide a measure of the internal success or congruence of the programme. The relationship between the descriptive matrix and the standards provides a basis for making judgements about the programme.

The evaluation model tests for logical consistency between the intended antecedents, transactions and outcomes. In other words, given the antecedents which exist when work begins and the transactions which will be undertaken, is it logical that the intended outcomes will eventuate? If not, why not? Furthermore, what is the degree of congruence between intended and observed variables? Finally, given the observed antecedents and transactions, is there an empirical consistency between the two and between the observed transactions and outcomes? Once this process has been undertaken the analyst may compare the observed variables with the standards and make judgements.

EXAMPLES OF THE USE OF A STAKE MODEL APPROACH IN SOCIO-ECONOMIC ACCOUNTING

As indicated above, socio-economic accounting is intended to be effective in evaluating short- and medium-term publicity-funded programmes, where a judgement must eventually be made about the continued operation of the programme. Examples could be taken from education, work experience and health programmes.

The work experience programme is perhaps a suitable example to consider. If a government agency arranges a work experience/training programme for young people presently unemployed, public funds are being expended which must have an alternative use elsewhere: there is an opportunity cost attached to the resources used. Such a programme will have a number of objectives and expected outputs that should be made explicit at some point in the planning process. The evaluation of a scheme such as work experience or a training programme could be carried out under existing government accounting systems. However, these systems would be mainly concerned with how much money was spent, compared to the amount authorized, and whether the spending took place in the approved accounts. A more modern approach, such as a planned programmed budgeting system, would still not view the input-output relationships in the same manner as does the Stake model. In this context the use of the Stake model would be, first, to examine the rationale for the programme, and then to consider in detail the descriptive and judgemental matrix. The descriptive matrix would be concerned with:

1. antecedents: what resources were planned or intended to be allocated to the programme, compared to those observed to be actually used in the operations;
2. transactions: did the processes and procedures which were originally intended or planned actually take place? To what extent did the observed procedures differ from those intended when the programme was planned?
3. outcomes: an outcome was planned. Perhaps in this example it was young people who were 'more employable' than before they started the programme. This concept would need to be operationalized and quantified in terms which could be measured. The observation would be of the number who did meet the criteria, compared to the number who did not and therefore remained unemployable.

The judgemental matrix compares what has been observed, with some sort of standard or expectation, in order to make a judgement about the event.

The Stake approach may be used to evaluate hospitals and medical services, provided that input and output measures can be agreed upon. Many factors which are left unexamined at the present time would be taken into account by the Stake model if it were applied to socio-economic accounting exercises. An important part of such an evaluation would be non-monetary quantitative measurements, which are frequently ignored by accounting-based evaluations at present. It is not suggested that this form of socio-economic accounting is appropriate to all circumstances, or that it should be used in place of more conventional forms of financial reporting. However, the added dimension is required to enable better decisions to be made and to monitor their implementation. The current pressure for greater accountability for public expenditure, which is being experienced in many countries, will require new systems similar to those described above.

INSTITUTIONAL PERFORMANCE EVALUATION

Socio-economic accounting is further exemplified by the literature dealing with institutional performance evaluation, which involves the use of financial and non-financial, qualitative and quantitative measures to evaluate the attributes of an educational institution. The specific area discussed is that of higher education, generally the university sector, which is suffering from reduced funding, often larger student inflows and a call from governments for more accountability. This area of research is quite compatible with the others in this chapter because non-traditional measurement methods are employed in evaluating a public-sector activity.

Sizer (1980, p. 5) noted the importance of measures of effectiveness as well as of efficiency:

> Is an institution of higher education effective if it achieves objectives which are appropriate to the economic, socio-political, technological, ecological, and educational environment in which it operates? Should its objectives be congruent with the long-term needs of society?

To agree on notions of effectiveness implies the acceptance of a common set of objectives, at least at the institutional level, and this would enable planning and evaluation by non-profit indicators to be undertaken. This has not been generally possible, and consequently the popularity of PPBS and CBA has declined. Sizer suggests that 'partial' performance may be used:

> Whilst it may not prove possible to agree objectives, measure outcomes and develop performance indicators for an institution as a

Table 7.1 Properties of performance indicators in higher education

Focus of measure	Conceptual content	Tells	Examples
Availability	Amount and type of course, research facility, or central service provided.	What can be obtained.	List of services available in Careers Advisory Service; list of facilities and opportunities available in academic department; number, capacities, and locations of lecture and seminar rooms.
Awareness Appropriateness	Knowledge of user population of existence; range and correct type and amount of service rendered, course offered, or research undertaken.	Who knows about what is available? Is quantity and/or quality of facility offered that required?	Knowledge of prospective students of courses offered by an academic department. Demand for courses: number and quality of applicants; mis-match between computing facilities required and available; comparison of class sizes to lecture and seminar room capacities.
Efficiency	Compares resource inputs with outputs.	How much resource was used such as: – how much did it cost per unit? – how much did it cost in total? – how much time did it take? – what grade of employee was used?	Cost per client service in medical centre. Cost per FTE student by course. Cost per literature search. Cost per meal served.

Effectiveness	Compares accomplishment with objectives (or what was intended) – qualitative – comparative	Characteristics Duration Content Effect Proportion served Variances from budgets, standards.	Comparison of planned with actual: % utilization of lecture and seminar rooms; number of students graduating; number of graduates employed; ratio of actual utilization to planned utilization of computer; comparison of budgeted cost of central service with actual cost; comparison of actual cost per FTE for course with planned cost; comparison of planned course content with actual course content; actual wastage rate compared with planned wastage rate.
Outcomes Benefits Impacts	Identifies social or economic benefits	Monetary effects. Non-monetary effects.	Increase in earnings arising from attendance at/graduating from course; benefits to society of successful research into previously incurable disease; benefits to local community of cultural programme; patents and copyrights registered.
Acceptability	Assess match of service/course/ research outcomes with user/ participant preference.	User satisfaction with service; Student satisfaction with courses; Client satisfaction with outcome of sponsored research.	Demand for courses; number of complaints to Librarian; course evaluation at end of lecture programme; repeat sponsoring of research.

Note: FTE denotes full-time equivalent student.
Source: Adapted from Sizer (1980).

Table 7.2 Process measures in higher education indicator system

I Institutional	II Subject grouping level	III Subject level
General data 1–1 Number of FTE students 1–2 Number of academic posts 1–3 Annual budget 1–4 Space provision	General data 1–9 Number of FTE students 1–10 Number of academic posts 1–11 Direct expenditure by subject grouping	General Data 1–13 Number of FTE students 1–14 Number of academic posts 1–15 Direct expenditure by subject 1–16 Total of teaching hours 1–17 Space provision
Structural data 1–5 Proportion of staff costs within the total budget 1–6 Amount of resources obtained from third parties in relation to the annual budget 1–7 Expenditure at subject grouping level within the annual budget 1–8 Academic orientation (proportion of liberal arts subjects (in terms of student numbers))	Expenditure indicator 1–12 Direct expenditure per FTE student	Expenditure indicators 1–18 Direct expenditure per FTE student 1–19 Indirect expenditure per FTE student Staff–student ratios 1–20 Relation of FTE students to academic posts 1–21 Relation of FTE students to teaching hours 1–22 Proportion of professorial posts within the total of academic posts 1–23 Proportion of professorial teaching hours within the total of teaching hours Space provision 1–24 Space provision per FTE student Staff structure 1–25 Proportion of expenditure on academic posts within the total expenditure on staff 1–26 Total of teaching hours realized by part-time teachers with limited contracts Student flow 1–27 Obligatory weekly seminar time 1–28 Study duration 1–29 Gross continuation rate

Note: FTE denotes full-time equivalent student.
Source: Adapted from Elstermann and Lorenz (1980).

whole, it often proves possible to do so for parts of the organisation; i.e., to develop performance indicators that relate physical and monetary inputs to physical and monetary outputs and outcomes, and to build these into the planning and reporting system.

Sizer (1980) developed partial performance indicators for institutions of higher education. This scheme, reproduced in Table 7.1, is based upon the characteristics for performance indicators developed by Sorenson and Grove (1977). These are: availability, awareness, accessibility, extensiveness, appropriateness, efficiency, effectiveness, outcomes/ benefits/impacts, and acceptability.

Although many of the partial performance indicators shown in Table 7.1 are process measures, Sizer argues for the development of progress measures which would assess the quality of institutions and programmes: 'At the present time there is a strong case for developing *progress measures* of performance in addition to *process measures* of outcomes/benefits/impacts' (Sizer, 1990, p. 22). Progress measures of performance are not confined to the evaluation of efficiency but are aimed at institutional effectiveness. An alternative set of process performance indicators, directed towards measuring institutional efficiency, have been produced by Elstermann and Lorenz (1981). They are shown in Table 7.2.

Sizer has asked whether the standards developed by the American Accounting Association could be applied to performance indicators in higher education. This is an important question, not only for higher education performance measures (both progress and process types) but for all measures which may be included in socio-economic accounting. Indeed, the author provides an interesting reference which may be applicable to all forms of measurement, traditional and non-traditional, financial and non-financial:

> The problems of agreeing objectives, identifying and measuring the component parts of the institutions, and of evaluation performance and effectiveness, suggests that only 'partial' measures of performance are possible and that a proper balance has to be struck between qualitative and quantitative aspects.   (Sizer, 1980, p. 45)

VALUE-FOR-MONEY (VFM) AUDITING

INTRODUCTION

Earlier sections of this chapter examined briefly CBA and PPBS. Each was found to be inadequate as a means of monitoring, controlling and reporting on short- and medium-term publicly funded activities. CBA is intended to facilitate decision-making by discounting future costs and benefits to the present in order to determine net cost or net benefit. In addition to the problems of making estimates and determining discount rates, decisions will be impacted by political expediency. Attempts to convert non-financial data to financial measurements involve subjectivity to perhaps an unacceptable degree. Furthermore, CBA has very little to say about the control of projects once they have been implemented. PPBS is intended to facilitate the control of projects, once a decision to implement them has been made by the political authorities. A number of deficiencies of this approach have already been discussed. In terms of the overall objective of this chapter it should be noted that PPBS is intended to control inputs in monetary terms without reference to outputs, which can be both monetary and non-monetary. The concept of socio-economic accounting is concerned with input-output relationships using both financial and non-financial quantification. This section examines value-for-money (VFM) audits to see if they are a viable alternative to the SEA model.

THE DEVELOPMENT OF VFM

Value-for-money auditing as a general practice has a relatively short history of some 15 to 20 years, which corresponds to that of most developments reviewed in this chapter. Although there are variations in approach from one country to another, which are described in the next· section, all are concerned with the review of publicly funded programmes from the perspective of the 'three Es'. These are economy, efficiency and effectiveness, and are defined in the following terms:

Economy   The acquisition of resources in appropriate quantity and quality at the lowest cost.

Efficiency   The relationship between the goods or services produced and the resources used to produce them.

Effectiveness The extent to which programmes or goods and services produced achieve their objectives.

The criticism levelled at VFM is that, although the reviews of economy and efficiency are thorough, those of effectiveness are often inadequate. Grimwood and Tomkins (1986), for example, question whether VFM audits do address the issue of effectiveness.

Before considering the strengths and weaknesses of this approach to evaluating publicly funded projects it is necessary to consider the origins of VFM and national variations in practice.

A COMPARISON OF VFM APPROACHES

Glynn (1985) has surveyed VFM auditing practices in six countries, thus providing a valuable introduction to the area. The countries are: the UK, Canada, Australia, New Zealand, the US and Sweden.

In the UK the Local Government Finance Act 1982 provided for the audit of publicly funded activities to determine 'that local authorities have made proper arrangements for securing economy, efficiency and effectiveness in the use of their resources; and to report on matters of public interest (undefined) which come to his attention' (Glynn, 1985, p. 114). A different part of the Act set up an Audit Commission to carry out most of these audits through the District Audit Service. A different but comparable operation is carried out in Scotland. There has been considerable criticism of the VFM audits of local government which are seen as part of the restrictive monetary policy operated by the central government and also because the audit is incomplete, since:

> In only a few years important moves have been made with respect to two important aspects of value for money: economy and efficiency. However, the third most important element, that of effectiveness, appears so far to be only of secondary importance. (Ibid., p. 113)

The Canadian VFM system originated earlier than that in the UK. It dates from developments in the mid–1970s which led to the appointment in 1979 of a Comptroller-General and a Royal Commission of Financial Management and Accountability, and subsequently to the development of the 'comprehensive' approach to auditing. The Canadian Federal Audit Office defines comprehensive auditing as:

> the term is used by the office of the Auditor-General and others to describe the broad-based auditing approach which is aimed at systematically reviewing and reporting on accountability relationships and on the supporting activities, systems and controls employed by management in fulfilling its responsibilities. (Office of the Auditor General of Canada, 1981, p. 42, cited by Glynn, 1985)

The Canadian Comprehensive Auditing Foundation (1983, cited by Glynn, 1985) has described comprehensive auditing as follows:

- financial, human and physical resources are managed with due regard to economy, efficiency and effectiveness; and
- accountability relationships are reasonably served. The comprehensive audit examines both financial and management controls, including information systems and reporting practices, and recommends improvements where appropriate.

This clearly extends the traditional transaction audit process to involve both physical resources and measures of effectiveness. Consequently, a link with socio-economic accounting may be discerned in this definition of VFM auditing.

The position of VFM audits in Australia is complicated by the federal system of government. The Auditor-General for the Commonwealth of Australia is appointed under the 1979 amendment to the Audit Act of 1901. Although efficiency and economy in the use of resources are included as part of the Act, there is no requirement to examine programme effectiveness, although this activity has not been overlooked:

> The review of effectiveness falls within the purview of the Department of the Prime Minister. The efficiency audits reported upon to date have been undertaken as discrete projects separate from any other audit coverage by specialist staff of the Efficiency Audit Division. (Glynn, 1985, p. 119)

The various Australian states also have the office of Auditor-General. At present no official holding that position enjoys an effectiveness review function, although New South Wales employs the Premier's Department for this purpose. The Auditor-General of Victoria is able to become involved in comprehensive auditing by virtue of the Audit Act 1958, which refers to effective and economic auditing although this does not appear to involve effectiveness auditing. However, it has been argued that efficiency and effectiveness are not so different and therefore the Act could be used or readily modified to permit or require effectiveness audits (Glynn, 1985, p. 120). Glynn reports that this position has not been resolved. In a review of the Australian VFM experience, Parker (1986, p. 82) noted that:

> The debates which have occurred in Australia over the role of the Auditor-General and the appropriate areas of responsibility for effectiveness reviews appear to suggest some level of political resistance to this concept . . . Of concern also is the fact that Canadian, U.K. and New Zealand interest in VFM auditing appears to have been initially sponsored by a politically motivated concern to restrict public sector expenditure and to reduce costs as far as possible.

VFM auditing is less developed in Australia than in Canada (and perhaps in the UK) and may have the same defects as are alleged to occur in the UK in terms of the extent of the programme evaluation process and concern that the process is subject to political influence.

In New Zealand the Audit Office has been set up under the Public Finance Act 1977 to provide for an independent audit agency, with personnel and an organization whose independent role is guaranteed.

The authority to conduct value-for-money audits is provided under Section 25(3). However, most of the work of the Audit Office is organized within a structure called CARE:

C   Control – the evaluation of management controls over the resources for which it is responsible;

A   Attest and Authority – the expression of an opinion on financial transactions;

R   Reporting – to Parliament, ministers and other external parties on matters arising from audits;

E   Effectiveness and Efficiency – the giving of an opinion on whether audited entities have applied their resources in an effective and efficient manner consistent with the policy of the governing body of that entity. (Glynn, 1985, p. 121)

Glynn notes the broad nature of the New Zealand mandate. The majority of the work of the Audit Office is concerned with the first three parts of the acronym. The audit of effectiveness and efficiency is undertaken on a project-by-project basis as time and staff are available. Suitably prepared staff are in short supply and Glynn notes that: 'The Audit Office has often acknowledged the fact that it cannot perform adequately in the value for money auditing area solely with accounting based skills' (ibid., p. 122).

The United States has several organizations concerned with the control and audit of public-sector accounts. These include the Office of Management and the Budget (OMB) which is responsible for the supervision, control and administration of the budget and the financial programmes of the government, and the General Accounting Office (GAO). The GAO is supportive of independent reviews of efficiency and effectiveness, which are termed 'program results reviews'. The review has been defined differently as demonstrated below. First, the GAO stated, in 1972, that there were three levels of audit:

Level I (Financial and compliance) – An examination of financial transactions, accounts and reports, including an evaluation of compliance with applicable laws and regulations. (Purpose: to evaluate whether operations and resources are properly accounted for and presented in reports and whether legal requirements are being met.)

Level II (Economy and efficiency) – A review of efficiency and economy in the use of resources. (Purpose: to evaluate whether the management operates with due regard to conserving its monetary, property and human resources.)

Level III (Program results) – A review to determine whether desired results are effectively achieved. (Purpose: to evaluate the extent to which statutory or other goals are being achieved and whether alternative methods of operation should be considered.) (Grimwood and Tomkins, 1986, p. 251).

Second, in a 1978 Exposure Draft entitled 'Comprehensive Approach for Planning and Conducting a Program Results Review', the GAO defined their approach:

> A program results review is a process or approach by which qualified individuals can determine the level of program effectiveness and, if necessary, identify areas for improved program performance.
>
> A program results review extends beyond traditional audit theory into the realm of activities commonly known as evaluation and analysis. Program results review activities are neither constrained to the conventional audit of information and control systems nor as pervasive as the wide range of activities associated with evaluation and analysis. (Glynn, 1985, p. 123)

Managers of particular projects are allowed to develop effectiveness measures within their organizations, and auditors are charged with satisfying themselves about the systems which are implemented. However, Glynn (1985, p. 24) has commented that many of the in-depth investigations are 'ad hoc' and 'atypical' of the GAO approach.

In Sweden, the main body dealing with VFM audits is the National Audit Bureau, which carries out both financial and effectiveness auditing. These audits have been defined by the Auditor General of Sweden as follows:

> Financial auditing of a government agency shall result in a professional and impartial opinion on the agency's financial statement and records.
>
> Effectiveness auditing in the central administration involves examining the effectiveness and productivity of an agency or an activity. One purpose of this is to check that activities are being carried out in a functional, systematic and economically satisfactory way. Effectiveness auditing should also give rise to ideas and incentives for improvements at all levels of the central administration. The ultimate goal of the audit is to promote effectiveness in public administration. (Ibid., p. 124)

There are clearly a number of similarities between the intentions behind the various approaches outlined above. Some of the difficulties (obtaining the necessary funds and staffing resources to carry out appropriate audits) and deficiencies (a tendency to concentrate on economy and efficiency to the detriment of effectiveness, and allegations of political interference) are also common to several of the examples. The next section considers these alleged deficiencies in greater detail.

DEFICIENCIES OF VFM AUDITS

Sherer (1984) has drawn attention to both conceptual and practical problems in respect of VFM audits of local authorities. The component parts of economy, efficiency and effectiveness are interrelated, with effectiveness the most important (in Sherer's view). Effectiveness is also the most difficult attribute to measure because of (1) the problem of finding suitable measures with which to evaluate the service under examination; and (2) the problem of commenting on the political decisions made by members of elected bodies, for example local councils. Sherer has noted that in response to these difficulties auditors tend to adopt narrow definitions of effectiveness which appear to be capable of verification, rather than broader definitions which impact on the final objectives of local authorities such as environmental health or the educational attainment of pupils: 'Indeed it may be thought that measures such as these can be interpreted as efficiency rather than effectiveness measures; at best they attempt only to quantify the intermediate outputs of a service'. (Sherer, 1984, p. 8)

Sherer has also objected to auditing the other attributes of economy and efficiency because the processes of VFM audits are dominated by the ideology of profit: 'The use of accounting technologies, including VFM audits for local authorities, introduces a 'bottom line' measure, equivalent to (and sometimes identical with) the net profit figure found in private sector financial accounts' (ibid., p. 18). This has an effect on employment policies and the willingness to provide public services despite the problematic nature of the profit determinations. McSweeney and Sherer (1985, p. 3) have made similar observations:

> Many of the reports published thus far demonstrate an asymmetry in the recommendations of VFM auditors. A great deal of attention is given to possible cost savings that can be made achieving the same or lower levels of service quality, if best management practice is adopted. In contrast much less attention is given to an evaluation of the effectiveness of local authority activities . . .

In the remainder of their paper McSweeney and Sherer reiterate many of the arguments against VFM audits: the difficulty of setting standards; a tendency to concentrate on economy and efficiency and not effectiveness as though these were separable; the fear that political and economic concerns are dominating technical concerns in the implementation of VFM.

Gray, Owen and Maunders (1987, p. 155) have noted that the VFM audit is:

> unlikely to provide a significant improvement in public account-ability. Its focus on spending – generally unrelated to performance measures – might improve the efficiency of services from local authorities etc., but appears to have little to do with the quality of service and virtually nothing to do with the broader issues of the community, the labour force, and general accountability.

The problems inherent in the term 'value for money' have been brought out by Jones and Pendlebury (1984, p. 10): 'Strictly speaking it relates output (value) to input (money) and is therefore another way of saying efficiency.'

The author has concluded that although the concept of VFM is much closer to the concept of SEA than the other monitoring and controlling systems examined earlier in the chapter, the reality of implementation means that the distance is still quite wide. SEA is envisaged as a system which monitors both inputs and outputs in financial and non-financial modes. The implementation of VFM, as reported in the literature, suggests that in practice a greater proportion of attention is given to the financial measurements and that effectiveness is not given the same degree of attention as economy and efficiency.

SUMMARY

This chapter has expanded the arguments used in support of socio-economic accounting by examining areas of measurement and disclosure which presently employ, or could employ, non-traditional techniques. Cost-benefit analysis and planned programmed budgeting systems have been examined and found wanting. The need for the conversion of costs and benefits into financial terms and subsequent discounting of present monetary values means that CBA is dependent upon a number of assumptions, such as which flows to include and the discount rate to be used. There is also the problem of data manipulation to suit decisions which have already been made. Planned programmed budgeting systems are also financially based and require agreement about objectives. Proponents of PPBS have already made exaggerated claims, and applications have been less than fully successful as a result of the defence-based model, which did not transfer easily to other fields, and the difficulty of reaching agreement on institutional objectives. Furthermore, PPBS does not provide for an examination of input-output relationships.

Socio-economic accounting has been placed into a different category to CBA and PPBS in this study, since it used Level I and II measurements as well as financial measures. SEA may be regarded as a form of social audit of publicly funded programmes, and prototype models may be found in the educational evaluation literature (the Stake model, for example), and the institutional performance evaluation indicators produced by Sizer and others. Value-for-money auditing was also examined, because this approach to programme evaluation appeared to be very close to the concept of SEA. However, a study of the literature revealed that in practice VFM often stops short of the end result envisaged for SEA. There is some concern that VFM is not leading to a more socially responsible accounting.

The area of government-funded programmes is seen as fertile ground for evaluation models, using both financial and non-financial measurements and criteria, aimed at promoting efficiency and effectiveness. The use of models developed by other disciplines is not considered a problem, since these would be modified by experience and adapted to the particular nature of the problem under examination. The importance of an earlier reference to partial performance indicators should not be underestimated. To a large extent all measurements result in partial indicators of performance. This applies to financial accounting reports as well as to less-traditional forms of reporting. The socio-economic accounting discussed in this chapter is an attempt to convert unreported performance to a partial reporting of performance by publicly funded organizations. As such, it would be a major advance in the overall usefulness of accounting to society, thus leading to a more socially responsible accounting.

Social indicators accounting (SIA)

8

INTRODUCTION

This chapter is concerned with the review of a further division of the social accounting field. Socio-economic accounting (the use of accountants and accounting techniques to improve project selection, operation and control, and output evaluation in the public sector) is at a micro level. The corresponding macro approach is referred to as social indicators accounting. Social indicators accounting may be applied where the stated objectives of a social system (expressed via the political process) are to have a healthier, wealthier and better-educated population. This is to be achieved by a series of public programmes (each perhaps influenced by socio-economic accounting), where progress towards these objectives ought to be capable of measurement. These measurements may vary in scope and time-scale, as outlined below; in particular there may be a distinction between national, regional and local measures.

Social indicators research may be tracked back at least as far as the work of Bauer (1966) and has generated a substantial volume of published material, only a small part of which may be regarded as belonging to the accounting area. Glatzer (1981) provided an overview of the development of social indicators, whilst Parke and Peterson (1981) discuss the development of social indicators in the United States. The remainder of this chapter on social indicators accounting will be devoted to an examination of the work of Terleckyj (1970) as an example of long-term social indicators accounting at the national level, and reviews of the contributions of Glatzer (1981), and Parke and Peterson (1981).

GOAL INDICATORS AND DATA DEFICIENCY

GOAL INDICATORS

In several important papers Terleckyj has addressed the problems of measuring social change directed towards specific goals. Terleckyj (1970) was concerned with measurement and the data needed for goal analysis. He provided a series of hypothetical national goals which were to be attained over a ten-year period. To achieve these goals a number of activities would have to be undertaken and these in turn should be monitored. It is the monitoring process, as well as the goal performance, with which SIA is concerned. In respect of goal analysis and the monitoring of activities Terleckyj (1970, p. 766) noted:

Two kinds of data are needed for this analysis:

1. the data defining and measuring the output indicators, and
2. the much more voluminous and complex data which would permit estimation of the effects of activities on output indicators and of the cost of the activities.

The goal output indicators developed by Terleckyj are given in Table 8.1. The areas shown are concerned with nationally determined goals in the fields of domestic concerns that are relevant to a ten-year programme. The process by which the goals are chosen is not within the control of the SIA system, but the majority of the areas of goal concern should be those acceptable to most people and arise out of the political process. However, the goal output indicators may be more difficult to define. This is accepted by Terleckyj (1970, p. 766): 'Identification of areas of goal concerns and the corresponding selection of output indicators are neither absolute nor immutable. The selections should vary with their purpose, and the time when they are made.'

DATA DEFICIENCY

When considering the availability of data in support of the principal indicators of goals output shown in Table 8.1, Terleckyj stated that the goals analysis was not supported by the statistical information system available at that time. The general impressions of data availability are summarized in Table 8.2. The view expressed by Terleckyj is in contrast to the review of data sources given by Glatzer (1981). The conflict can be resolved in terms of the availability of data to enable an accounting-type examination of goals and degrees of achievement.

The principal indicators shown in Table 8.2 are assisted by auxiliary indicators, which clarify the significance of changes in the principal indicators and also help to explain the reasons for the changes. In

Table 8.1 A summary list of areas of national goals concern and the corresponding principal indicators of goals output

Area of goals concern		Principal indicators of goals output
I	Freedom, justice & harmony	Not yet defined.
II	Health and safety	
	Health	Mean life expectancy at birth
		Number of persons with chronic disability conditions
	Public safety	Violent crime rate
III	Education, skills and income	
	Basic schooling	Index of average achievement and mathematics, grade 12
	Advanced learning	Percent of age group completing college
	Skills	Average earnings
		Number of persons outside mainstream of the labour force
	Adequacy and continuity of	Number of persons below poverty standard
	income	Number of persons in near-poverty conditions
		Number of persons with permanent losses in levels of living over 30%
IV	Human Habitat	
	Homes	Proportion of persons living in inadequate housing
	Neighbourhoods	Proportion of persons living in satisfactory neighbourhoods
	Access	Index of cost of travel and transportation
	Quality of environment	Percent of persons exposed to bothersome pollution
	Recreation	Percent of persons regularly taking part in recreation
V	Finer things	
	Beauty of nature	Number of areas of preservation of beauty
	Sciences	Number of scientists active in basic science
	Arts	Number of active artists
	Leisure	Average time free from work and chores
VI	Economic base	GNP

Note: These categorizations are being used in the ongoing study and are subject to change. The choice of indicators describing comparative conditions of people between the absolute number and proportion of population was based on judgement regarding which formulation corresponds better to the actual goals concern.

Source: Adapted from Terleckyj (1970, p. 770).

Table 8.2 Checklist for selected goals orientated output indicator statistics

Goal output indicator	Existence of national-level statistics	Local area availability	Quality of analytical information	Principal source of federal statistics
Health and safety				
life expectancy	yes	yes	Good	National Centre of Health Statistics
disability	yes	yes	Fair	National Centre of Health Statistics
violent crime	yes	yes	Fair	Federal Bureau of Investigation
Education, skills & income				
education index	no	no	Fair	Office of Education
college completion	yes	yes	Fair	Office of Education
ability to earn	no	no	Fair	Manpower Administration
average earnings	yes	yes	Fair	Office of Business Economics
number of poor	yes	yes –	Good	Social Security Administration
number of near-poor	yes	yes –	Good	Social Security Administration
number with income loss	no	no	Fair	Social Security Administration
Human habitat				
houses	yes –	yes –	Poor	Bureau of the Census
neighbourhoods	no	no +	Poor	Bureau of the Census
access	no	no +	Fair	Bureau of Labour Statistics and Interstate Commerce Commission
pollution	no	no	Poor	Departments of the Interior and Health Education and Welfare
Recreation	no	no +	Poor	Bureau of Outdoor Recreation
Finer things				
science	yes	yes	Fair	National Science Foundation
art	no	no	Poor	Natl. Foundation on Arts and Humanities
nature	no	no	Poor	Department of the Interior
leisure	no	no	Poor	None
Economic base				
GNP or local indicator	yes	yes	Good	Office of Business Economics

Source: Terleckyj (1970, p. 771).

addition, Terleckyj noted that all indicators have differing degrees of usefulness at national and local levels.

In conclusion, Terleckyj (1970, pp. 775–6) referred to five specific points:

(i) Articulation of social goals is important for ascertaining whether they are being reached, and even for reaching them.

(ii) The existing statistical systems are not geared to articulating and reporting social goals, either nationally or locally.

(iii) Development of simple systems which would reflect progress towards some of the generally accepted goals is feasible locally as well as nationally.

(iv) If such systems are to serve as aids in policy information or as vehicles of information for the general public, they have to be simple and clear-cut.

(v) Development of larger systems, encompassing a larger variety of indicators and aiming at consistency or compatibility of data systems developed and used by different policy units, depends on progress in basic work that remains to be done.

The papers reviewed above form an important contribution to an understanding of SIA and the extent of potential involvement for social accountants. There are a number of aspects to the logical sequence described by Terleckyj where accounting principles and techniques may be employed: determination of goals; selection of principal and auxiliary output indicators; and the organization of data collection and aggregation. The involvement of accountants in social indicators research needs to be selective, because the area covered by SIA is only a part of the total area devoted to social indicators research. This is evident from an examination of the literature and is confirmed by the particular use of 'social accounting' by Parke and Peterson (1981).

MACRO-SOCIAL INDICATORS – AN INTERNATIONAL OVERVIEW

Glatzer (1981) has provided an extensive review of the work on social indicators in several countries. In contrast to Terleckyj (1970), who referred to data deficiency, Glatzer has compiled a list of references which amounts to almost an oversupply of data. However, relatively little of the data is intended for use by accountants, although some aspects of the social indicators movement are probably appropriate for exploration by those in the profession who are seeking to develop a more socially responsible accounting. Glatzer (1981, p. 219) stated that: 'The dominating interest of social indicators research is social reporting, involving the provision of descriptive, normative, evaluative and explanatory knowledge about societal problems and developments for social guidance', and progress may be distinguished in three areas. These are: measurement of quality of life and welfare; the monitoring of social change and socio-economic development; and the conduct of evaluations and forecasts.

Measurement of the development of quality of life and welfare requires agreement on a number of normative positions. The subjective nature of this area of study suggests that there is not a major role for any form of accounting, whether dealing with the quality of life and welfare of the whole population or of specific groups of disadvantaged persons. The area of social indicators research which is concerned with monitoring social change and socio-economic development might provide an opportunity for the application of accounting techniques. However, Glatzer (1981) reports that social indicators are used without a goal or output orientation, which would make the application of achievement measures very difficult.

The most important area of social indicators research for accountants would appear to be the work on forecasting and evaluating the results of social policies. The effect of public-policy decisions on the social fabric of the country should be evaluated:

> evaluation research is interested in the ways in which specific amounts of public expenditure (the 'input') contribute, through the additional provision of goods and services (the 'output') to the achievement of objectives and goals (the 'outcome'). (Glatzer, 1981, p. 226)

This aspect of social indicators research has also been commented on by Sheldon and Parke (1975, p. 695) in a manner which suggests that they do not want to see too much work devoted to this form:

> One view sees social indicators as providing a basis for the evaluation of government programs. However, the development of evaluation research, particularly social experimentation, of social research as a distinct type has attenuated the expectation that social indicators are to serve the purpose of program evaluation.

Attention to this area would, presumably, draw resources away from another major area, that of measuring social change itself without any reference to goals. Glatzer (1981, p. 228) listed the characteristics which he discerned as belonging to social indicators research in the following way:

- An empirical and quantitative interest rather than a purely theoretical interest in societal phenomena; a tendency to investigate problems which are of interest within the context of a broad political perspective rather than a purely scientific one; a readiness for interdisciplinary work on problems which transcend the traditional boundaries of scientific disciplines; and

● A concern for communicative and cooperative relationship between social science and public policy, the administration of government and public opinion.

Interestingly, Glatzer concluded that because social indicators research is very diverse it is unlikely to continue as an independent field, but is most likely to be divided and become part of diverse research traditions. There is, therefore, the possibility that the parts of social indicator research which are concerned with the setting of goals and the measurement of their achievement through social policies could become part of a social accounting development.

THE DEVELOPMENT OF CHANGE INDICATORS

Parke and Peterson (1981) noted that the term 'social indicators' became widely used after the work of Bauer (1966), and that a frequently used definition is that of the US Department of Health Education and Welfare, which described social indicators as: 'in all cases . . . direct measure(s) of welfare' (Parke and Peterson, 1981, p. 225). This description is not considered satisfactory by Parke and Peterson because it does 'not include many of the variables central to an understanding of changes taking place in the society' (ibid., p. 236).

There is a major difference of approach between those researchers of social indicators, who would confine their attention to direct measures as far as possible, and the users of those indicators. The users would accept data obtained indirectly and by inference, if they cannot obtain them directly. SIA is usually concerned with direct measures of social activity.

Parke and Peterson (1981) is divided into three sections: social measurement, social accounting, and social reporting. In the area of social measurement, at a macro social indicators level, researchers are attempting to develop a series of quantitative measures of social change, since 'a prerequisite to the advancement of social indicators, however defined, is the quantitative measurement of social change. Such measures make possible empirical findings about current social conditions and social processes' (ibid., p. 236).

The specific examples of categories in which data collection is proceeding are: social mobility; educational achievement; victimization by crime; and the subjective well-being of individual respondents. However, the authors comment:

Impressive as these data collection efforts are, they do not by themselves produce the indicators that are needed. For this, we need improvement of instrumentation, improvement of access to data, and assessment of the value of the data as a measure of phenomena of interest. (Ibid., p. 238)

From an examination of their section on the subject, it is evident that Parke and Peterson use the term 'social accounting' in a different context from that in which the same term is used in this book and in the accounting literature. They refer to four areas: an expansion of the national income accounts to include externalities such as the value of household production as a part of gross national product; time-based accounts, a concept of social accounts incorporating time as an expenditure; national goals accounting, including the work of Terleckyj; and finally, demographic accounts. It appears that only the work of Terleckyj is really a study of macro measures using accounting techniques, and it is work of this type which fits into the framework of this book.

There has been, according to Parke and Peterson, little interrelationship between the social measurement and social accounting research work: 'the interests of those engaged in social measurement and those working in social accounting have led to little joint work' (ibid., p. 241). Their section on social reporting refers to notable reports on social indicators that have been published in the United States since 1933. The discussion included the manner in which findings are communicated to a wider public. The authors noted that: 'Significant improvements in social reporting, beyond those already in evidence, must depend first of all on improvements in the indicator measures themselves and this will be accomplished primarily by social scientists' (ibid., p. 243). Parke and Peterson concluded that careful measurement is needed, supported by appropriate instruments and processing, together with suitable reporting.

It is evident, from an examination of this and other survey articles, that only a small part of the literature of social indicators research is relevant to a study of social indicators accounting as the term is used here. Furthermore, a lengthy time-period for measurement may be involved, together with a regional dimension or scale. All these factors contribute towards making this an area which is, apparently, of less interest to accounting researchers than those considered in the earlier chapters. However, the potential fragmentation of the social indicators research area referred to by Glatzer (1981) cannot be ignored.

LINKING MACRO AND MICRO INDICATORS

The two areas of socio-economic accounting and social indicators accounting are related, in that SEA refers to short-term disclosures and

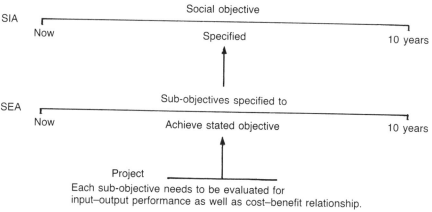

Figure 8.1 Relating SEA and SIA.

SIA to long-term goals and supporting social measurements of a macro (public) nature.

A suitable example might be education, which features in both of the schedules taken from Terleckyj. National education programmes which state goals for long-term achievements have to be supported by shorter-term goals (interim achievement points) which may be monitored by the use of socio-economic accounting and institutional performance evaluation. The link between the two levels is explored in Figure 8.1.

SUMMARY

It is evident that SIA means many things to many people, possibly to a greater extent than the other categories or divisions of social accounting with which this book has been concerned so far. The literature on social indicators does not belong primarily, or even mainly, to social accounting but to sociology and welfare economics. Indeed, one point made in the paper by Parke and Peterson (1981) is that in their scheme only one-quarter of 'social accounting' corresponds to the use of social indicators accounting in this chapter.

The paper by Terleckyj (1970) illustrated clearly both the promise and the problems of social indicators accounting. The need for better data collection and processing systems is universal, but the paucity of non-financial information, as a basis for some of the indicators which government agencies might want to use, was seen as a serious problem. The case for the involvement of accountants and accounting procedures in the development of social indicators (that is, the basis of SIA) is less easily established than the arguments for the forms of social accounting set out in previous chapters.

Societal accounting　9

INTRODUCTION

A number of writers in the area of social accounting have adopted a larger dimension than any of the others considered previously. This wider view is termed 'societal accounting' and takes a 'global' view of the relationship of society and accounting, tempered by the recognition that any accounting system must be related to the society in which it exists, and is therefore nationally or culturally dependent.

THE GLOBAL VIEW

MATTESSICH

One theorist who has attempted to construct an integrated overarching theory of accounting is Mattessich. In an early work Mattessich (1957, p. 330) referred to the search for a general theory of accountancy:

> the next step would be to bring all existing and imaginable accounting systems to a common denominator. This process would mean developing a general basis valid for all these systems, out of which the features and peculiarities of any individual system could be derived through the introduction of additional axioms and definitions.

The axiomatic foundation of accountancy, it was argued, underlies all those accounting systems shown in Figure 9.1. The scheme was viewed as incomplete, since 'even the possibility of creating new accounting systems for specialised purposes can be expected' (ibid., p. 331). Presumably this statement refers to the area designated 'non-monetary accounting' which corresponds to the social responsibility accounting and other disclosures already discussed. In the context of Figure 9.1,

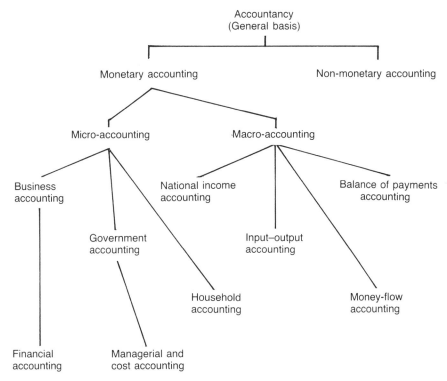

Figure 9.1 Accounting systems and their relationships. Adapted from Mattessich (1957, p. 331).

Mattessich acknowledged the incomplete nature of his model at the same time as he indicated the directions in which accounting may develop.

In a much later work Mattessich (1972) continued the task of developing a general theory of accounting. The spread of accounting research was acknowledged, together with the potential dangers inherent in this development:

> If the many fugitive parts and pieces of our discipline can be held together and integrated, accounting as an academic discipline will survive, if not it might dissolve, and be absorbed by neighbouring fields.   (Mattessich, 1972, p. 482)

This warning may be applied in exactly the same way to the constituent parts of social accounting. Mattessich concluded with a reference to the need for developing and testing alternative theoretical structures by reference to empirical verification:

> This testing of a general accounting theory by way of the empirical

verification or reputation of its interpreted systems, seems to me the only way of conforming to the requirements of an empirical discipline.   (Ibid., p. 486)

GAMBLING

The global view has also been expressed by Gambling (1974, p. 9): 'What is needed is nothing less than the redefinition or clarification of "accounting" as the data base for *all* aspects of social measurement and control.'

Recognition of the cultural basis of accounting may be seen in the following statement by the same writer:

> Even between societies whose values are not dissimilar, it is possible to find basically different approaches to income recognition; primarily between those who are prepared to [take] account of managerial attentions (as in Germany and the Netherlands) and those who seek some internal accounting standards (as in Great Britain and the United States).   (Ibid.)

Gandhi (1976, p. 199) has expressed similar views: 'On a larger scale, accounting seeks to clarify for the society as a whole a certain dimension of societal properties which are under the process of decision-making.'

Gambling (1974, p. 208) discusses the need for an overarching theory of accounting, and some of the reasons why we do not have one at the present time:

> Just as the present day aversion to 'overarching theories' prevents the useful further development of social indicators the absence of such theories provides a justification for continuing to use the self-financing corporation. Any thinking man can see that a firm's activities have social costs and social effects that feed back to the firm itself: it is very hard to present absolutely convincing estimates of what those effects might be precisely because we do not have theories about how the whole society works . . . If one did attach credence to any one overarching theory, one could then proceed to product a comprehensive taxonomy of the variables needed to describe the issues facing society, and so produce accounting statements that would tell us more clearly how existing institutions were supposed to be affecting that society.

The global nature of societal accounting means that all time-scales and all forms of ownership and enterprise must be included in the model. This all-embracing theory is required to supplement the shorter-term processes which are more easily defined, and which make up the first four categories of activities embraced by social accounting in this book.

Thus, societal accounting may be regarded as an abstract intellectual phenomenon, rather than a concrete activity, and must be accepted as such. It should be noted that societal accounting, according to Gambling, attempts to view the activities of the individual (mini-accounting), the firm (micro-accounting) and the public-enterprise or government activity (macro-accounting), within an interlocking framework, whereby the interrelationships are noted and in some way measured.

The sheer magnitude of such a data collection and measurement/ aggregation task ensures that we are examining a theoretical model in order to gain insight into the overall complexity of the accounting process. Gambling (1985) has acknowledged that the search for an understanding of the complexities of the model will need to be continued. The implications for what we normally regard as accounting will be far reaching.

ACCOUNTING AND SYSTEMS THEORY

Gambling's interrelated macro-micro-mini accounting system appears to be strongly related to general systems theory which views the world as a series of systems: supra-system, system and subsystem. These systems are open in the societal accounting approach and interrelated across their boundaries. Each system may be seen as containing strategic, co-ordinating and operating subsystems or levels, together with inputs and outputs across the organization boundary to the environment or to other subsystems. The role of internal (management) accounting may be seen as providing the information system for the co-ordinating and operating subsystems. The specialist information systems for marketing management, capital budgeting and financial management assist the strategic subsystem. The intrusion of environmental forces is best viewed in terms of external regulation by government agencies requiring information, or even specific action, at any or all of the subsystem levels. The role of internal accounting may be easily reconciled with Figure 9.2.

The societal accounting theorist has a view of accounting in which all economic activity (and a great deal of social activity as well) forms a vast supra-system. Systems (or industries?) operate within the supra-system and individual enterprises form subsystems (and within them even smaller divisions exist). These diverse units are linked together by inputs and outputs of resources which include various kinds of information. The interaction of the system with the environment (or supra-system) is only partly demonstrated by existing systems of financial accounting. The current environment towards which information is directed is frequently limited to shareholders, debt-holders and government. This restricted list of stakeholders is gradually being wid-

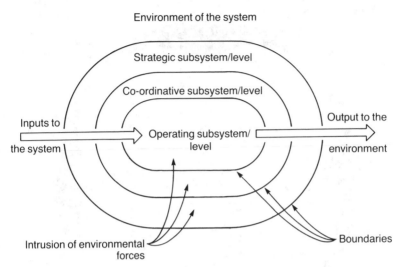

Environment of the system

Strategic subsystem/level

Co-ordinative subsystem/level

Inputs to

the system

Operating subsystem/
level

Output to the

environment

Intrusion of environmental
forces

Boundaries

Figure 9.2 The organization as a composite of strategic, co-ordinative and operating subsystems/levels. Source: Kast and Rosenzweig (1974, p. 120).

ened to include customers, employees, trade unions and the general public, as recorded in previous chapters. The relationships of the organization subsystems with the system, and the system with the supra-system or environment, are shown in Figure 9.3.

The range of information types adds to the difficulty in explaining the role of social accounting to most accountants. Theoretical models of societal accounting are necessarily complex and may be of most use in a teaching programme or as an aid to further theorizing. They are not intended to be of immediate use in attempting to develop pragmatic reporting systems.

SUMMARY

This chapter has introduced the concept of societal accounting as seen by a few accounting theoreticians. The value of this category may be seen in its all-inclusive nature which marks the large-scale, long-term boundary to social accounting. Societal accounting in the global sense would involve the tracking of all financial and non-financial resource flows within society. Gambling (1974) has expressed the overarching theory by reference to mini-accounts, which are the product of individual household accounts, micro-accounts relating to individual organizations, and macro-, or national-scale accounts. Gandhi (1976) has visualized accounting on the societal scale as assisting decision-making by society as a whole. Mattessich (1957) sought a general theory of

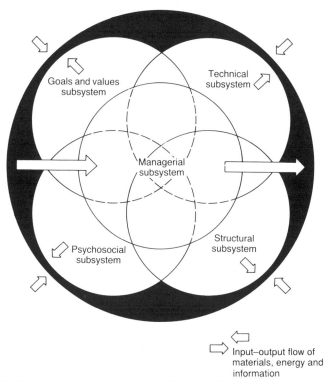

Figure 9.3 The organizational system. Source: Kast and Rosenzweig (1974, p. 112).

accounting which integrated all aspects of the discipline, although this view did not appear to be inclusive of non-monetary flows at the time.

Societal accounting can perhaps be better described by reference to systems theory, which views the world as a series of subsystems, systems and supra-systems, all interacting to a greater or lesser extent, according to the degree of openness or closedness of the system. The subsystem, consisting of strategic, co-ordinating and operating activities, is maintained by the use of the internal accounting and information systems, which are entitled the management accounting, capital budgeting and financial management functions, and decision support systems. The relationships between systems (other organizations) and between the system and the supra-system (society) is indicated through financial accounting and forms of statutory reporting, which may also extend back into the subsystem. The basis of societal accounting is the recognition that there are non-financial flows involved and that the system currently in use is therefore partial and incomplete. The different categories used in the previous chapters recognized that the process of intra- and inter-system resource movements may be better visualized through smaller-scale specific techniques. The systems-theory view of societal accounting puts the various techniques in perspective as part of an overall resource-flow monitoring system. Consequently, the notion of societal accounting is basically an intellectual extension of all the other conceivable forms of social and conventional accounting processes and techniques for resource flow identification and measurement, and not a blueprint for system implementation.

Concluding comments and directions for future research

10

This book has investigated two of the major issues of contemporary social accounting, namely, the justification of further expenditure of resources on additional disclosures (Chapters 1–3) and the provision of a structure to aid research and implementation (Chapters 4–9).

CONCLUDING COMMENTS ON CHAPTERS 1–3

Before developing the framework which forms the major part of the book it was necessary to address the basic issue of what justifications may exist for extending accounting measurements and disclosures beyond traditional limits. Three forms of justification were suggested.

First, it was proposed that there is a market-related consideration that disclosures of a socially relevant nature may have information content for use in the market place. Shareholders and other market participants, it was argued, could benefit from the increased amount of information available. Although a large number of studies have been undertaken using data from both social responsibility accounting reports and that supplied by independent bodies such as the CEP, few are decisive in their conclusions. The data sources, degree of aggregation and disaggregation, tests performed and overall statistical manipulation employed are all open to challenge. Although on balance it may be argued that there is some evidence that social responsibility disclosures have information content in the capital markets, because above- or below-standard returns may be obtained it has been concluded that there is insufficient certainty to put this forward as a major justification for new forms of accounting.

Secondly, it was argued that wider audiences (employees, customers, suppliers and the general public) were entitled to information about the operations of the enterprise because of the existence of a social contract between business and society. A number of the philosophical issues were examined, including varieties of social permission theory (social contract, organizational legitimacy) and individual contract theory, which is offered as a justification for a free-market, non-interventionist model.

Social permission theory, in its various forms, provides a firmer conceptual foundation for social accounting developments than either the earlier literature, which asserted that social accounting was 'a good thing to do', or some of the literature relating to markets and information content, which has been referred to above. Social permission theory lays the groundwork from which to develop non-traditional forms of measurement and reporting in both the private and public sectors. The social contract approach enables a justification to be put forward for many types of disclosure on the grounds that the basis for the contractual relationship is changing. The organizational legitimacy view justifies the development of social accounting disclosures by management to protect the interests of the shareholders, and not because of any philosophical commitment to a social contract between business and society.

The social permission theory approach provides a justification for developing social accounting disclosures which is part of the current organizational and societal structure. This approach seeks to modify and amend our present systems of private and public control and associated reporting practices. It does not seek to replace them in the manner advocated by adherents of the radical paradigm. It supports evolution rather than revolution. This partial support for the status quo is both a strength and a weakness of the social permission theory approach. It is a strength because a large number of groups in society can accept this position to a greater or lesser extent. These include managers, shareholders, many employees and customers. It is a weakness because existing wealth endowments are taken as given and power relationships are viewed as unproblematic. Those groups not involved in society as employees or customers (such as the very poor) tend to be ignored.

Thirdly, the radical paradigm was examined because, although regarded by the author as inappropriate as a justification for the adoption of social accounting at the present time, there is no doubt of the powerful intellectual qualities of the arguments put forward by radical advocates. The radical view is that accounting acts to support the status quo and social accounting should move away from this position. In particular, the acceptance of marginalist economic positions, the use of an efficient market model, and a lack of recognition of the pre-disposition of wealth endowments are of concern to these theorists. Whilst there is no doubt of the intellectual challenge, there are considerable problems inherent in getting non-traditional accounting disclosures accepted. An acceptance of radical approaches by social accountants would only exacerbate the position. The challenge of the radical paradigm is strong when confronting issues of wealth endowments, power relationships and the hierarchical nature of Western capitalism. However, most radical theorists have not put forward models of their own to set against those reviewed in many of the sections of this book. The theoretical proposals discussed in a number of recent papers do not generally provide any critique of what current social accounting in its various forms is trying to do, except to say that it defends the status quo (in whole or in part) and is therefore unacceptable. This book has taken what the author thinks to be a more positive approach by describing and critiquing what has been attempted in this field.

CONCLUDING COMMENTS ON CHAPTERS 4–9

Chapters 4–9 have considered developments in social accounting by dividing the total range of activities into the following areas:

1. social responsibility accounting;
2. total impact accounting;
3. socio-economic accounting;
4. social indicators accounting;
5. societal accounting.

The second major objective of this book has been to provide a framework which might assist researchers in the area of social accounting. The approach to policy formation set out by McDonald (1972) indicated that normative frameworks require a clarification of values, a means-end analysis and the incorporation of all relevant data. The division of 'social accounting' into social responsibility accounting, total impact accounting, socio-economic accounting, social indicators accounting and societal accounting assists in the identification of the ends, and consequently of the means.

Social responsibility accounting (Chapters 4 and 5) was shown to have been the most active dimension of social accounting, with a large number of both conceptual and operational models available to theoreticians and practising accountants. A number of organizations have employed SRA in their annual reports to shareholders or employee reports to employees or to works councils. The use of SRA varies in both type and extent from country to country, and this variation may be partly the result of cultural factors as well as the relative stage of development.

Social responsibility accounting is the area most widely researched and practised. SRA research exhibits many of the characteristics of descriptive (theories of) accounting. This may be a productive approach, given the amount of data available. However, it is suggested that further research should concentrate on the extent of disclosure, relationships between the size and type of industry and SRA disclosures, the audit of disclosures, disclosures and security market prices, and the views of the participants. Currently, the work is frequently deficient because of the subjectivity of many of the measures used. Any form of non-traditional disclosures made by a private-sector organization has the prospect of being a social responsibility accounting disclosure as defined in the literature. However, there is often a fine dividing line between those disclosures which may be included as SRA, because they have many of the characteristics of accounting data, and those which should be excluded because they are self-serving or uncritical in approving of company policy.

Much of the analysis completed to date is likely to be incapable of replication because the precise details of the techniques employed have not been disclosed. There are exceptions which have been noted in the test. However, even though the techniques have been imperfect and the analysis suspect, it is hoped that the examination of reported SRA disclosures will continue.

Total impact accounting (Chapter 6) involves the addition of externalities to private costs to yield the costs of operations. An examination of the early literature revealed relatively little use of this form of accounting, even by theoreticians. Clearly, there are empirical difficulties connected with identification, measurement and, finally, the valuation of externalities. However, one of the major issues appears to be a philosophical one: should accountants be involved in this area at all? Opinions are sharply divided on this issue, although those in favour appear to be gaining in strength. In dealing with total impact accounting we must confront the philosophical debate over whether shareholders are being required to pay for social responsibility or, on the other hand, whether the general public is entitled to protection from externalities. Identifying the ends (in this case the valuation of externalities to convert public costs to private costs) does not immediately indicate the means to be employed. Although data on general externalities may be available, the isolation and valuation of special enterprise-related externalities is more problematic. Research into this area may begin by looking at the externalities attached to single-enterprise communities. However, the issue of the valuation of externalities must still be addressed. The degree of pollution in some parts of the industrialized world demands that action of some sort be taken to repair the damage because the market model cannot cope with externalities. There are legislative and administrative solutions, such as legal sanctions against the discharge of externalities and licensed discharge under limiting conditions. In both cases there is a need to monitor discharges and consequently for work in the area of total impact accounting. It is extremely probable that a financial dimension would be recognized and attached to the organization in order that the total cost would be the same in both private and public calculations. In many ways, the likely outcome of the recognition, measurement, valuation and attachment of externalities is closest to the experience of accountants in the industrial sector. Recent developments in this area include the work of environmental economists who have drawn attention to intergenerational effects and sustainable development, and environmental accountants (Gray, 1990, 1991) with recommendations for new disclosures.

Socio-economic accounting (Chapter 7) was the term used to cover the evaluation of publicly funded projects. Although there have been attempts to provide for improved decision-making, implementation and control of the work of the public sector using CBA, PPBS and, latterly, VFM audits, so far the problems involved have not been overcome, in particular, the problem of measuring and evaluating effectiveness (in comparison with economy and efficiency). The end to be addressed by socio-economic accounting is the evaluation of publicly funded programmes by techniques other than those used at present. The main problem (of means) is an almost complete lack of accounting models that enable the analyst to deal with financial, non-financial and qualitative inputs and outputs. Research in this area must begin with the development of the models themselves. Some assistance may be obtained from other areas such as the institutional performance indicators research in education. Socio-economic accounting will require a new institutional performance indicators research in education. Socio-economic accounting will require a new institutional relationship to replace that which currently persists in the public service. The experience which government accountants are having with value-for-money (VFM) audits may provide a good training ground from which models for SEA may be developed. Value-for-money audits make some progress towards finding models, but the implementation is often inadequate because effectiveness is frequently not evaluated. The lack of specific models will slow the development of this important area.

The study of social indicators accounting (Chapter 8), which is concerned with short- and medium-type publicly funded activity, is complementary to social indicators accounting which takes the longer-term perspective. The literature relating to social indicators was found to be largely in the hands of non-accountants. However, it may be argued that there is a place for accounting in an area which is concerned with recording data, making comparisons with plans and reporting outcomes. Social indicators accounting has, as an 'end' product, data from which the progress towards socially agreed goals may be determined. The area appropriate to accounting involvement must be delineated and the goals identified; the goals indicators may then be developed. The processing of the indicators will be dependent on the availability of the underlying data. Research is needed into both of these 'means', the data to develop the indicator and the indicators themselves.

Finally, the endeavours of a number of accounting theoreticians to develop an overarching theory of accounting, was examined in the chapter dealing with societal accounting (Chapter 9).

Although SRA is currently the most 'populated' area, the other areas are deserving of support, because therein lie some of the most important challenges for academic accountants. There is considerable scope since, as Gandhi (1976, pp. 199–200) has expressed it:

> Accounting as an information system transfers images which are a necessary precondition to any individual or collective behaviour. These images constitute a knowledge structure which included inputs and outputs of information, symbols and language. By providing such knowledge structures of various economic entities accounting furthers the societal process of adaption in which the society tries to adapt itself to its larger ecological environment. Simultaneously, it also adapts that environment.

This statement sums up the larger approach of societal accounting. However, accounting at present is still very much on a micro scale, whether it is for a business enterprise, a local authority or a government department. It is micro in the sense of small, but also narrow in the degree to which it recognizes information as a suitable input to the system. One of the purposes of this book has been to review some of the attempts to broaden the view of accountants towards information which should be available to government departments and social programmes.

This book has examined some of the newer ideas in accounting, many of which are usually discussed under the general heading of social accounting, and others which are not discussed in the mainstream accounting literature. The intention has been to show how these ideas are different and a scheme is presented which relates the new ideas to each other and to present-day accounting. Recent work on the disclosure of socially relevant information is described. The pursuit of many of the issues covered in this book would indeed result in a more socially responsible accounting.

It is apparent that to combine these areas into a coherent whole would require the amalgamation of the public and private sectors, macro- and micro-scale activities, and monetary and non-monetary measurements. It must also be recognized that some data will be 'hard' and some 'soft'.

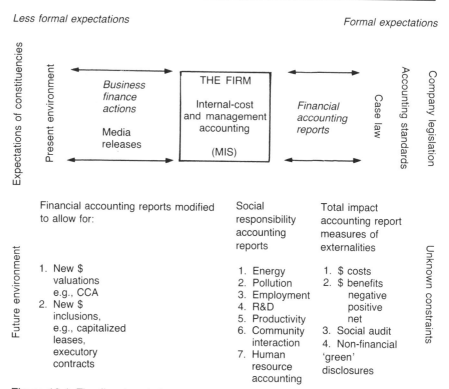

Figure 10.1 The firm in relation to present and future accounting requirements.

TOWARDS REINTEGRATION

Reconciliation of these complex and conflicting developments has been attempted in Figures 10.1 and 10.2. Figure 10.1 shows the impact of social responsibility accounting and total impact accounting on individual organizations. The individual organization is represented by the rectangle called 'The Firm' which employs some form of cost and management accounting process, or even a management information system, to maintain internal control. The firm operates within an environment affected by company legislation, accounting standards and case law, as well as less-formalized expectations held by customers, shareholders, employees and government agencies. The firm interacts with the formal constraints through financial accounting reports, and with the less formal expectations of other constituencies by means of financial actions in the market-place and by means of media releases. Conformity with other legal restraints on employment practices and the discharge of waste is assumed.

The future environment is unknown, in respect of both formal and less-formal expectations, although it is reasonable to speculate that

	MACRO	MICRO
P R E S E N T	Financial budget allocation and control	Cost–benefit analysis Political decision processes Public activities ◄——— PPBS Social benefit programmes ◄——— ZBB Internal control ◄——— MBO Systems Conventional
F U T U R E	Social indicators accounting 1. Goal concerns articulated 2. Output measures identified 3. Output measures quantified 4. Evaluation of the extent of achievement of goals 5. Formulation of new goals and measures Mainly non-financial	Socio-economic accounting* 1. Evaluation of costs and benefits 2. Evaluation of outputs 3. Statement of achievements 4. Evaluation of total project *ex-post* 5. Use of data in new cost–benefit analyses of subsequent projects * Mixed financial and non-financial

Note: PPBS Planned Programmed Budgeting System
ZBB Zero Based Budgeting
MBO Management by Objectives

Figure 10.2 The possible extension of accounting reports in respect of public-sector activities.

present constraints will not be reduced and that the expectations of the various constituencies are likely to increase over time.

In the lower part of Figure 10.1 the three possible areas of increased reporting are given under appropriate headings. Thus increased reporting, which might be required in conventional annual reports, includes (as examples only) new valuations of existing disclosures and new inclusions valued in dollar amounts. Social responsibility accounting reports, written in both financial and non-financial terms, would disclose a whole range of items not included at the present time. Some suggestions about content are given in the figure. The total impact accounting report would provide for measures of positive and negative externalities, converted where possible into financial quantities.

Figure 10.2 illustrates the place which might be occupied by socio-economic and social indicators accounting in the evaluation of publicly funded activities. The shorter-term micro social indicators accounting tends to be similar to socio-economic accounting, although the latter would be concerned with a specific programme, rather than the measurement of a general phenomenon, which would provide indicators for future action in respect of a number of programmes. The figure should be viewed as follows: the public activities represented by the upper-right rectangle are instituted as a result of a political decision process which may be influenced by using cost-benefit analysis in a particular situation. The decision-making processes may be sharply influenced by political factors. However, once instituted, the programme is controlled both internally and externally. The external control may be by a conventional fund accounting system or a later type, such as a planned programmed budgeting system. In all cases the control system is financially based and concentrates on the input of resources in financial terms while tending to ignore non-fictional inputs and outputs. Future control processes, it is argued, should take the form of mixed financial and non-financial measurements of inputs and outputs for individual projects. This process has been termed socio-economic accounting and the process is given in the lower right-hand quadrant of the figure.

On a macro scale, as shown on the left of the figure, control is exercised at the present time by means of a financial budget and fund accounting system. There is little or no measure of overall effectiveness of the macro programme (examples might be health and education). It is suggested that the use of social indicators accounting would assist in determining the overall effectiveness of programmes in achieving socially determined objectives.

IMPLICATIONS FOR ACCOUNTANTS, ACCOUNTING STUDENTS AND ACCOUNTING EDUCATORS

Even if we confine our attention to the three most likely developments – social responsibility accounting, total impact accounting and socio-economic accounting – it is most unlikely that the present structure of the profession could cope with the changes that acceptance of these new techniques would bring. It would be necessary to incorporate new material into existing academic and professional development programmes to allow for areas of knowledge in which accountants would initially be deficient. For social responsibility accounting, it would be necessary for future accountants to be less reliant upon monetary quantification and to move into wider areas of non-monetary quantification. An awareness of the measures used by the social and physical sciences may also be necessary. Auditing of the new measures would eventually be needed, and this too would either require a wider expertise from the auditor or place reliance upon specialist personnel, a social audit specialist for example.

In the area of total impact accounting, the future accountant will not have to forgo monetary measurement, but it may be a new type of accounting based upon the valuation of externalities that requires expertize in econometrics, sampling theory and the construction of models. Once again, the audit problem will be of the same magnitude and nature. Gray (1990, 1991) and Owen (1992) have given some indication of a system of additional disclosures which would be based upon non-financial statements.

It is probably the area of socio-economic accounting which brings the greatest challenge to theorists and teachers of accounting and to their students. It is clear that this area of evaluation and control is not being pursued by accountants at present. To come to grips with the problems involved, the accountant will require specialist training. The socio-economic accountant will require a good knowledge of government policy-making and administration, business accounting and investment management, the social sciences in general and social statistics in particular. However, the rewards will be commensurate with the difficulties, since increasing the efficiency of government spending and programme formulation and control is something from which all taxpayers should benefit. There is an opportunity for accountants to exert a major influence upon the efficiency and effectiveness of government operations.

FUTURE DIRECTIONS

The wide-ranging contents of this book mean that a large number of relatively discrete areas may be identified for further research. These are listed below using the same format as is employed for the structure of the book:

1. Additional market-related studies are needed to establish whether relationships exist between specific disclosures and the reactions of market participants. At present the results of such studies are equivocal.
2. The philosophical arguments which may underlie additional disclosures (such as social permission theory, the social contract between business and society, and organizational legitimacy) provide opportunities for further research. At present the normative-deductive arguments are unsupported by empirical research into the motivation of those managers who use annual reports to provide non-traditional disclosures to a variety of audiences. Also, the reaction of users of annual reports needs to be considered, although this is done to some extent through the market studies referred to above.
3. Social responsibility accounting disclosures are currently made

by a number of organizations, and there is a literature relating to the measurement of the type and extent of these disclosures. As noted elsewhere, the research methods employed require further refining in order to provide for greater replicability of results by independent researchers. In addition, there are a number of specific SRA-related issues that need further attention, including human resource accounting, employee reports and industrial democracy/power sharing, and the means by which pollution may be recorded.

4. Total impact accounting, involving the identification, measurement and valuation of externalities, is considerably underdeveloped at the present time. Consequently, opportunities exist for further research into the means by which externalities may be measured and valued. The problems associated with a compensation system using non-market mechanisms, whereby parties affected by externalities can seek redress, is a difficult but necessary research area which may be pursued. The recently developed areas relating to the division of capital between man-made and natural offer challenges to accounting theorists.

5. Socio-economic accounting provides for the integration of non-financial quantification and financial measurements in the evaluation of publicly funded projects. The search for measures of effectiveness in areas where there is no market for the end product/service offers many opportunities for research, especially in areas which are politically sensitive, such as educational systems and the provision of health care. Models to assist in the evaluation of the wider aspects of these activities have yet to be developed.

6. In the area of social indicators accounting, further work is needed to map out specific problems of measurement and reporting which may be assisted by an accounting approach. The databases currently available may be deficient and unable to support the type of information which is considered necessary in order to measure progress towards agreed socially desirable goals.

7. The macro aspects of accounting systems, which were referred to under the heading of societal accounting, are culturally determined or, at least, strongly influenced by the national culture. Consequently, research may be undertaken to compare systems with each other and to investigate what are the main factors impacting upon a particular national accounting system.

References

1: Introduction to socially responsible accounting

Accounting Standards Steering Committee (1975) *The Corporate Report*, ICAEW, London.

American Accounting Association (1971) *Supplement to the Accounting Review*, 46 (Report of the Committee on Accounting Theory and Construction and Verification), AAA, Sarasota, Fla.

Barnet, A. H. and Caldwell, J. C. (1974) Accounting for corporate social performance: a survey. *Management Accounting*, 23–6.

Baxter, W. T. and Davidson, S. (eds) (1977) *Studies in Accounting*, Chapel River, Andover.

Beams, F. A. and Fertig, P. E. (1971) Pollution control through social costs conversion, *Journal of Accountancy*, **132**, 37–42.

Chatfield, M. (1977) *A History of Accounting Thought*, Kreiger, New York.

Crossman, P. (1953) The genesis of cost control, *Accounting Review*, **28**(4), 522–7.

Estes, R. W. (1972) Socio-economic accounting and external diseconomies, *Accounting Review*, **47**, 284–90.

Financial Accounting Standards Board (1978) *Statement of Financial Accounting Concepts. No. 1: Objectives of Financial Reporting by Business Enterprises*, FASB, Stamford.

Fu, P. (1971) Government accounting in China during the Chou dynasty (1122 BC to 256 BC), *Journal of Accounting Research*, **9**(1).

Galbraith, J. K. (1958) *The Affluent Society*, Houghton Mifflin, Boston, Mass.

Goldberg, L. (1971) The development of accounting, in C. T. Gibson, G. G. Meredith and R. Peterson (eds), *Accounting Concepts Readings*, Cassell, Melbourne, pp. 4–37.

Gray, R., Owen, D. and Maunders, K. (1987) *Corporate Social Reporting: Accounting and Accountability*, Prentice-Hall, London.

Gray, R. H. (1990) *The Greening of Accountancy: The Profession after Pearce*, Certified Record Report no. 17, Chartered Association of Certified Accountants, London.

HMSO (1977) *The Future of Company Reports: A Consultative Document*, HMSO, London.

Keister, O. R. (1965) The mechanics of Mesopotamian record-keeping, *National Association of Accountants Bulletin*, pp. 18–24.

Likierman, A. and Creasey, P. (1985) Objectives and entitlements to rights in government financial information, *Financial Accountability and Management*, **1**(1), 33–50.

Littleton, A. C. (1966) The antecedents of double-entry bookkeeping, in A. C. Littleton (ed.), *Accounting Evolution to 1990* [1933], Russell and Russell, New York, pp. 13–21.

Mathews, M. R. and Gordon, I. M. (1984) Social responsibility accounting disclosures: differential responses as a function of professional body membership, *Working Paper no. 8*, Public Interest Section, American Accounting Association.

Mathews, M. R. and Perera, M. B. H. (1991) *Accounting Theory and Development*, Thomas Nelson, Melbourne.

Mayston, D. J. (1985) Non-profit performance indicators in the public sector, *Financial Accountability and Management*, **1**(1), 51–74.

Sombart, W. (1924) *Der Modern Kapitalismus*, 2.1 (6th edn), Munich and Leipzig, p. 118.

Stiner, F. M. Jr (1978) Accountants' attitudes toward social accounting, *Mid-Atlantic Journal of Business*, **16**(2).

Winjum, J. O. (1970) Accounting in its age of stagnation, *Accounting Review*, **45**(4), 743–61.

Winjum, J. O. (1971) Accounting and the rise of capitalism: an accountant's view, *Journal of Accounting Research*, **9**(2), 333–50.

Yamey, B. S. (1949) Scientific bookkeeping and the rise of capitalism, *Economic History Review*, second series, **1**(1–2), 99–113.

Yamey, B. S. (1964) Accounting and the rise of capitalism: Further notes on a theme by Sombart, *Journal of Accounting Research*, **1** (2), 117–36.

2: Justifications for additional disclosures

Abbot, W. F. and Monsen, R. J. (1979) On the measurement of corporate social responsibility: self-reported disclosures as a method of measuring corporate social involvement, *Academy of Management Journal*, **22**(3), 501–15.

Accounting Standards Steering Committee (1975) *The Corporate Report*, ICAEW, London.

Alexander, J. J. and Bucholz, R. A. (1978) Corporate social responsibility and stock market performance, *Academy of Management Journal*, **21**(3), 479–86.

American Accounting Association (1971) *Supplement to the Accounting Review, 46* (Report of the Committee on Accounting Theory and Construction and Verification), AAA, Sarasota, Fla.

American Accounting Association (1972) *Supplement to the Accounting Review, 47* (Report of the Committee on Measures of Effectiveness for Social Programs), AAA, Sarasota, Fla, pp. 336–96.

American Accounting Association (1973a) *Supplement to the Accounting Review, 48* (Report of the Committee on Environmental Effects of Organizational Behavior), AAA, Sarasota, Fla, pp. 72–119.

American Accounting Association (1973b) *Supplement to the Accounting Review,*

47 (Report of the Committee on Human Resource Accounting), AAA, Sarasota, Fla, pp. 532–54.

American Accounting Association (1974) *Supplement to the Accounting Review, 49* (Report of the Committee on the Measurement of Social Costs), AAA, Sarasota, Fla, pp. 98–113.

American Accounting Association (1975) *Supplement to the Accounting Review, 50* (Report of the Committee on Social Costs), AAA, Sarasota, Fla, pp. 51–89.

American Accounting Association (1976) *Supplement to the Accounting Review, 51* (Report of the Committee on Accounting for Social Performance), AAA, Sarasota, Fla, pp. 38–69.

American Institute of Certified Public Accountants (1973) *Objectives of Financial Statements*, AICPA, New York.

Arlow, P. and Gannon, M. (1982) Social responsiveness, corporate structure and economic performance, *Academy of Management Review,* 7(2) 235–41.

Belkaoui, A. (1976) The impact of the disclosure of the environmental effects of organizational behaviour on the market, *Financial Management,* 26–31.

Belkaoui, A. (1980) The impact of socio-economic accounting statements on the investment decision: an empirical study, *Accounting, Organizations and Society,* 5(3), 263–83.

Bowen, H. R. (1953) *Social Responsibilities of the Businessman*, Harper and Row, New York.

Bowman, E. H. and Haire, M. (1975) A strategic posture toward corporate social responsibility, *California Management Review,* 18(2), 49–58.

Burchell, S., Clubb, C. and Hopwood, A. G. (1985) Accounting in its social context: towards a history of value added in the United Kingdom, *Accounting, Organizations and Society,* 10(4), 381–413.

Chen, K. H. and Metcalf, R. W. (1980) The relationship between pollution control record and financial indicators revisited, *Accounting Review,* 60(1), 168–77.

Chua, W. F. (1986) Theoretical considerations of and by the real, *Accounting, Organizations and Society,* 11(6), 583–98.

Cooper, D. J. and Sherer, M. J. (1984) The value of corporate accounting reports: arguments for a political economy of accounting, *Accounting, Organizations and Society,* 9(3/4), 207–32.

Dalton, R. and Cosier, R. A. (1982) The four faces of social responsibility, *Business Horizons,* 19–27.

Davis, K. (1973) The case for and against business' assumption of social responsibilities, *Academy of Management Journal,* 16(2), 312–22.

Davis, K. (1976) Social responsibility is inevitable, *California Management Review,* 19, 14–20.

Den Uyl, D. J. (1984) The new crusaders: the corporate social responsibility debate, *Studies in Social Philosophy and Policy, no. 5*, Social Philosophy and Policy Center, Bowling Green State University, Ohio.

Donaldson, T. (1982) *Corporate Morality*, Prentice-Hall, Englewood Cliffs, N.J.

Dowling, J. and Pfeffer, J. (1975) Organizational legitimacy: social values and organizational behavior, *Pacific Sociological Review,* 123.

Eberstadt, N. (1973) What history tells us about corporate responsibilities. *Business and Society Review,* 7 76–81.

Financial Accounting Standards Board (1978) *Statement of Financial Accounting*

Concepts no. 1: Objectives of Financial Reporting by Business Enterprises, FASB, Stamford.

Fitch, H. G. (1976) Achieving corporate social responsibility, *Academy of Management Review*, 38–46.

Folger, H. R. and Nutt, F. (1975) A note on social responsibility and stock valuation, *Academy of Management Journal*, 155–160.

Freedman, M. and Stagliano, A. J. (1984) The market impact of social information: investor reaction to public disclosure, in AAA Mid-Atlantic Regional Meeting, Baltimore, *Proceedings*.

French, P. (1979) The corporation as a moral person, *American Philosophical Quarterly*, **16**, 207–15.

Friedman, M. (1962) *Capitalism and Freedom*, University of Chicago Press, Chicago.

Galbraith, J. K. (1974) *Economics and the Public Purpose*, Andre Deutsch, London.

Gambling, T. E. (1977) Magic, accounting and morale, *Accounting, Organizations and Society*, **2**(2), 141–51.

Gambling, T. E. and Karim, R. A. A. (1986) Islam and social accounting, *Journal of Business Finance and Accounting*, **13**(1), 39–59.

Gray, R. H. (1990) The greening of accountancy: the profession after Pearce, *Certified Research Report 17*, Chartered Association of Certified Accountants, London.

Gray, R., Owen, D. and Maunders, K. (1987) *Corporate Social Reporting: Accounting and Accountability*, Prentice-Hall, London.

Gray, S. J. (1985) Cultural influences and the international classification of accounting systems, *Working Paper 85–7*, University of Glasgow.

Grcic, J. M. (1985) Democratic capitalism: developing a conscience for the corporation, *Journal of Business Ethics*, **4**, 145–50.

Heald, M. (1970) The social responsibilities of business, company, community, 1900–1960, Case Western University Press, Cleveland, Ohio.

Henderson, V. E. (1984) The spectrum of ethicality, *Journal of Business Ethics*, **3**, 163–9.

Hofstede, G. (1983a) Dimensions of national cultures in fifty countries and three regions, in J. B. Dregowski, S. Dziurauriec and R. C. Annis (eds), *Expectations in Cross Cultural Psychology*, Swets and Zeitlinger, Amsterdam.

Hofstede, G. (1983b) The cultural relativity of organisational practices and theories, *Journal of International Business Studies*.

Hopper, T., Cooper, D. J., Lowe, E. A., Capps, T. M. and Mouritsen, J. (1986) Management control and worker resistance in the national coal board: financial controls in the labour process, in H. C. Wilmott and D. Knights (eds), *Managing the Labour Process*, Gower, Aldershot.

Ingram, R. W. (1978) An investigation of the information content of (certain) social responsibility disclosures, *Journal of Accounting Research*, **16**(2), 270–85.

Johnson, S. B. (1986) Review of Tony Tinker's Paper Prophets, *Accounting Review*, **61** (3), 563–4.

Ladd, J. (1970) Morality and the ideal of rationality in formal organizations, *Monist*, **54**, 488–516.

Laughlin, R. C. and Puxty, A. G. (1986) The socially conditioning and socially conditioned nature of accounting: a review and analysis through Tinker's Paper Prophets, *British Accounting Review*, **18**(1), 77–90.

Laughlin, R. C., Lowe, E. A. and Puxty, A. G. (1986) Designing and operating a course in accounting methodology: philosophy, experience and some preliminary empirical tests, *British Accounting Review*, **18**(1), 17–42.

Lawrence, M. (1982) How companies become involved in their communities. *Personnel Journal*, 502–10.

Lehman, C. R. (1983) Stalemate in corporate social responsibility research, *Working Paper no. 3*, Public Interest Section, American Accounting Association.

Lehman, C. R. (1988) Accounting ethics: surviving survival of the fittest, *Advances in Public Interest Accounting*, **2**, 71–82.

Likierman, A. and Creasey, P. (1985) Objectives and entitlements to rights in government financial information, *Financial Accountability and Management*, **1**(1), 33–50.

Lindblom, C. E. (1984) The accountability of private enterprise: private – no, enterprise – yes, in A. M. Tinker, (ed.), *Social Accounting for Corporations*, Marcus Weiner, New York.

Loft, A. (1986) Towards a critical understanding of accounting: the case of cost accounting in the UK, 1914–1925, *Accounting, Organizations and Society*, **11**(2), 137–69.

Mahapatra, S. (1984) Investor reaction to a corporate social accounting, *Journal of Business Finance and Accounting*, **11**(1), 29–40.

Manning, R. C. (1984) Corporate responsibility and corporate personhood, *Journal of Business Ethics*, **3**, 77–84.

Mathews, M. R. and Perera, M. H. B. (1993) *Accounting Theory and Development*, Thomas Nelson, Australia.

Merino, B. D. and Neimark, M. D. (1982) Disclosure regulation and public policy: a socio-historical appraisal, *Journal of Accounting and Public Policy*, **1**, 33–57.

Nader, R. (1973) *The Consumer and Corporate Accountability*, Harcourt Brace Jovanovich, New York.

National Association of Accountants (1974a) Report of the Committee on Accounting for Corporate Social Performance, *Management Accounting*, 39–41.

National Association of Accountants (1974b) Report of the Committee on Accounting for Corporate Social Performance, *Management Accounting*, 59–60.

Neubauer, J. C. (1971) The accounting aid society, *Journal of Accountancy*, 55–9.

Owen, D. (ed.) (1992) *Green Reporting*, Chapman & Hall, London.

Parker, I. R. and Eilbert, H. (1975) Social responsibility: the underlying factors, *Business Horizons*, **18**(4), 5–10.

Perera, M. H. B. (1985) The relevance of international accounting standards to developing countries, Research monograph, University of Glasgow.

Perera, M. H. B. and Mathews, M. R. (1990) The cultural relativity of accounting and international patterns of social accounting, in K. S. Most (ed.), *Advances in International Accounting*, **3**, JAI Press, New York.

Prakash, S. S. (1975) Dimensions of corporate social performance: an analytical framework, *California Management Review*, **17**(3), 58–64.

Preston, L. E. and Post, J. (1975) *Private Management and Public Policy*, Prentice Hall, Englewood Cliffs, N.J.

Shane, P. B. and Spicer, B. H. (1983) Market response to environmental information produced outside the firm, *Accounting Review*, **58**(3), 521–38.

Shocker, A. D. and Sethi, S. P. (1974) An approach to incorporating social preferences in developing corporate action strategies, in S. P. Sethi (ed.), *The Unstable Ground Corporate Social Policy in a Dynamic Society*, Melville, California.

Skousen, C. R. (1982) Public interest accounting: a look at the issues, *Accounting, Organizations and Society*, **7**(1), 79–85.

Spicer, B. H. (1978a) Accounting for corporate social performance: some problems and issues, *Journal of Contemporary Business*, 151–70.

Spicer, B. H. (1978b) Investors, corporate social performance and information disclosure: an empirical study, *Accounting Review*, **53**(1), 94–111.

Spicer, B. H. (1980) The relationship between pollution control record and financial indicators revisited: further comment, *Accounting Review*, **55**(1), 178–85.

Stevens, W. P. (1982) Market reaction to corporate environmental performance, a paper presented at the American Accounting Association Annual Conference, San Diego.

Sturdivant, F. D. and Ginter, J. L. (1977) Corporate social responsiveness: management attitudes and economic performance, *California Management Review*, **19**(3), 30–9.

Tinker, A. M. (1985) *Paper Prophets*, Praeger, New York.

Tinker, A. M., Merino, B. D. and Neimark, M. D. (1982) The normative origins of positive theories: ideology and accounting thought, *Accounting, Organization and Society*, **7**(2), 167–200.

Valone, J. J. (1985) A review of D. J. Den Uyl, *The New Crusaders: The Corporate Social Responsibility Debate*, *Journal of Business Ethics*, **4**, 384, 408, 424.

Vance, S. C. (1975) Are socially responsible corporations good investment risks? *Management Review*, **64**(8), 18–24.

Wartick, S. L. and Cochran, P. L. (1985) The evolution of the corporate social performance model, *Academy of Management Review*, **10**(4), 758–69.

Willmott, H. C. (1986) Organising the profession: a theoretical and historical examination of the development of the major accountancy bodies in the UK, *Accounting, Organizations and Society*, **11**(6), 555–80.

Zeisel, G. and Estes, R. W. (1979) Accounting and public service, *Accounting Review*, **54**(2), 402–8.

3: The classification of social accounting

American Accounting Association (1975) *Supplement to the Accounting Review, 50* (Report of the Committee on Social Costs), 51–89.

Lindblom, C. E. (1959) The science of muddling through, *Public Administration Review*, **19**(2).

Mathews, M. R. (1984) A suggested classification for social accounting research, *Journal of Accounting and Public Policy*, 199–222, Fall.

McDonald, D. L. (1975) *Comparative Accounting Theory*, Addison Wesley, Cambridge, Mass.

4: Social responsibility accounting

Accounting Standards Steering Committee (1975) *The Corporate Report*, ICAEW, London.

Anderson, R. H. (1976) Social responsibility accounting: what to measure and how, *Cost and Management*, 34–8.

Anderson, R. H. (1977) Social responsibility accounting: evaluating its objectives, concepts and principles, *CA Magazine*, 32–5.

Anderson, R. H. (1978) Social responsibility accounting: how to get started, *CA Magazine*, 46–51.

Anderson, R. H. (1980) Attitudes of chartered accountants to social responsibility disclosure in Australia, *Chartered Accountant in Australia*, 12–16.

Anderson, R. H., Brooks, L. J. and Davis, W. R. (1978) *The Why, When and How of Social Responsibility Accounting*, CICA, Toronto.

Barnett, A. H. and Caldwell, J. C. (1974) Accounting for corporate social performance: a survey, *Management Accounting*, 23–6.

Benjamin, J. J., Stanga, K. G. and Strawser, R. K. (1977) Corporate social responsibility: the viewpoint of CPAs, *National Public Accountant*, 18–22.

Bougen, P. D. and Ogden, S. G. (1985) Joint consultation and the disclosure of information: an historical perspective, a paper presented to the *Interdisciplinary Perspectives on Accounting Conference*, Manchester.

Brooks, L. J. (1986) *Canadian Corporate Social Performance*, Society of Management Accountants of Canada, Toronto.

Burchell, S., Clubb, C. and Hopwood, A. G. (1985) Accounting in its social context: towards a history of value added in the United Kingdom, *Accounting, Organizations and Society*, 10(4), 381–413.

Burke, R. C. (1980) The disclosure of social accounting information, *Cost and Management*, 221–4.

Burke, R. C. (1984) *Decision Making in Complex Times: The Contribution of a Social Accounting Information System*, Society of Management Accountants of Canada, Ontario.

Chan, R. S. (1975) Social and financial stewardship, *Accounting Review*, 50(3), 533–43.

Cheng, P. (1976) Time for social accounting, *Certified Accountant*, 285–91.

Choi, F. D. S. and Mueller, G. G. (1984) *International Accounting*, Prentice-Hall, Englewood Cliffs, N.J.

Chye, M. (1982) Employee reports: another channel of communication, *Occasional Paper no. 42*, Faculty of Business, Massey University.

Craig, R. and Hussey, R. (1981) *Employee Reports: An Australian Study*, Enterprise Australia, Sydney.

Davey, H. B. (1985) Corporate social responsibility disclosure in New Zealand: an empirical investigation, *Occasional Paper no. 52*, Department of Accounting and Finance, Massey University.

Demers, L. and Wayland, D. A. (1982a) Corporate social responsibility: is no news good news?, part 1. *CA Magazine*, 42–6.

Demers, L. and Wayland, D. A. (1982b) Corporate social responsibility: is no news good news?, part 2, *CA Magazine*, 56–60.

Department of Trade, United Kingdom (1977) *Report of the Committee of Enquiry on Industrial Democracy* (Bullock Report), Cmnd 6707, HMSO, London.

Dierkes, M. (1979) Corporate social reporting in Germany: conceptual developments and practical experience, *Accounting, Organizations and Society*, **4**(1/2), 87–107.

Epstein, M., Flamholtz, E. and McDonough, J. J. (1976) Corporate social accounting in the United States of America: state of the art and future prospects, *Accounting, Organizations and Society*, **1**(1), 23–42.

Ernst and Ernst (1972–8) *Social Responsibility Disclosure: Surveys of* Fortune 500 *Annual Reports*, Ernst and Ernst, Cleveland.

Flamholtz, E. G. (1974) *Human Resource Accounting*, Dickenson, Belmont, Cal.

Flamholtz, E. G. (1985) *Human Resource Accounting*, Jossey-Bass, San Francisco.

Gartenberg, M. (1980) How Dow accounts for its energy usage, *Management Accounting*, 10–12.

Gray, R., Owen, D. and Maunders, K. (1987) *Corporate Social Reporting: Accounting and Accountability*, Prentice-Hall, London.

Gray, R. and Perks, R. (1982) How desirable is social accounting?, *Accountancy*, 101–2.

Gray, S. J. and Maunders, K. T. (1980) *Value Added Reporting: Uses and Measurement*, Association of Certified Accountants, London.

Guthrie J. E. (1982) Social accounting in Australia: social responsibility disclosure in the top 150 listed Australian companies, 1980 annual reports, unpublished Masters dissertation, Western Australia Institute of Technology, Perth.

Guthrie, J. E. and Mathews, M. R. (1985) Corporate social accounting in Australasia, in L. E. Preston (ed.), *Corporate Social Performance and Policy*, JAI Press, New York, 251–77.

HMSO (1977) *The Future of Company Reports: A Consultative Document*, HMSO, London.

Hussey, R. (1979) *Who Reads Employee Reports?*, Touche Ross, Oxford.

Hussey, R. (1981) Developments in employee reporting, *Managerial Finance*, **7**(2), 12–16.

Hussey, R. and Craig, R. (1979) Employee reports – what employees think, *Chartered Accountant in Australia*, **49**(10).

Jackman, C. J. (1982) An accountant's view of social accounting and social disclosure, a paper presented at an Institute of Chartered Accountants (NSW) Professional Development Course on Social Accounting and Social Disclosure.

Jackson-Cox, J., Thirkell, J. E. M. and McQueeny, J. (1984) The disclosure of company information to trade unions: the relevance of the ACA's code of practice on disclosure, *Accounting, Organizations and Society*, **9**(3/4), 253–73.

Jefferis, K. and Thomas, A. (1985) Measuring the performance of worker co-operatives, a paper presented to the *Interdisciplinary Perspectives on Accounting Conference*, Manchester.

Jones, M. and Blunt, P. (1981) Industrial democracy and accountants' attitudes, *Chartered Accountant in Australia*, **51**(11), 42–6.

Kelly, G. J. (1981) Australian social responsibilities disclosures: some insights into contemporary measurement, *Accounting and Finance*, **21**(2), 97–107.

Lessem, R. (1977) Corporate social reporting in action: an evaluation of British, European, and American practice, *Accounting, Organizations and Society*, **2**(4), 279–94.

Lewis, N. R., Parker, L. D., Pound, G. D. and Sutcliffe, P. (1983) An analysis of accounting report readability: corporate financial reports to employees, 1977–1980, A paper presented to the AAANZ Conference, Brisbane.

Lewis, N., Parker, L. D. and Sutcliffe, P. (1982) Financial reporting to employees: towards a research framework, *Working Paper no. 7*, Department of Accounting and Finance, Monash University.

Logsdon, J. M. (1985) Organisational responses to environmental issues: oil refining companies and air pollution, in L. E. Preston (ed.), *Research in Corporate Social Performance and Policy*, vol. 7, JAI Press, New York.

Mathews, M. R. and Gordon, I. M. (1984) Social responsibility accounting disclosures: differential responses as a function of professional body membership, *Working Paper no. 8*, Public Interest Section, American Accounting Association.

Mathews, M. R. and Heazlewood, C. T. (1983) Accountants' attitudes to new developments in accounting, *Occasional Paper no. 46*, Faculty of Business, Massey University.

Mathews, M. R. and Perera, M. B. H. (1991) *Accounting Theory and Development*, Thomas Nelson, Melbourne.

Maunders, K. T. (1984) *Employment Reporting – An Investigation of User Needs, Measurement and Reporting Issues and Practice*, ICAEW, London.

Morley, M. F. (1978) *The Value Added Statement*, ICAS, Edinburgh.

Ng. L. W. (1985) Social responsibility disclosures of selected New Zealand companies for 1981, 1982 and 1983, *Occasional Paper no. 54*, Faculty of Business, Massey University.

Pang, Y. H. (1982) Disclosures of corporate social responsibility, *Chartered Accountant in Australia*, 53(1), 32–4.

Pound, G. D. (1980) Employee reports – readability, *Australian Accountant*, 50(11), 775–9.

Preston, L. E. (1981) Research on corporate social reporting: directions for development, *Accounting, Organizations and Society*, 6(3), 255–62.

Purdy, D. (1981) The provision of financial information to employees: a study of the reporting practices of some large public companies in the United Kingdom, *Accounting, Organizations and Society*, 6(4), 327–38.

Ramanathan, K. V. (1976) Toward a theory of corporate social accounting, *Accounting Review*, 51(3) 516–28.

Ray, F. (1978) Corporate social responsibility and social reporting in France, in H. Schoenfeld (ed.), *The Status of Social Reporting in Selected Countries*, University of Illinois Press, Urbana, Ill.

Renshall, M., Allan, R. and Nicholson, K. (1979) *Added Value in External Financial Reporting*, ICAEW, London.

Robertson, J. (1976) When the name of the game is changing, how do we keep the score?, *Accounting, Organizations and Society*, 1(1), 91–5.

Robertson, J. (1977) Corporate social reporting by New Zealand companies, *Occasional Paper no. 17*, Faculty of Business, Massey University.

Robinson, C. (1980) Efficient markets and the social role of accounting, *CA Magazine*, 21–4.

Ross, G. H. B. (1971) Social accounting: measuring the unmeasurables, *Canadian Chartered Accountant*, 46–54.

Roth, H. P. (1981) A new outlet for energy audit data – reporting energy usage as social accounting information, *Journal of Accountancy*, 68–78.

Schafer, E. L. and Mathews, M. R. (1984) The management accountant and social responsibility disclosures, *Mississippi Business Review*, 46(3), 3–6.

Scudiere, P. M. (1980) Justifying proposals to save energy, *Management Accounting*, 42–8.

Smith, A. and Firth, M. (1986) Employee reporting in New Zealand – what employees think, *Accountants Journal*, **65**(10), 24–6.

Stiner, F. M. Jr (1978) Accountants' attitudes toward social accounting, *Mid-Atlantic Journal of Business*, **16**(2).

Taylor, D. W., Webb, L. and McGinley, L. (1979) Annual reports to employees – the challenge to the corporate accountant, *Chartered Accountant in Australia*, **49**(10), 33–9.

Thompson, E. R. and Knell, A. (1979) *The Employment Statement in Company Reports*, ICAEW, London.

Tomlinson, J. (1985) Accounting for feasible socialism: accounting, industrial democracy and the theory of the firm, a paper presented to the *Interdisciplinary Perspectives on Accounting Conference*, Manchester.

Trotman, K. T. (1979) Social responsibility disclosures by Australian companies, *Chartered Accountant in Australia*, **49**(8), 24–8.

Trotman, K. T. and Bradley, G. W. (1981) Associations between social responsibility disclosure and characteristics of companies, *Accounting, Organizations and Society*, **6**(4), 355–62.

UEC Working Party on Social Reporting (1983) *Socio-economic Information*, a report prepared for the 9th UEC Congress, Strasburg.

Unruh, A. R. and Mathews, M. R. (1992) Human resource accounting: an important topic revisited, *Accounting Forum* **16**(3), 47–63.

Wartick, S. L. and Cochran, P. L. (1985) The evolution of the corporate social performance model, *Academy of Management Review*, **10**(4), 758–69.

Webb, L. and Taylor, D. W. (1980) Employee reporting – don't wait for it, *Australian Accountant*, **50**(1), 30–4.

Wiseman, J. H. (1982) An evaluation of environmental disclosures made in corporate annual reports, *Accounting, Organizations and Society*, **7**(1), 53–63.

5: Social responsibility accounting in practice

Abel, R. (1971) The impact of environment on accounting practices: Germany in the thirties, *International Journal of Accounting Education and Research*.

Arpan, J. S. and Radebaugh, L. H. (1985) *International Accounting and Multinational Enterprises*, John Wiley, New York.

Bakker, P. A. H. (1975) Het sociaal jaarverslat in oponars, *Intermediair*, **121**.

Barrett, V. M. E. (1977) The extent of disclosure in annual reports of large companies in seven countries, *International Journal of Accounting Education and Research*,

Belkaoui, A. (1983) Economic, political and civil indicators and reporting and disclosure adequacy: empirical investigation, *Journal of Accounting and Public Policy*,

Benston, G. J. (1982a) Accounting and corporate accountability, *Accounting, Organizations and Society*, **7**(2), 87–105.

Benston, G. J. (1982b) An analysis of the role of accounting standards for enhancing corporate governance and social responsibility, *Journal of Accounting and Public Policy*, 5–17.

Benston, G. J. (1984) Rejoinder to 'Accounting and corporate accountability: an extended comment', *Accounting, Organizations and Society*, **9**(3/4), 417–19.

Brockhoff, K. (1979) A note on external social reporting by German companies: a survey of 1973 company reports, *Accounting, Organizations and Society*, **4**(1/2), 77–85.

Bromwich, M. and Hopwood, A. G. (1983) *Accounting Standard Setting: An International Perspective*, Pitman, London.

Brooks, L. J. (1986) *Canadian Corporate Social Performance*, Society of Management Accountants of Canada, Toronto.

Burchell, S., Clubb, C. and Hopwood, A. G. (1985) Accounting in its social context: towards a history of value added in the United Kingdom, *Accounting, Organizations and Society*, **10**(4), 381–413.

Burke, R. C. (1980) The disclosure of social accounting information, *Cost and Management*, 221–4.

Burke, R. C. (1984) *Decision Making in Complex Times: The Contribution of a Social Accounting Information System*, Society of Management Accountants of Canada, Ontario.

Buzby, S. L. (1974) Selected items of information and their disclosure in annual reports, *Accounting Review*, 423–35.

Choi, F. D. S. and Mueller, G. G. (1984) *International Accounting*, Prentice-Hall, Englewood Cliffs, N.J.

Da Costa, R. C., Bourgeois, J. C. and Lawson, W. M. (1978) A classification of international financial accounting practices, *International Journal of Accounting Education and Research*,

Davey, H. B. (1985) Corporate social responsibility disclosure in New Zealand: an empirical investigation, *Occasional Paper no. 52*, Department of Accounting and Finance, Massey University.

de Gier, E. (1976) Sociaal verslag gepunt, Zeggenschap. 3.

Dekker, H. C. and van Hoorn, Th.P. (1977) Some major developments in social reporting in The Netherlands since 1945, unpublished discussion paper, Department of Economics, University of Amsterdam.

Delmot, A. (1982a) Social written information in Belgian enterprises: results of a survey, *Working Paper*, Department of Accountancy, University of Mons.

Delmot, A. (1982b) Social written information in Belgian enterprises: results of a survey, a paper presented at the *Workshop on Accounting in a Changing Social and Political Environment*, Brussels.

Demers, L. and Wayland, D. A. (1982a) Corporate social responsibility: is no news good news?, part 1, *CA Magazine*, 42–6.

Demers, L. and Wayland, D. A. (1982b) Corporate social responsibility: is no news good news?, part 2, *CA Magazine*, 56–60.

Dierkes, M. (1979) Corporate social reporting in Germany: conceptual developments and practical experience, *Accounting, Organizations and Society*, **4**(1/2), 87–107.

Ernst and Ernst (1972–8) *Social Responsibility Disclosure: Surveys of Fortune 500 Annual Reports*, Ernst and Ernst, Cleveland.

Feenstra, D. W. and Bowma, J. L. (1975) Human resource accounting: some tentative statements and a preliminary examination concerning the presentation of non-accounting information in external reporting of some selected Dutch companies over 1970–73, a paper presented at the EIASM *Workshop on Human Resource Accounting*, Brussels.

Frank, W. G. (1979) An empirical analysis of international accounting principles, *Journal of Accounting Research*,

Goodrich, P. S. (1982) Accounting and political systems, *Discussion Paper no. 109*, School of Economic Studies, University of Leeds.

Gray, R., Owen, D. and Maunders, K. (1987) *Corporate Social Reporting: Accounting and Accountability*, Prentice-Hall, London.

Gray, S. J. (1985) Cultural influences and the international classification of accounting systems, *Working Paper 85–7*, University of Glasgow.

Gray, S. J., McSweeney, I. B. and Shaw, J. C. (1984) *Information Disclosure and the Multinational Corporation*, John Wiley, Chichester,

Gröjer, J. E. and Stark, A. (1977) Social accounting: a Swedish attempt, *Accounting, Organizations and Society*, **2**(4), 349–86.

Gul, F. A. K., Andrew, B. H. and Teoh, H. J. (1984) A content analytical study of corporate social responsibility accounting disclosures in a sample of Australian companies (1983), *Working Paper*, University of Wollongong.

Guthrie, J. E. (1982) Social accounting in Australia: social responsibility disclosure in the top 150 listed Australian companies, 1980 annual reports, unpublished Masters dissertation, Western Australia Institute of Technology, Perth.

Guthrie, J. E. and Mathews, M. R. (1985) Corporate social accounting in Australasia, in L. E. Preston (ed.), *Corporate Social Performance and Policy*, JAI Press, New York, pp. 251–77.

Hofstede, G. (1983a) Dimensions of national cultures in fifty countries and three regions, in J. B. Dregowski, S. Dziurauriec, and R. C. Annis (eds), *Expectations in Cross-Cultural Psychology*, Swets and Zeitlinger, Amsterdam.

Hofstede, G. (1983b) The cultural relativity of organisational practices and theories, *Journal of International Business Studies*,

Hofstede, G. (1985) The ritual nature of accounting systems, a paper presented at an EIASM *Workshop on Accounting and Culture*, Amsterdam.

Holzer, H. P. (ed.) (1984) *International Accounting*, Harper and Row, London.

Hopwood, A. G. and Schreuder, H. (eds) (1984) *European Contributions to Accounting Research: The Achievement of the Last Decade*, Free University Press, Amsterdam.

Ingram, R. W. (1978) An investigation of the information content of (certain) social responsibility disclosures, *Journal of Accounting Research*, **16**(2), 270–85.

Jackman, C. J. (1982) An accountant's view of social accounting and social disclosure, a paper presented at an Institute of Chartered Accountants (NSW) Professional Development Course on Social Accounting and Social Disclosure.

Jaruga, A. A. (1984) Social responsibility of accountants in Poland, *Working Paper*, Accounting Department, University of Lodz.

Jonson, L. C., Jonson, B. and Svenson, G. (1978) The application of social accounting to absenteeism and personnel turnover, *Accounting in Organizations and Society*, **3**(3–4), 261–8.

Kelly, G. J. (1979) Measurement of selected social responsibility disclosure items in Australian annual reports and their relations to temporal changes, corporate size and industry, Dissertation, University of New England.

Lafferty, M. (1975) *Accounting in Europe*, Woodhead-Faulkner, London.

Lee, T. A. and Tweedie, D. P. (1977) *The Private Shareholder and the Corporate Report*, ICAEW, London.

Low Aik Meng, Koh Hian Chye and Yeo Hian Heng (1985) Corporate social responsibility and reporting in Singapore: a review, *Singapore Accountant*, 1(8), 7–13.

Lyal l, D. (1982) Disclosure practices in employee reports, *Accountants Magazine*, 246–8.

Marsh, A. and Hussey, R. (1979) Survey of employee reports, *Company Secretary's Review*, Tolley.

Mathews, M. R. and Perera, M. B. H. (1991) *Accounting Theory and Development*, Thomas Nelson, Melbourne.

Most, K. S. (1977) Corporate social reporting – 'Model' report by Deutsche Shell, *Accountant*, 164–7.

Mueller, G. G. (1967) *International Accounting*, Macmillan, New York.

Mueller, G. G. (1968) Accounting principles generally accepted in the United States versus those generally accepted elsewhere, *International Journal of Accounting Education and Research*,

Mueller, G. G. (1976) *International Accounting*, Macmillan, New York.

Mueller, G. G. (1985) Is accounting culturally determined? A paper presented at an EIASM *Workshop on Accounting and Culture*, Amsterdam.

Nair, R. D. and Frank, W. G. (1980) The impact of disclosure and measurement practices on international accounting classification, *Accounting Review*,

Ng. L. W. (1985) Social responsibility disclosures of selected New Zealand companies for 1981, 1982, and 1983, *Occasional Paper no. 54*, Faculty of Business, Massey University.

Nobes, C. W. (1983) A judgemental international classification of financial reporting practices, *Journal of Business Finance and Accounting*,

Nobes, C. W. (1984) *International Classification of Financial Reporting*, Croom Helm, London.

Nobes, C. W. and Parker, R. H. (1981) *Comparative International Accounting*, Philip Allan, Oxford.

Oldham, K. M. (1981) *Accounting Systems and Practices in Europe*, Gower, London.

Organization for Economic Cooperation and Development (OECD) (1980) *Accounting Practices in OECD Member Countries*, OECD, Paris.

Pang, Y. H. (1982) Disclosures of corporate social responsibility, *Chartered Accountant in Australia*, 32–4.

Perera, M. H. B. (1985) The relevance of international accounting standards to developing countries, *Research Monograph*, University of Glasgow.

Perera, M. H. B. and Mathews, M. R. (1990) The cultural relativity of accounting and international patterns of social accounting, in K. S. Most (ed.), *Advances in International Accounting, 3*, JAI Press, New York.

Radebaugh, L. H. (1975) Environmental factors influencing the development of accounting objectives, standards, and practices in Peru, *International Journal of Accounting and Research*,

Riahi-Belkaoui, A., Perochin, C. and Mathews, M. R. (1991) Report on the cultural studies and accounting research committee, *Advances in International Accounting*, **4**,

Robertson, J. (1977) Corporate social reporting by New Zealand companies, *Occasional Paper no. 17*, Faculty of Business, Massey University.

Rockness, J. W. (1985) An assessment of the relationship between US corporate environmental performance and disclosure, *Journal of Business Finance and Accounting*, **12**(3).

Schoenfeld, H. M. (1978) The status of social reporting in selected countries, *Contemporary Issues in International Accounting, Occasional Paper no. 1*, University of Illinois, Urbana.

Schreuder, H. (1979) Corporate social reporting in the Federal Republic of Germany: an overview, *Accounting, Organizations and Society*, **4**(1/2), 109–22.

Stevens, W. P. (1982) Market reaction to corporate environmental performance, a paper presented at the American Accounting Association Annual Conference, San Diego.

Teoh, H. Y. and Thong, G. (1984) Another look at corporate social responsibility and reporting: an empirical study in a developing country, *Accounting, Organizations and Society*, **9**(2), 189–206.

Theunesse, H. (1979) Corporate social reporting in Belgium, *Working Paper 79–08*, Faculty of Applied Economics, University of Antwerp.

Tinker, A. M. (1985) *Paper Prophets*, Praeger, New York.

Tokutani, M. and Kawano, M. (1978) A note on the Japanese social accounting literature, *Accounting, Organizations and Society*, **3**(2), 183–8.

Trotman, K. T. (1979) Social responsibility disclosures by Australian companies, *Chartered Accountant in Australia*, 24–8.

Trotman, K. T. and Bradley, G. W. (1981) Associations between social responsibility disclosure and characteristics of companies, *Accounting, Organizations and Society*, **6**(4), 355–62.

Van den Bergh, R. (1976) The corporate social report: the Deutsche Shell experience, *Accountancy*, 57–61.

Van Ommeren, A. W. (1974) Het Sociaal Jaavuerslag. Informatiebron of verantwoordingstuk, Personeels beleid. 293.

Violet, W. J. (1983) The development of international accounting standards: an anthropological perspective, *International Journal of Accounting Education and Research*,

Wiseman, J. H. (1982) An evaluation of environmental disclosures made in corporate annual reports, *Accounting, Organizations and Society*, **7**(1), 53–6.

Zeff, S. A. (1973) *Forging Accounting Principles in Australia*, Australian Society of Accountants, Melbourne.

6: Total impact accounting (TIA)

Abt, C. C. (1977) *The Social Audit for Management*, Amason, New York.

Accounting Standards Steering Committee (1975) *The Corporate Report*, ICAEW, London.

American Accounting Association (1975) *Supplement to the Accounting Review, 50*, (Report of the Committee on Social Costs), 51–89.

Beams, F. A. and Fertig, P. E. (1971) Pollution control through social costs conversion, *Journal of Accountancy*, **82**, 37–42.

Benston, G. J. (1982a) Accounting and corporate accountability, *Accounting, Organizations and Society*, **7**(2), 87–105.

Benston, G. J. (1982b) An analysis of the role of accounting standards for enhancing corporate governance and social responsibility, *Journal of Accounting and Public Policy*, 5–17.

Brooks, L. J. (1980) An attitude survey approach to the social audit: the Southam Press experience, *Accounting, Organizations and Society*, **5**(3), 341–55.

Brooks, L. J. (1986) *Canadian Corporate Social Performance*, Society of Management Accountants of Canada, Toronto.

Burke, R. C. (1984) *Decision Making in Complex Times: The Contribution of a Social Accounting Information System*, Society of Management Accountants of Canada, Ontario.

Dierkes, M. and Preston, L. E. (1977) Corporate social accounting reporting for the physical environment: a critical review and implementation proposal, *Accounting, Organizations and Society*, **2**(1), 3–22.

Dilley, S. C. and Weygandt, J. J. (1973) Measuring social responsibility – an empirical test, *Journal of Accountancy*, 62–70.

Donaldson, T. (1982) *Corporate Morality*, Prentice-Hall, Englewood Cliffs, N.J.

Estes, R. W. (1973) Accounting for social costs, in R. W. Estes (ed.), *Accounting and Society*, Melville, Los Angeles, pp. 248–55.

Estes, R. W. (1976) *Corporate Social Accounting*, John Wiley, New York.

Estes, R. W. (1977) The corporate social accounting model: an information system for evaluating the impact of corporations on growth, resource use and specific constituent groups within society, in L. A. Gordon (ed.), *Accounting and Corporate Social Responsibility*, Proceedings of a Symposium, University of Kansas.

Filios, V. P. (1985) Social process auditing: a survey and some suggestions, *Journal of Business Ethics*, **4**, 477–85.

Gray, R. H. (1990) The greening of accountancy: the profession after Pearce, *Certified Research Report 17*, Chartered Association of Certified Accountants, London.

Gray, R. H. (1991) The accountancy profession and the environmental crisis, *Discussion Paper ACC/9102*, University of Dundee.

Gray, R., Owen, D. and Maunders, K. (1987) *Corporate Social Reporting: Accounting and Accountability*, Prentice-Hall, London.

Harte, G. F. and Owen, D. L. (1986) Fighting de-industrialisation: the role of local government social audits, *Accounting, Organizations and Society*.

Heard, J. E. and Bolce, W. J. (1981) The political significance of corporate social reporting in the United States of America, *Accounting, Organizations and Society*, **6**(3), 247–54.

Lindblom, C. E. (1983) The concept of organizational legitimacy and its implications for corporate social responsibility disclosure, *Working Paper no. 7*, Public Interest Section, AAA.

Linowes, D. F. (1972) Socio-economic accounting, *Journal of Accountancy*, 37–42.

Marris, R. (1964) *The Economic Theory of Managerial Capitalisation*, Free Press, New York.

Mathews, M. R. (1991) A limited review of the green accounting literature, *Accounting, Auditing and Accountability Journal*, **4**(3), 110–21.

Owen, D. (ed.) (1992) *Green Reporting*, Chapman & Hall, London.

Owen, D. L. and Harte, G. F. (1984) Reporting on corporate accountability to the workforce, *Accountants Magazine*, 184–7.

Pearce, D., Markandya, A. and Barbier, E. B. (1989) *Blueprint for a Green Economy*, Earthscan, London.

Ramanathan, K. V. (1976) Toward a theory of corporate social accounting, *Accounting Review*, **51**(3), 516–28.

Ramanathan, K. V. and Schreuder, H. (1982) The case for social accounting and reporting: a macro-perspective, paper presented at a *Workshop on Accounting in a Changing Social and Political Environment*, EIASM, Brussels.

Schreuder, H. (1979) Corporate social reporting in the Federal Republic of Germany: an overview, *Accounting, Organizations and Society*, 4(1/2), 109–22.

Schreuder, H. and Ramanathan, K. V. (1984a) Accounting and corporate accountability: an extended comment, *Accounting, Organizations and Society*, 9(3/4), 409–15.

Schreuder, H. and Ramanathan, K. V. (1984b) Accounting and corporate accountability: a postscript, *Accounting, Organizations and Society*, 9(3/4), 421–3.

Sellers, J. H. (1981) A conceptual model for the social audit, *Singapore Accountant*, 24–9.

Siebert, H. and Antal, A. B. (1979) *The Political Economy of Environmental Protection*, JAI Press, New York.

Taylor, K. (1975) Social accounting: whose responsibility?, *Management Accounting*, 361–4.

Tinker, A. M. and Lowe, E. A. (1980) A rationale for corporate social reporting: theory and evidence from organisational research, *Journal of Business Finance and Accounting*, 7(1), 1–15.

Ullman, A. A. (1976) The corporate environmental accounting system: a management tool for fighting environmental degradation, *Accounting, Organizations and Society*, 1(1), 71–9.

United Nations (1975) *Towards a System of Social and Demographic Statistics*, Studies in Methods, series 1, no. 18, United Nations, New York.

Williamson, O. E. (1964) *The Economics of Discretionary Behaviour*, Prentice-Hall, Englewood Cliffs, N.J.

7: Socio-economic accounting (SEA)

Birnberg, J. G. and Gandhi, N. M. (1976) Toward defining the accountants' role in the evaluation of social programs, *Accounting, Organizations and Society*, 1(1), 5–10.

Bogue, E. G. and Brown, W. (1982) Performance incentives for state colleges, *Harvard Business Review*, 123–8.

Churchman, C. W. (1971) On the facility, felicity, and morality of measuring social change, *Accounting Review*, 30–5.

Commission on the Third London Airport (Roskill Commission) (1970), *Report*, HMSO, London.

Corson, J. J. and Steiner, G. A. (1974) *Measuring Business Social Performance: The Corporate Social Audit*, Committee for Economic Development, New York.

Dasgupta, A. and Pearce, D. W. (1972) *Cost Benefit Analysis: Theory and Practice*, Macmillan, London.

Dennison, W. F. (1979) Management developments in government resource association: the example of the rise and fall of PPBS planning programming budgeting system, *Journal of Management Studies*, 270–82.

Elsterman, G. and Lorenz, W. (1980) Financing universities on the basis of performance indicators?, a paper to the Ninth Special Topic Workshop of the IMKE Programme, OECD/CERI, Paris.

Estes, R. W. (1973) Accounting for social costs, in R. W. Estes (ed.), *Accounting and Society*, Los Angeles, Melville, pp. 248–55.

Francis, M. E. (1973) Accounting and the evaluation of social programs: a critical comment, *Accounting Review*, 245–57.

Glynn, J. J. (1985) Value for money auditing: an international review and comparison, *Financial Accountability and Management*, **1**(2), 113–28.

Gray, R., Owen, D. and Maunders, K. (1987) *Corporate Social Reporting: Accounting and Accountability*, Prentice-Hall, London.

Grimwood, M. and Tomkins, C. (1986) Value for money auditing: towards incorporating a naturalistic approach, *Financial Accountability and Management*, **2**(4), 251–72.

Gul, F. A. K. (1981) Zero-based budgeting (revisited), *Australian Accountant*, 121–6.

Jones, R. and Pendlebury, M. (1984) *Public Sector Accounting*, Pitman, London.

Linowes, D. F. (1968) Socio-economic accounting, *Journal of Accountancy*, 37–42.

McSweeney, B. and Sherer, M. J. (1985) Value for money auditing: some observations on its origins and theory: a paper presented at the *Interdisciplinary Perspectives on Accounting Conference*, Manchester.

Mishan, E. J. (1972) What is wrong with Roskill?, in R. Layard (ed.), *Cost Benefit Analysis*,

Mobley, S. C. (1970) The challenges of socio-economic accounting, *Accounting Review*, 762–8.

Parker, L. D. (1986) Towards value for money audit policy, *Australian Accountant*, 79–82.

Prest, A. R. and Turvey, R. (1965) Cost-benefit analysis: a survey, *Economic Journal*, 682–735.

Provus, M. (1971) As reported in D. D. Mackay and M. Maguire, *Evaluation of Instructional Programs*, Alberta Human Resource Research Council, Alberta, pp. 40–9.

Pyhrr, P. A. (1970) Zero-based budgeting, *Harvard Business Review*, **48**(12), 111–21.

Sellers, J. H. (1981) A conceptual model for the social audit, *Singapore Accountant*, 24–9.

Sherer, M. J. (1984) The ideology of efficiency: a critical evaluation of value for money auditing, *Discussion paper series no. 241*, Department of Economics, University of Essex.

Sizer, J. (1980) Performance assessment in institutions of higher education under conditions of financial stringency, contraction, and changing needs: a management accounting perspective; a paper presented to the Third Annual Congress of the European Accounting Association.

Small, J. R. and Mansfield, R. (1978) Zero base budgeting – theory and practice, *Accountants' Magazine*, 191–6.

Sorenson, J. R. and Grove, H. D. (1977) Cost-outcome and cost-effectiveness analysis: emerging non-profit performance evaluation techniques, *Accounting Review*, **52**(3).

Stake, R. E. (1967) The countenance of educational evaluation, *Teachers College Record*, 523–40.

Stufflebeam, D. (1968) Towards a science of educational evaluation, *Educational Technology*, 6–12.

8: Social indicators accounting (SIA)

Bauer, R. A. (ed.) (1966) *Social Indicators*, MIT Press, Cambridge, Mass.

Glatzer, W. (1981) An overview of the international development in macro social indicators, *Accounting, Organizations and Society*, **6**(3), 219–34.

Mathews, M. R. (1984) Towards a more socially relevant accounting, *Occasional Paper no, 51*, Faculty of Business, Massey University.

Parke, R. and Peterson, J. L. (1981) Indicators of social change: developments in the United States of America, *Accounting, Organizations and Society*, **6**(3), 235–46.

Sheldon, E. B. and Parke, R. (1975) Social indicators, *Science*, 693–9.

Terleckyj, N. E. (1970) Measuring progress towards social goals: some possibilities at national and local levels, *Management Science*, 765–78.

9: Societal accounting

Accounting Standards Steering Committee (1975) *The Corporate Report*, ICAEW, London.

Enthoven, A. J. H. (1985) Mega accounting trends, *Accountancy Research Monograph no. 5*, University of Texas at Dallas.

Gambling, T. E. (1974) *Societal Accounting*, Allen and Unwin, London.

Gambling, T. E. (1985) The accountants' guide to the galaxy, including the profession at the end of the universe, Valedictory Lecture, University of Birmingham (1984); reproduced in *Accounting, Organizations and Society*, **10**(4), 42–5.

Gandhi, N. M. (1976) The emergence of the post-industrial society and the future of the accounting function, *Journal of Management Studies*, 199–212.

Kast, F. E, and Rosenzweig, J. E. (1974) *Organization and Management: A Systems Approach*, 2nd edn, McGraw Hill, New York.

Mattessich, R. (1957) Towards a general and axiomatic foundation of accountancy, *Accounting Research*, **8**, 328–55.

Mattessich, R. (1972) Methodological preconditions and problems of a general theory of accounting, *Accounting Review*.

10: Concluding comments and directions for future research

Gandhi, N. M. (1976) The emergence of the post-industrial society and the future of the accounting function, *Journal of Management Studies*, 199–212.

Gray, R. H. (1990) The greening of accountancy: the profession after Pearce, *Certified Research Report 17*, Chartered Association of Certified Accountants, London.

Gray, R. H. (1991) The accountancy profession and the environmental crisis, *Discussion Paper ACC/9102*, University of Dundee.

McDonald, D. L. (1972) *Comparative Accounting Theory*, Addison Wesley, Cambridge, Mass.

Owen, D. (ed.) (1992) *Green Reporting*, Chapman & Hall, London.

Author index

Subject index